Ideology, Politics,
and Government in
the Soviet Union

Ideology, Politics, and Government in the Soviet Union

AN INTRODUCTION

THIRD EDITION

John A. Armstrong

PRAEGER PUBLISHERS
New York • Washington

Published in the United States of America in 1974
by Praeger Publishers, Inc.
111 Fourth Avenue, New York, N.Y. 10003

This is the third edition, revised and expanded, of the book published
in 1962 by Frederick A. Praeger, Inc., Publishers.

© 1962, 1967 by Frederick A. Praeger, Inc.
© 1974 by Praeger Publishers, Inc.

Library of Congress Catalog Card Number: 72-91711

Printed in the United States of America

To Roy and Leona Taylor

PREFACE
TO THE THIRD EDITION

When I wrote the first edition of this book twelve years ago, I believed there was a need for a brief, simplified survey of the main features of the Soviet political system. Since that time, the reception given the book suggests that it has, indeed, served a purpose. I am convinced that a good part of the book's utility has been due to its timeliness. The first edition appeared less than a year after the Twenty-second Congress of the Soviet Communist Party; Nikita Khrushchev was then apparently at the height of his power. Two years later he was overthrown, and the oligarchical leadership which succeeded him systematically demolished his ideological and institutional innovations. By 1967, when the second edition of this book appeared, it was already clear that the confident progress toward Communism which the Twenty-third Congress had proclaimed was at an end. Except in the foreign policy sphere, changes since 1967 have not been so spectacular. Instead, minor institutional reorganizations, subtle ideological re-emphases, and gradual shifts in methods of social and economic control have occurred. Paralleling these changes has been a notable increase in the amount of information about the nature of the Soviet system. The cumulative impact of systemic changes and new information is so great that a new look at the Soviet polity is imperative.

The third edition has been almost completely revised so as to provide an introduction focusing on *current* Soviet politics. As with the first edition, for the sake of brevity I have omitted

almost all history of Soviet institutional development and political rivalry from this volume. Government in the Soviet
Union is no longer a curiosity, and only in a very special sense
can one describe it as an experiment. Consequently, a preliminary look at the system may well take for granted its relative
stability, its capacity as a going concern. It seems to me that the
historical examination of political institutions and behavior
can reasonably be postponed. The great danger of this type of
approach is the loss of historical perspective. I have tried to
avoid, or at least limit, this danger by treating the more remote
background of present-day Soviet society in the opening chapter. Furthermore, while institutions and behavior can be presented out of their historical context, the same does not hold
true for Soviet ideology, which is incomprehensible except in
its developmental framework. Consequently, Chapter 2, though
not chronological in organization, contains numerous refer-
ences to the precursors of the present Soviet ideologues.

Discussion of foreign policy also requires attention to the
radical transformations in the international environment
within which the Soviet regime operates. Increasingly over the
past decade, it has become apparent that Soviet foreign and
domestic policies are so closely related that consideration of
the latter is hardly possible without a close if brief examination of foreign affairs. In earlier editions, this examination
was attempted in the form of brief interpolations, especially
in the concluding chapter. Now, it seems to me, a more systematic consideration of the interpenetration of foreign and
domestic policy, as presented in Chapter 8, is the most effective way to sum up the underlying factors affecting the evolution of Soviet policy during the 1970's.

Both the pre-Soviet background treated in Chapter 1 and
the effects of ideology discussed in Chapter 2 are part of what
social science theorists increasingly agree on calling "political
culture." During the past twelve years, the conceptual frame-

work and vocabulary of systems analysis and structural functionalism have rapidly become part of the common fund of knowledge of social science students. Even those who do not intend to acquire specialized competence in analytic social science have frequently obtained at least a general familiarity with the approaches. Apart from certain general difficulties involved in applying "whole-system" approaches, there are special difficulties involved in adapting them to the examination of Soviet politics.

I think there is widespread agreement that, of all major categories of political systems, the totalitarian type is least readily susceptible to systems analysis and still less to structural functional analysis. Both approaches were developed primarily from the consideration of pluralist societies like the United States or from the adaptation of anthropological perspectives on traditional societies. The application of these approaches to an extremely centralized political system, dominated by a small, relatively homogeneous elite adhering to an ideology demanding the complete transformation of human nature, requires fundamental reconsideration. The organic analogies behind some of the newer social science models, which tend to assume the existence of unconscious social processes tending toward an equilibrium state, are particularly hard to relate to the highly self-conscious goal orientation of a Communist elite. On the other hand, such approaches make it equally difficult to place adequate conceptual emphasis on the high degree of intra-elite conflict in Communist systems. For the time being, therefore, it seems to me preferable to use an eclectic approach, employing a "rational actor" model to interpret much of the ideological development and policy formation in the U.S.S.R. and a "conflict model" to examine elite political processes. As a heuristic device, a systems conceptual point of view that does not imply the assumption that there are systemswide functions is used throughout. In specific sections—especially

the nationalities question and its relation to foreign policy—
a modified systems model with explicitly functionalist characteristics is utilized. Hopefully this eclectic treatment will
suggest the relevance of the newer social science approaches
and some of their vocabulary, without attempting what I
regard as the premature application of a single conceptual
framework.

I hope that the material presented on the nationalities
question, particularly, will be stimulating in a methodological
as well as a conceptual sense. Increasingly, quantitative comparison of political and social units has become a significant
exercise for undergraduate students as well as an important
tool for more advanced researchers. Like language study,
training in statistical techniques and computer programing
becomes immensely more challenging for the social science
student if exercises utilize substantively significant contemporary materials. While the usual approach is correlation
analysis of data relating to independent countries, comparative
quantitative analysis of sub-national units (as several excellent
studies of differences among American states demonstrate) is
equally appropriate. Ordinarily, the unspecialized student
wishing to pursue such analyses finds it difficult to obtain
reliable data standardized for comparable aspects of each
subdivision of any national political system other than the
United States. Data on major Soviet nationalities (or on the
Union republics, which usually constitute their "home territories") are becoming increasingly available. These data are
highly standardized across nationality units. Nevertheless,
specific problems such as access to scattered sources in Russian
and other Soviet languages and the need for specialized
evaluation and interpretation of the Soviet data have prevented their utilization in general comparative data books.
Recently Ellen P. Mickiewicz and her collaborators have provided an impressive compilation of data on all facets of Soviet

society, *Handbook of Soviet Social Science Data* (Riverside, N.J.: The Free Press, 1973). However, most of her data on ethnic factors were—unavoidably—derived from the 1959 Soviet census, whereas the very recent appearance of 1970 census data calls for a fundamental reappraisal of Soviet nationalities. The Table of Major Nationalities in Chapter 7 of my book provides fully evaluated data, including the results of the 1970 census. I hope that readers may find these data useful not only for systematic comparison of Soviet units but also in extending the universe of the readers' general comparative investigations, particularly in the sphere of social mobilization. Consequently, while the data are presented in a form suitable for quantitative manipulation, I have by no means exhausted the potential for analysis in my verbal interpretation.

While expressing certain reservations concerning the use of a single social science approach, I must emphasize, as I did in the earlier editions of this book, that a dominantly legal or institutional approach to the study of the Soviet system would be utterly misleading. Emphasis on the constitutional system of Soviet government, or even on the formal structure of the Communist Party of the Soviet Union, would be inappropriate. Consequently, I have confined myself to brief explanations of what I consider to be the significance of formal structure in both government and Party. Additional details on these structures are contained in the organizational charts accompanying the text. These charts are not confined to the formal structures of Party and government, but attempt to suggest the dynamics of power relations as well as formal lines of subordination. In a short book, illustrations of this kind are exceptionally important. But even the most penetrating elucidation of structural features could not furnish complete insight into the extent of Soviet totalitarianism. Such insight requires an understanding of the complex nationality question, earlier police terror as a background to contemporary repression, and the pervasive control of the economy. Brief as my treatment is, I have felt it essential to devote nearly a third of the book to these subjects.

I hope that this work will serve as a useful elementary guide to the Soviet political system; it is not a compendium of the opinions of others or even an abridgment of my own. Today, excellent specialized studies on nearly all aspects of the Soviet system are very numerous. Consequently, although "Suggested Readings" in the present edition contain nearly twice as many items as in the first edition, a comprehensive bibliography would be impracticable. I can only plead that those books I do list seem to me to be most useful for the general reader and the nonspecialized student. While I rely on these works, the emphasis and many of the conclusions I advance are my own; no other writer on the Soviet system will accept all of them without reservation. I am convinced that it is impossible to avoid a personal approach if one is to present a coherent analysis of Soviet politics, particularly in the international sphere, and it should be pointed out that much of what is said in this book is not established beyond dispute. I have tried to indicate the most important points where the accuracy of available data is doubtful or where divergence of informed opinion exists, but conciseness of expression may, at times, have led to unwarranted generalizations. Some readers may question my evidence for certain statements. Elaborate footnotes seemed out of place in so brief a survey. Where feasible, I have indicated my sources, such as the proceedings of the Soviet Communist Party Congresses, in the text. Because the Nationalities Table, as indicated above, is intended to be a data resource, I have provided precise footnote indications of its sources.

Probably the general reader is more likely to be concerned with over-all information about the workings of the Soviet political system than with my particular sources. A major portion of our information on Soviet politics and government is derived from "overt" Soviet sources—for the most part Soviet publications. Even the neophyte will find that the Soviet press provides a revealing, if distorted, reflection of the system at work. The reader who wishes to cover a comprehensive range of Soviet publications must know Russian (and, if possible, some of the other languages of the U.S.S.R.). Fortunately, the weekly *Current Digest of the Soviet Press* (2043 Millikin Road, Columbus, Ohio 43210) provides English-language translations from an immense range of Soviet publications. The coverage provided by the *Current Digest*, which a single scholar can hardly match, has been indispensable in preparing this book. But I cannot stress too strongly that the beginning student of Soviet affairs should not overrate his ability to understand and appraise Soviet press reports, whether in Russian or in translation. Soviet writings on general subjects, and particularly articles on political affairs, while somewhat more candid in recent years, are geared to propaganda. After a time, the student readily recognizes the propaganda "line" and learns to discount it. It is not so easy to detect the bias of factual "examples" or statistics carefully selected for their propaganda effect. As a rule, only specialists, after painstaking comparative analysis of Soviet materials appearing at different times and places, can extrapolate the facts behind such distorted selection. But the Soviet press is not only a propaganda medium; it is also a functional medium of communication in a highly complex technological society. There are facts to be discovered behind the distortion, for there is a limit to the extent to which Soviet readers can be misled without reducing the effectiveness of their service to the regime. Increasingly, the Soviet regime appears to recognize the significance of this limit; as a result, published information on economic, social, and demographic subjects has become more abundant and diversified as well as more candid. It is significant that the severe restrictions imposed on literary expression (discussed in Chapter 5) since Khrushchev's ouster have not been accompanied by a return to the moratorium on sociological and economic publication which characterized Stalin's rule. Instead, major Soviet studies on social science topics, including several employing sophisticated techniques like survey research, increased markedly in the late 1960's and early 1970's.

When internal political rivalries are at issue, however, the Soviet propagandist continues to put up a second screen between the reader and significant developments. This screen consists of "esoteric language"—the use of terms and allusions that the uninitiated fail to understand. In order to grasp the importance of esoteric language, one must have an extensive detailed knowledge of Communist history from before the Revolution to the present. Even with such knowledge, unraveling the meaning of esoteric language is often a matter of educated guess; but such guesses are crucially important in understanding Soviet political developments.

Our ability to penetrate the Soviet communication screens has been immensely helped by occasional access to hidden sources of information. During World War II, the Germans captured a number of extremely important secret documents, including the economic plan for 1941, the archives of a provincial Party organization, and thousands of political directives to guerrillas and regular military units. In 1945, the United States forces seized these materials. Since the end of the war, only a few Soviet secret documents have come to light, but, on occasion, Soviet defectors who had memorized fairly extensive outlines of major documents—such as the secret letters of the Party's Central Committee—have furnished valuable information. Naturally, defectors were most numerous during the war, when the Soviet control system was disrupted. Social scientists (of the Harvard Project on the Soviet Social System) could even construct a sample reflecting the attitudes and backgrounds of the general Soviet population on the basis of interviews with defectors. While defectors have been fewer recently, dissidents remaining inside the U.S.S.R. have been able to send out a wide variety of manuscripts commenting on the social and political situation. In some recent years hundreds of such "samizdat" manuscripts have reached Western countries.

Since the 1950's foreigners, including specialists on Soviet affairs from the United States and Western Europe, have been allowed some direct access to the Soviet Union. While all such visitors have been restricted to a considerable degree, they have obtained a "feel" for the Soviet system, which has helped them draw conclusions from the other sources described above. Exchange students have been able to study series of local newspapers unavailable outside the U.S.S.R. and, sometimes, even to interview Soviet officials. No one who studies the Soviet system intensively would claim that any one of these sources, or even all of them taken together, are fully satisfactory. The social scientist dealing with the U.S.S.R. lacks many "tools," such as survey research on public opinion, that his counterparts concerned with the United States and Western Europe have developed to a high degree. Yet in some ways, the Soviet specialist has an advantage, for he is dealing with a system where decisions are highly centralized and where all general media reflect, however obscurely, the central manipulation. If one can but find the clue, Soviet totalitarian politics may become easier to interpret than the baffling flux that culminates in the expression of the popular will under democratic pluralism.

It should be clear by this point that my principal debt is to the objective scholars and observers who have sifted the great mass of material dealing with Soviet political affairs. Without the numerous systematic studies that already exist, no summary treatment could even be attempted. I am particularly indebted to my colleagues in the University of Wisconsin Russian Area Studies Program for suggestions, and to those elsewhere who have used and criticized the first two editions of this book. I am grateful to Murray Feshbach and Brian Silver for help with the 1970 Soviet census data. Again, however, I must stress that the manner of the treatment and the conclusions are my own, and I must consequently bear full responsibility for them. Frederick A. Praeger first suggested the writing of a concise study of this type. To him and the competent editorial staff of Praeger Publishers, particularly Denise Rathbun, the work owes a great deal indeed. I am indebted to Mildred Busse for typing the complicated manuscript. Lastly, I must acknowledge my great debt to my wife, who made innumerable improvements in both text and illustrations of all three editions.

J.A.A.

Department of Political Science
University of Wisconsin
1973

CONTENTS

MAPS, CHARTS, AND TABLES

Ideology, Politics,
and Government in
the Soviet Union

MAP OF

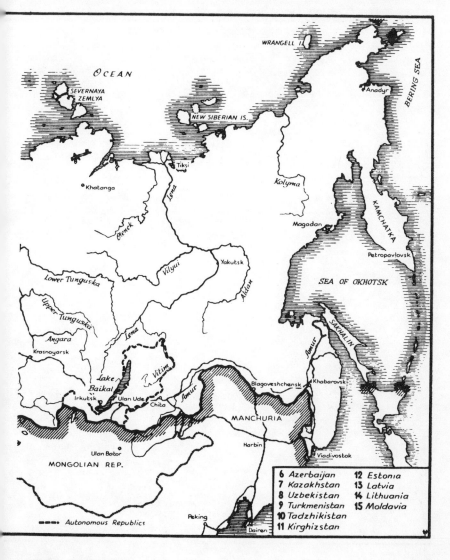

The U.S.S.R. map labels:

OCEAN

SEVERNAYA ZEMLYA

WRANGELL I.

BERING SEA

NEW SIBERIAN IS.

Anadyr

Tiksi

Khatanga

Kolyma

Lena

KAMCHATKA

Olenek

Magadan

Vilyui

Yakutsk

Petropavlovsk

Lower Tunguska

Aldan

SEA OF OKHOTSK

Upper Tunguska

Angara

Lena

Krasnoyarsk

SAKHALIN

Vitim

Amur

Lake Baikal

Blagoveshchensk

Khabarovsk

Irkutsk

Ulan Ude

Chita

Amur

MANCHURIA

Ulan Bator

Harbin

MONGOLIAN REP.

Vladivostok

Peking

Dairen

- - - - Autonomous Republics

6 Azerbaijan	12 Estonia
7 Kazakhstan	13 Latvia
8 Uzbekistan	14 Lithuania
9 Turkmenistan	15 Moldavia
10 Tadzhikistan	
11 Kirghizstan	

THE U.S.S.R.

1

THE BACKGROUND

At the heart of all political systems is a paradox: political power is based on, and in fact requires, the monopoly of force in a given territory, yet force alone is an inadequate basis for a political system. The paradox is frequently resolved by explaining that the monopoly entails only the *legitimate* exercise of force. But what is legitimate depends on the attitudes of the population of the territory, or at least on the attitudes of a dominant element among the population. Attitudes reflect widely held expectations concerning proper political behavior. Taken together, customs and beliefs constitute the political culture of a society. Ordinarily, the effort to determine the political culture involves direct surveys of the attitudes of the population. In a closed system like the Soviet, this approach is rarely available. Instead, one must rely on two indirect sources for understanding Soviet political culture. To a far greater extent than most political systems, the Soviet system is the creation of a consciously articulated body of ideas—the ideology. We shall look at this ideology in Chapter 2 and, at many points in this book, we shall try to assess its influence on the political culture. But political culture, like most popular beliefs and customs, is extremely persistent. The Soviet ideology has enjoyed a near monopoly in public expression for more than fifty years. Nevertheless, it is highly likely that earlier influences, transmitted by word of mouth, by reading the classic Russian literature, and by unconscious family customs, continue to permeate political culture in the U.S.S.R.

In the following pages, those elements of the Russian past

that seem to be related to present Soviet political culture will
be described. It is impossible to establish direct connections
between these aspects of Russian history and Soviet behavior,
particularly since the regime explicitly disavows the connection in most instances. Until the mid-1930's, Communist writers maintained that nearly all Russian development before the
Bolshevik Revolution of 1917, though a necessary stage of social evolution, was nevertheless an outworn and often shame-
ful memory rather than a proud heritage. Since the mid-1930's,
the Soviet regime has been more selective in its evaluation of
pre-Revolutionary history; but the essential break with the past
remains a major element of Soviet Communist thought. The
outside observer, on the other hand, is immediately struck by
the similarities as well as the differences between the Soviet
system and the Czarist regime that prevailed in much the same
territory for centuries prior to the establishment of the U.S.S.R.
Since Czarism was essentially a Russian phenomenon, and the
Russians remain dominant in the U.S.S.R., this chapter will
concentrate on the Russian heritage. Chapter 7 will treat the
significantly different heritages of the large non-Russian minorities.

ABSOLUTISM

One of the most striking parallels between Czarism and Bolshevism is the existence of an unusual measure of centralized,
unrestricted power in both systems. To the student of government at the beginning of this century, Czarist rule was synon-
ymous with autocracy, as indeed it was in the official parlance
of the old regime. It is true that in the twelve years immediately preceding the Bolshevik Revolution, some modifications
were introduced in the autocratic system. Although the institution of an elected legislative assembly (Duma) did enable
public opinion to exercise some pressure upon the Czar, the

government of the Russian Empire remained responsible to him alone. Similarly, if one goes back far enough in the history of the East Slavs—from whom the Russians, along with other nationalities, descended—one finds evidence of embryonic democratic institutions. On the whole, however, Russia has probably had less experience with limited government or representative institutions than any other European country.

Orthodox Church and Czarist State

Prominent among the factors contributing to the absolutistic nature of Russian government was the relation between church and state. The Orthodox faith, to which traditionally an overwhelming majority of Russians have adhered, has been an extremely important element in the country's history—so important, indeed, that some historians (notably Arnold Toynbee) class the Russian Orthodox society as a civilization distinct from that of Western Europe. In the Byzantine Empire, from which the Russians obtained their Christian faith in the late tenth century, Orthodoxy had developed the peculiar institution of "Caesaropapism." In this system, the emperor was both autocratic ruler of the state and supreme head of the church. Consequently, the separation of ecclesiastical and temporal power—whether between Pope and Holy Roman Emperor, or between secular state and church—did not exist. The tension, latent or visible, between these two powers in the West, which prevented either from assuming control of all aspects of life, was largely absent in Byzantium. The Orthodox Church might admonish the ruler, but it had to submit to him and support him, evil though he may have been. This doctrine, transplanted to the East Slavic lands, made the church a bulwark of absolute monarchy, especially after the Czars, in the fifteenth century, proclaimed themselves to be the successors of the Byzantine emperors.

No one has depicted the relationship between Caesaropapism and governmental absolutism more poignantly than the contemporary Russian Nobel Prize novelist, Alexander Solzhenitsyn. During Lent in 1972, in a letter to the official head of the Russian Orthodox Church, Patriarch Pimen, Solzhenitsyn wrote: "A study of Russian history in the last few centuries will show that it might have been incomparably more humane and harmonious if the church had not surrendered its independence and the people had listened to its voice, as for example, in [Roman Catholic] Poland. Alas, with us it has been different for a long time." Solzhenitsyn saw a direct connection, moreover, between the subordination of the Orthodox Church to the Czars and its present manipulation by the Soviet regime: "The entire administration of the church, the appointment of priests and bishops (including even sacrilegious churchmen who make it easier to deride and destroy the church), all of this is secretly managed by the [Soviet] Council for Religious Affairs. A church dictatorially ruled by atheists is a sight not seen in two thousand years." *

The Influence of Mongol Rule

A second major influence in the development of absolutism —some historians consider it to have been more important than the Orthodox doctrine—was the Mongol invasion of the thirteenth century. Living in the broadest portion of the great Eurasian plain, almost unprotected by natural barriers, the East Slavs were easily subjected by the Mongol cavalry. Aside from destroying or dispersing much of the old East Slavic civilization (which for some time had been on the wane), the Mongol invasion gave rise to new distributions of power in Eastern Europe. Indirectly, the principal Russian beneficiaries of Mongol rule were the princes of Moscow, who became the vassals and lieutenants of the khans. While it is not altogether clear

* Translated by Ludmilla Thorne, *New York Times*, April 9, 1972.

where the Mongol khans found their patterns of rule, they required a degree of self-abasement from their subjects commonly associated with Oriental despotisms. The Muscovite princes adopted many of the despotic attitudes and practices of the Mongol rulers, and these attitudes and practices persisted after the princes obtained a position of equality with the surviving Mongol (or Tatar) khans and ultimately subjugated them.

Western Theories of the Divine Right of Kings

In noting these peculiarly Russian experiences that influenced the rise of Czarist absolutism, one should not lose sight of the importance of Western ideas in the establishment of absolute rule. Probably the high-water mark of Czarist autocracy came under Catherine II (the Great) in the eighteenth century. Catherine was German by birth, and most of the intellectual underpinning for her rule was provided by West Europeans. The era was the culmination of the "divine right" theory of monarchy in the West, a justification for absolute rule that had been developed quite apart from the above-noted influences on Russia. In "perfecting" autocracy in the Russian Empire, Catherine and her immediate predecessors were following the almost predominant model of European statecraft. But the special features of the Russian heritage enabled Czarist reality to approach the model more closely than almost any other European country—and to last far longer.

THE "CLASSLESS" SOCIETY

There is a second feature of the Russian heritage that is not nearly so obvious as absolutism. For centuries, most men took social inequality for granted. Distinctions of wealth, rank, even legal privilege, were widespread. One of the most signifi-

cant developments of the nineteenth century was the concern
with such social stratification. As a rule, the phenomenon was
described as a "class" structure, though social thinkers presented, and continue to present, widely varying definitions of
"class." To the casual Western observer, the Czarist Empire
seems almost the epitome of social stratification. The superficial impression is of a glittering, if rather irresponsible, aristocracy; an intense but morbid intellectual milieu; and a
downtrodden though enduring peasantry. There is considerable validity in this picture, but it does not necessarily add
up to a class society in the traditional pattern of Western
Europe. In fact, a whole school of Russian thinkers of the
nineteenth century, the Slavophiles, sharply rejected the idea
that Russia had classes at all comparable to those of the West,
and many Western historians share this viewpoint.* The Slavophiles, indeed, considered the absence of classes in the Russian Empire to be a significant indication of the superiority
of the Russian social order over that of the West, a proof of
Russian Orthodoxy's devotion to human brotherhood.

The Nobility

In Western Europe, so the Slavophiles argued, the nobility
considered itself to be a true aristocracy. Though usually of
the same race and nationality as the rest of its country's population, the nobility had for centuries enjoyed the status of a
hereditary privileged class. As a result, the nobles regarded
themselves as wholly distinct and superior, entitled to rule
and to enjoy the fruits of rule. No doubt there is much that
is exaggerated in this argument. But it does seem to reflect a
fairly common attitude among a group of West European

---

* The Slavophile school, as the name indicates, fervently admired Slavic
(in fact, mainly Russian) traditional culture. It contrasted sharply with the
"Western-oriented" school of nineteenth-century Russian thinkers, which
regarded emulation of Western Europe as a major basis for progress.

nobles with whom the Russians were in close contact. Since the early part of the eighteenth century, the Russian Empire had included the Baltic provinces, where a small ruling class of German origin dominated a Latvian and Estonian peasantry. There, to quote a Baltic German noble of a later generation,

> The person of the peasant, as such, was completely in the background. If one considered him at all, for the most part one did so with the sort of inquisitive interest with which one today examines some interesting species of man or beast from unknown lands.*

Such a concept of class differentiation, while extreme, no doubt influenced the Slavophiles' view of the West European nobility's mentality.

In the Russian lands of the Empire, the position of the upper stratum was different. The nobles were indeed legally and factually distinct from the remainder of the population, and they enjoyed many privileges. Unlike the typical Western noble, however, the Russian noble was essentially a servant of the autocracy. No traditions of family honor or class autonomy shielded him from the full force of absolute rule. Historically, the Czars had made and remade the nobility in accordance with the exigencies of their struggle to strengthen and extend their power. Ivan IV (the Terrible) slaughtered many of the nobles, filling their posts with loyal members of his bodyguard and entourage. Later Czars were somewhat less ruthless, but constantly raised large numbers of new men to the nobility. On the other hand, surviving descendants of the princely families of medieval Russia frequently lived as obscure rustics scarcely distinguishable from the peasants. During the last century of Czarist rule, the equation of nobility

---

* Astaf von Transehe-Roseneck, *Die Reform der bäuerlichen Verhältnisse in Livland, 1765–1804* (Strasbourg: Karl J. Trubner, 1890).

with service to the regime was codified by regularly conferring patents of nobility upon all who had attained high rank in the civil or military hierarchy. Those who had attained top ranks were entitled to pass on their noble status to their sons. Thus Ilya Ulyanov, Lenin's father,* became a hereditary noble on attaining the post of school superintendent.

Lenin's career, though extreme, suggests the lack of regard for hereditary class status common among all but a small group of "great" families in the Russian Empire. Instead of a self-conscious ruling group, attached to the sovereign by concepts of feudal loyalty but jealous of their rights even as against the crown, the Russian nobles constituted essentially a bureaucratic order, though initially they derived their material support from landed estates rather than salaries. In the latter part of the nineteenth century, the nobles' importance even as landlords diminished, and except for a select group who turned to social welfare and educational work in the "zemstvos" (provincial boards with limited legal authority), the landowners as a group did not constitute a decisive factor in the operation of the imperial regime. The real core of the Czarist system was the great bureaucracy of the capital, St. Petersburg (now Leningrad), the military commanders in the field, the governors and police chiefs of the provinces, and the church hierarchy. These officials maintained order, secured obedience to the Czar's commands (which, of course, they often inspired), and even supervised much of the social and economic development of the country. These bureaucrats (the term is used in the sociological rather than the pejorative sense) were often recruited from older noble families, but they were shaped by their careers rather than by their origins; and, as noted above, "new men" were constantly wending their way upward via the bureaucratic system.

* Vladimir Ilich Ulyanov has gone down in history under the name of "Lenin," originally an underground pseudonym.

The Peasantry

Juxtaposed to the bureaucratic nobility was the vast mass of peasants, three-quarters of the entire population. These were "the nation" (*narod*), the "dark people" indeed in the sense of ignorance, but still, as the Russian word for "peasant" (*krestyanin*) suggests, the Christians par excellence. The special regard, almost awe, in which the peasant masses were held indicates the strong populist trend in Russian thought. However, there was a chasm between the idealized image and reality. Until 1861, most of the peasants in the Russian Empire were serfs, the property of noble landlords or (almost as frequently) of the crown. Under Catherine the Great, the peasant had been little better than a chattel slave, subject to removal from his ancestral farm, to almost unrestricted sale as property, and to arbitrary and brutal chastisement. "Emancipation," following some minor reforms earlier in the century, ameliorated the peasant's position, but still his freedom was restricted from two directions. The government kept close watch over his activities through the "land captains." Primary control of the peasant's movement was left to the village community, or *mir*, which, because it was collectively responsible for the tax and redemption payments for the land allotted the peasants at the time of emancipation, would not let its members leave freely. Thus the peasant was subject to the group pressure of his peers as well as to the authority of the government. The power of the *mir* over the individual was by no means a wholly spontaneous development; for centuries, the Czarist regime had in various ways strengthened the *mir* as a convenient instrument of control. But long-established custom also played a vital role.

In many areas of the Russian Empire, the practice of "repartitional tenure" meant that each village commune periodically redistributed its land among the member families. As a result, the individual or the family group had little incentive to undertake long-range improvement of the land. Methods of cultivation tended to be set by custom rather than economic calculation. To a considerable extent, this was the case even in those territories where repartitional tenure did not prevail, for even there the family's allotment of land usually consisted of scattered strips. The size and location of these fragmented holdings required that many of the farming operations be conducted in unison, ordinarily in accordance with long-established patterns. Where new decisions were required, they were made by the *mir* as a collective body in which the less efficient or enterprising members were at least as influential as those who favored modern innovations.

In spite of these circumstances, peasant institutions underwent considerable change in the last years of the Czarist regime. From 1907 on, the government itself fostered these changes in an effort to create a class of "yeomen" farmers attached to the principles of social stability as guarantees for their own property and profits. Measures were envisaged, and to some extent implemented, to break up the *mir,* consolidate the scattered holdings of each peasant family, and thus give fuller scope to the initiative of the individual. There is no doubt that many peasants were eager to become fully independent farmers. By 1917, the less fortunate or less enterprising peasants were beginning to become differentiated in status and attitudes from their more successful brethren, and in some ways this development was accelerated during the confused situation immediately following the revolutions of that year. The more a peasant had, and the more enterprising—and possibly unscrupulous—he was, the more he was apt to receive in the breakup of the nobles' estates. Nevertheless, the peasant whom the Bolsheviks confronted was still deeply immersed in the customary life of his village community.

The Workers

By 1917, the peasants no longer comprised the entire lower stratum. A few million industrial workers gained an inordinately important role in revolutionary activity, both because of their strategic location in the metropolitan centers and railroad junctions and because of the importance ascribed to them by revolutionary doctrine. In the general perspective of pre-Revolutionary history, however, the "proletariat" was relatively insignificant; this was all the more true because the industrial worker was often really a peasant recently, perhaps only temporarily, transplanted to an urban environment.

The Intelligentsia

The rudimentary nature of the middle class was in some ways a more striking difference between pre-Revolutionary Russia and the more advanced Western lands than the lack of individualist farmers, numerous workers, or an independent aristocracy. While the exact relationship between the rise of the European middle classes and the growth of limited, representative government is uncertain, the reciprocal influence of these developments is incontestible. Historically, the middle classes were based on commerce and industry. In the Czarist Empire, however, commercial activities were relatively poorly developed, especially by members of the dominant Russian national group. The post-1890 period saw phenomenal industrial development, exceeding in proportional growth (though not, of course, in absolute increment) that of most of the Western countries. A large part of the industry, however, was controlled by Western investors, and much of the remainder consisted of government enterprises. To the extent to which a Russian commercial and entrepreneurial class had emerged by 1917, it was a new social element, uncertain of its position, relatively unsophisticated, and narrow in its attitudes.

Alongside the businessman, the professional has constituted an essential element of the Western middle class. The usual liberal professions were, of course, represented in the Czarist Empire. Physicians, lawyers, and teachers were numerous and increasingly important. Without the support—economic and psychological—of an independent aristocracy or a self-reliant farmer or business group, however, the professionals tended to become absorbed in the governmental bureaucracy or to spend their lives in frustrating, if altruistic, efforts to improve the lot of the peasantry. Because their professional skills, based on Western experience, provided them with an image of a more rationally organized society, the conditions of Czarist Russia seemed the more repugnant to them. In particular, the illiteracy and high mortality of the peasants appalled the professional groups. Many of those with the most useful skills, such as physicians and teachers (engineers and agricultural technicians, who might have been even more useful in the long run, were scarce and often hardly regarded as professionals), devoted themselves to work in the zemstvo. Others took more revolutionary steps.

Most of the professionals constituted a part of a social group that had no precise Western counterpart, as our very use of the Russian term—intelligentsia—indicates. Generally speaking, membership in the intelligentsia was a matter of self-identification. The highly educated bureaucrat or businessman might or might not regard himself as a member. A half-educated but articulate clerk might aspire to membership. More important than its precise composition was the fact that the intelligentsia, as a comparatively self-conscious and active element, occupied the place between the government and the inarticulate lower classes held by the middle class in Western Europe. The student (including many middle-aged men like Chekhov's "perpetual student"), the scholar, the artist, the professional, tended to constitute the intelligentsia proper. For the most part they were discontented with the situation in the Russian Empire, embarrassed at the "backwardness" of its economic and political development compared to the West (though often simultaneously extolling the inherent superiority of Russian traditions), and ashamed of the oppression and neglect of the peasantry. These attitudes were combined with feelings of frustration over their inability to exert influence on the autocracy, resentment against curbs on intellectual activity, and, often, the bitterness engendered by poverty. Instead of a stabilizing element, the intelligentsia tended to be the spearhead of the forces working for profound disruption of the Czarist order.

THE INTELLECTUAL CLIMATE

The importance of the intelligentsia's dissatisfaction as an element in the climate of opinion favorable to revolution is obvious. But there are other, more subtle ways in which the attitudes of Imperial society seem to have prepared for subsequent developments. The collectivist aspects of the village community hampered individual economic development, and the pressures of conforming to the peer group discouraged independent attitudes. Particularly interesting in this connection is the stress put on unanimous decisions in the rural community. While a considerable measure of discussion took place in village meetings, where all heads of households were, theoretically at least, equal, a decision by majority vote was unacceptable. Instead, village opinion demanded unanimity in the final decision, even if physical coercion was required to secure the minority's assent.

Pressure for Unanimity

At higher levels of Russian society, the demand for unanimity in the village took the form of pervasive censorship of expression. The most obvious side of this censorship was the official one; with varying scope and effectiveness, the regime sought to suppress ideas hostile to it. In some respects, the "censorship of the Left," however, was more effective and more interesting during the last years of the nineteenth century.* The writer or artist who failed to express the concepts of protest and revolt dominant among the intelligentsia was subjected to a type of unofficial ostracism and criticism few could withstand. While the vectors of official and unofficial pressure represented opposing camps, both failed to honor the inviolability of intellectual freedom.

Rejection of Systematic Rationality

The lack of concern on both Right and Left for fixed principles of civil liberties was characteristic of the fragmentary reception in Russia of Western ideas. The Slavophiles, and some of their successors, explicitly rejected the systematic rationality of Western thought. They argued that one of the great merits of Orthodoxy, in contrast to both Catholicism and Protestantism in the West, was its stress upon mystic experience rather than rationalized philosophy. The piety of the cloister rather than the systems of the scholastics was the glory of Orthodox monasticism. To some extent, the intellectual attitudes that underlay this position were shared by the secular intelligentsia. As mentioned earlier, many Russian intellectuals envied Western rationality. Yet, while German and French (less often British) philosophers were widely read in nineteenth- and early twentieth-century Russia, systematic indigenous philosophy developed only haltingly. Ideas were plentiful, and frequently highly original; but they served as spurs to the sentiments and activities of the intelligentsia rather than as starting points for great integrated systems of thought.

---

* Its effectiveness declined in the last two decades of Czarist rule.

In a somewhat related fashion, legal principles remained peripheral to Russian intellectual development. The autocracy provided a system of courts that, after the 1860's, provided for juries in criminal cases—sometimes with startling results. However, since the police possessed the administrative right to exile political offenders, the concept of inviolable rights under law inherent in Western legal systems did not exist. And it is notable that, in protesting the policies of the regime, the Russian intelligentsia laid little stress upon establishment of the rule of law as a safeguard against tyranny.

Intellectual Progress

Again, one should not exaggerate the extent of differences between Western and Russian intellectual achievement. Legal scholarship in the last years of the Czarist Empire was impressive, and one might well have expected it to have a strong impact upon social thinking in the next generation. The rapid growth of scientific thought in Russia, marked by the emergence of figures of world importance such as the chemist Dimitry I. Mendeleyev, the psychologist Ivan P. Pavlov, and the mathematician Nikolai I. Lobachevsky, indicates the acceptance of a kind of rationality that would inevitably have induced more systematic approaches to general problems of knowledge. The very considerable progress in general education, which promised to reduce illiteracy to modest levels within a generation following the reforms of 1905, might have provided a solid foundation for liberal institutions and social progress.

Messianism

One more aspect of the climate of ideas in the Czarist Empire must be mentioned: the tendency toward messianic conceptions of Russia's role in world history. The Slavophile conviction of the superiority of Orthodoxy in the social and intellectual spheres formed one foundation for this view. The Slavophiles' more militant successors, the Panslavs, envisaged a secular mission for the Russian nation—that of uniting all the Slavic peoples, assuming a dominant position in Europe, and reforming the "decadent" West. Except for brief intervals, such radically ethnocentric and expansionist ideas had little influence on official foreign policy. The concept of the civilizing mission of Russia—not basically different from the theories influencing contemporary West European imperialism—was more important. By the end of the nineteenth century, the Russian Empire embraced over 166 million inhabitants in an area of 8 million square miles. Over half of the population was non-Russian. True, many of the remainder were East Slavs, closely related to the Russians, and most of the others were Europeans living in the border areas. The greatest expansion of the Empire had taken place in Asia, however, and there the Czarist proconsuls believed that they were entitled to impose the benefits of Russian culture and material progress.

The Absence of Racist Attitudes

It should be pointed out that the Russians, on the whole, did not share the rigid attitudes of racial superiority and segregation that characterized many West European colonizers. Unlike the West European colonial empires, separated by thousands of miles of ocean from their home countries and inhabited by peoples whose physical characteristics differentiated them from the Europeans, the Russian Empire stretched in an unbroken mass across Eurasia. To a considerable degree, the physical characteristics of the Empire's population represented a series of gradual changes from the blond, semi-"Nordic" types of the Baltic coast to the darker, flatter Mongol features of the Altai. Then, too, in contrast to the dramatic "expansion of Western Europe" in the sixteenth century, Russian contact with non-Europeans had lasted for more than a millennium, involving relationships of subjection as well as ascendancy. Some observers would also ascribe part of the differences in Russian racial attitudes to Orthodox influence, especially as contrasted to northwest European Calvinism. But whatever the reasons, this aspect of Russian heritage—the combination of strong national pride, to the point of a messianic complex, and a relatively tolerant attitude toward racial differences—has exerted an important influence on more recent Soviet contacts with the non-European world.

THE REVOLUTION AND AFTER

It would be fascinating to trace both the constant and the changing aspects of Russian thought and practice under the impact of revolution. Here, however, we can only note the most essential facts of Soviet history; brief as it is, this summary should provide the reader with a sense of chronological development.

The first revolution of 1917, in March, was quite unplanned. Under the terrible strain of World War I, the rigid and inefficient structure of the Czarist regime broke down. For a few months, liberals and moderates imbued with Western concepts of governmental and social order maintained a precarious grip on the central authority. In November, they were swept away, almost without bloodshed, by the Bolshevik Revolution. A few thousand determined revolutionists, guided by the ideological and organizational theories that we shall examine in the next chapter, inherited the place of the Czarist bureaucracy. Among the main reasons for their success was their willingness to promise immediate distribution of land to the peasants (with covert reservations concerning the more distant future) and immediate peace negotiations with Germany.

Within a few months, however, the Bolsheviks were engaged in a desperate struggle against a variety of domestic "counter-

revolutionary" movements, which were sporadically and inef-
fectively supported by the Central Powers and the Western
Allies. By 1920, the Bolsheviks had triumphed fully, except in
some outlying areas of the former Empire, but they did so at a
terrible cost. Millions had died in battle or as a result of famine, and the relatively small industrial and transportation
capital of the country had been largely dissipated. A large part
of the old nobility, intelligentsia, and bureaucracy had fled or
died. These catastrophic events made it easier for the Bolsheviks to carry out the remodeling of Russian society, for much
of the old social fabric had disintegrated. In the early 1920's,
their most urgent need, however, was to ensure a minimal
livelihood for the surviving population and to maintain a
modicum of national strength. The long period of the "New
Economic Policy" (1921–28) was essentially a holding operation in which the Bolshevik leadership sought time to prepare
for the next stage.

Stalin

At the beginning of this period, Lenin, a truly charismatic
figure, became incapacitated (he died in early 1924), and leadership was gradually assumed by one of his less prominent
lieutenants, Joseph V. Stalin. In a series of crafty and ruthless
maneuvers, Stalin defeated and discredited his rivals in the
Communist Party (as the Bolshevik group called itself after
March, 1918). By 1928, Stalin ruled supreme. He then launched
a crash program of industrialization, the so-called Five-Year
Plans. Simultaneously, he carried out the collectivization of
agriculture, forcing the individual peasant-farmers into large
kolkhozes (collective farms). Collectivization was achieved at
the cost of several million lives and a catastrophic drop in food
production; as we shall see, its results are still by no means certain. It did, however, give the Soviet regime complete physical
control of the countryside. The more clear-cut successes of the

Five-Year Plans greatly increased the industrial basis for Soviet military power. In the period between 1934 and 1938, Stalin consolidated his absolute dictatorship by a vast blood purge of the Communist Party, which brought in its wake the destruction of most of the old Bolshevik leadership.

The Crisis of World War II

Scarcely had this crisis passed before the U.S.S.R. was involved in World War II, first as a quasi-ally of the Axis powers, then (when Hitler turned on the U.S.S.R.) as a member of the anti-Axis coalition. The war, which at one point saw Hitler's forces occupying territory that had sheltered more than one-third of the Soviet population, wrought enormous destruction. The Soviet death toll—in the neighborhood of 20 million—was greater than that of any other belligerent, even the defeated powers, and the per-capita death rate higher than that of any other country with the possible exception of Poland and Yugoslavia. Economic losses were also enormous, though the amazing success of Soviet evacuation and rebuilding of industry in the Urals and other regions prevented complete economic collapse. The Nazi invasion revealed that a large proportion of the Soviet population was so alienated from its own government that it welcomed foreign "deliverance." But the cruel policies of the Nazis, combined with the strength of the Communist apparatus and residual Russian patriotism, enabled the Soviet regime to maintain enough popular support to win. It may, perhaps, never be possible to estimate the exact measure in which each member of the anti-Axis coalition contributed to the final victory; but unquestionably, the U.S.S.R.'s contribution was enormous. Consequently, and also as a result of Germany's and Japan's elimination, the prestige of the Communist regime greatly increased, though (as Stalin privately admitted) its material strength had been sapped. The Soviet rulers have since taken advantage of this circumstance to claim that the superiority of the Soviet system has been proved in the test of war.

Khrushchev and His Successors

For seven and one-half years after the end of World War II, Stalin retained his undisputed dictatorial powers. While the U.S.S.R. rebuilt its physical plant, Stalin rigidly maintained barriers to intercourse between the Soviet population and the outside world. His death in March, 1953, unleashed a period of sharp struggle among his lieutenants, culminating in Nikita Khrushchev's victory at the Party meeting in January, 1955, which ordered his rival Georgi Malenkov's resignation. In June, 1957, Khrushchev succeeded in removing his principal rivals (the "anti-Party" group) from all major posts. But he never acquired the undisputed authority that Stalin had enjoyed; and in October, 1964, Khrushchev himself was ousted.

Since 1964, the idea of "collective leadership," frequently proclaimed under Lenin, Khrushchev, and even Stalin, has acquired more significance. Gradually the Party chief, Leonid Brezhnev, has acquired a degree of pre-eminence, but he has carefully avoided (or been obliged to avoid) the personal assertiveness which Khrushchev displayed, to say nothing of the real despotism which Stalin exercised. For a full decade, the Soviet regime has continued, therefore, without an individual dictatorship; it seems safe to assume that the particular brand of government established in the U.S.S.R. does not *require* highly personalized authority.

SUGGESTED READING · CHAPTER 1

The following general histories of Russia are especially valuable.

CLARKSON, JESSE D. *A History of Russia.* New York: Random House, 1961.

ELLISON, HERBERT J. *History of Russia.* New York: Holt, Rinehart, & Winston, 1964.

FLORINSKY, MICHAEL T. *Russia: A History and an Interpretation.* 2 vols. New York: The Macmillan Company, 1953.

PARES, BERNARD. *A History of Russia.* New York: Alfred A. Knopf, 1953.

RIASANOVSKY, NICHOLAS. *A History of Russia.* London and New York: Oxford University Press, 1963.

SETON-WATSON, HUGH. *The Russian Empire, 1801–1917.* Oxford: Clarendon Press, 1967.

SUMNER, B. H. *A Short History of Russia.* New York: Harcourt, Brace & Company, 1949; Harvest paperback, 1962.

THADEN, EDWARD C. *Russia Since 1801: The Making of a New Society.* New York: John Wiley, 1971.

VERNADSKY, GEORGE. *A History of Russia.* New Haven, Conn.: Yale University Press, 1954.

Very competent surveys of the Soviet period of Russian history and its immediate background of revolutionary ferment are:

RAUCH, GEORG VON. *A History of Soviet Russia.* 6th ed. New York: Praeger Publishers, 1972.

TREADGOLD, DONALD W. *Twentieth Century Russia.* Chicago: Rand McNally & Company, 1964.

Those deeply interested in the Bolshevik Revolution and its immediate aftermath should read:

CARR, EDWARD HALLETT. *A History of Soviet Russia.* 6 vols. New York: The Macmillan Company, 1950–64.

CHAMBERLIN, WILLIAM HENRY. *The Russian Revolution.* 2 vols. New York: The Macmillan Company, 1960.

DANIELS, ROBERT V. *Red October: The Bolshevik Revolution of 1917.* New York: Scribners, 1967. A thorough, up-to-date narrative of the principal events of the Revolution.

FISCHER, LOUIS. *The Life of Lenin.* New York: Harper Colophon Paperback, 1964. The most up-to-date and comprehensive Lenin biography, strong on the events of the Revolution, rather weak on ideological development.

SCHAPIRO, LEONARD. *The Origin of the Communist Autocracy.* Cambridge, Mass.: Harvard University Press, 1955; New York: Praeger paperback, 1965.

WOLFE, BERTRAM. *Three Who Made a Revolution.* New York: The Dial Press, 1948; Boston: Beacon Press paperback, 1955.

More specialized works on earlier Russian history of particular interest are:

BILLINGTON, JAMES H. *The Icon and the Axe: An Interpretative History of Russian Culture.* New York: Knopf, 1966. A fresh review stressing religious, intellectual, and artistic factors.

BLACK, CYRIL E. (ed.). *The Transformation of Russian Society.* Cambridge, Mass.: Harvard University Press, 1960. An impressive collaborative effort to compare pre-Revolutionary and Soviet society.

KORNILOV, A. A. *Modern Russian History.* New York: Alfred A. Knopf, 1943. A brilliant treatment of eighteenth- and nineteenth-century Russia by a nineteenth-century Russian historian.

MASARYK, THOMAS G. *The Spirit of Russia.* 2 vols. New York: The Macmillan Company, 1955. A penetrating analysis of Russian thought in the nineteenth century by a great Czechoslovak statesman.

MAVOR, JAMES. *An Economic History of Russia.* 2 vols. New York: E. P. Dutton & Company, 1914. The only comprehensive treatment of economic development under the Czars.

MAYNARD, JOHN. *Russia in Flux.* New York: The Macmillan Company, 1947. A controversial but stimulating interpretation of the main currents of Russian history.

PETROVICH, MICHAEL B. *The Emergence of Russian Panslavism, 1856–1870.* New York: Columbia University Press, 1956. A penetrating study of a crucial period in the development of Russian ideology.

PIPES, RICHARD (ed.), *The Russian Intelligentsia.* New York: Columbia University Press, 1961. An important collection of essays on the situation of the intelligentsia under the Czarist regime and the Soviet system.

ROBINSON, GEROID T. *Rural Russia under the Old Regime.* New York: The Macmillan Company, 1949. A masterful description of the peasant base of old Russia.

WALLACE, DONALD MACKENZIE. *Russia.* New York: Henry Holt & Company, 1905. In spite of its early date, this work has remained unsurpassed for its insight into Russian social conditions.

2

THE IDEOLOGY

In all societies, political culture is an amalgam of traditional, often subconscious, influences, and deliberate indoctrination by dominant institutions. In *The American Dilemma,* Gunnar Myrdal was able to identify an "American Creed," which included those democratic principles inculcated by the schools, the churches, the mass media, and other institutions, as well as those traditions transmitted from generation to generation. Similar political-cultural (deliberate-traditional) amalgams have been detected in most other modern societies. As we have seen, the traditional element is strong in the U.S.S.R., too. What distinguishes the Soviet political system is the near monopoly over the means of overt inculcation of political culture that is held by a single institutional complex, which we may call the "regime." The Soviet regime claims to exercise its monopoly in favor of a single body of ideas, the Communist ideology. Using this ideology, the regime seeks not merely to influence a limited range of political behavior but to remake the entire society. In order to carry out this totalitarian transformation, a new human personality must, according to the ideology, develop. Moreover, the ideology claims to be a systematic, indeed a scientific, doctrine capable of guiding the process of human transformation. An examination of this supposed scientific approach to social problems is the prerequisite to understanding the present Soviet system. For, whether or not the regime has followed its purported blueprint, a doctrine given such intense overt allegiance must, inevitably, exert a strong psychological influence.

THEORETICAL FOUNDATIONS

Officially, the body of Communist ideology is called "Marxism-Leninism."* As the name indicates, the ideology is not an indigenous Russian growth, for Karl Marx and his collaborator, Friedrich Engels, were German by birth. Their works and Lenin's constitute the "classics" of present-day Soviet ideology. Although Lenin built upon the basic Marxist structure, he modified it in many respects—rarely admitting that he had done so, however. His successors have introduced additional modifications, but "Leninism," to a much greater extent than "Marxism," remains the foundation of Soviet ideological thinking. Indeed, several of the most far-reaching modifications of Leninism made by Lenin's immediate successor, the Georgian Stalin, have been disavowed or allowed to fall into disuse. This circumstance is important, not least because it represents a return to the peculiarly Russian aspect of Communism. For Lenin (though of mixed ethnic descent) was Russian to the core, and many of the changes he introduced in Marx's doctrine reflect the influence of the Russian heritage. The return to Lenin promoted by Nikita Khrushchev and his successors (most of whom are Russians) bears the stamp of an earthy Russian mentality. Still, it may be argued, these national influences are secondary; for, through all changes, Marx's aim —the creation of the "new man"—has remained.

Materialism

Materialism, probably the most fundamental premise of the doctrine, has also remained essentially unchanged since Marx. According to Marxism-Leninism, all being is determined by

---

* This chapter draws heavily upon Communist terminology. Its connotation to the Western reader is often quite different from the real meaning of the terms—sometimes designedly so, for Communists are skilled in using words to convey one meaning to the unaware outsider, another to the initiated. To avoid misunderstanding, such terms will be enclosed in quotation marks when first used, and their implications explained.

the nature of the material "base." The situation of mankind is said to depend upon the "relationships of production." In each epoch of human history, given types of tools (using the term in a broad sense) are available, and human labor utilizes them in a certain way. The nature of this relation of man to his tools requires a special form of social organization—"the relationship of production," or "base." All other aspects of human society—family relations, religion, government, law, art, philosophy, literature—are included in the "superstructure." The elements of the superstructure are reflections of the base and change in their nature as man's organized relationship to his tools changes.

Expressed in these simple terms (avoiding the numerous complications and qualifications that Soviet and non-Soviet Marxists have discussed), materialism seems either self-evident or absurd, depending on the philosophical premises of the observer. Accepted implicitly by the Soviet Communist (and apparently by most educated Soviet citizens outside the Party), however, materialism has tremendous psychological implications. The world, all of human existence, is "explained" without reference to God. Consequently, Marxism-Leninism has always been rigorously atheistic, not merely agnostic. No religious influence can encroach (so long as the doctrine is accepted) upon the Communist's loyalty to the ideology and its spokesmen. The world, in both its physical and its human aspects, is explained "scientifically." As a result, the discoveries of the natural sciences receive enormous emphasis in the U.S.S.R. Except in more or less isolated cases—when it seems to conflict with Leninist principles or with the personal interests of a leader of the regime—scientific investigation receives great support. It seems probable, however, that materialism itself (as well as practical necessity) encourages emphasis upon the more immediate aspects of scientific work—those permitting immediate technical application—rather than upon the more abstract elements of scientific thought. Thus, the stress in Soviet activity and publicity is upon the conquest of nature, whether by Sputnik or polar exploration, rather than, for example, on the theory of relativity. Basic theory is often accepted ready-made from foreign sources.

Dialectic

The striking and readily comprehended successes of Soviet science and technology in conquering nature have unquestionably deepened popular confidence in the ability of science to explain and accomplish everything. In turn, this confidence strengthens the ideological teaching of materialism. To many foreign observers it has seemed that the young Soviet-trained citizens are indeed attached to a materialism based principally, if not exclusively, upon the kind of natural scientific materialism known (though not dominant) in the West for two centuries. To the official Communist ideologist, such a view is anathema, for by omitting the second basic aspect of Marxist-Leninist doctrine, the "dialectic," it reduces the system to "vulgar materialism." According to Marx (whom Lenin ostensibly fully accepted on this count), "dialectical materialism" is an indivisible whole. Unfortunately, the dialectic aspects of the doctrine are very difficult to explain concisely—and indeed there appears to be considerable confusion among its adherents (including Marx) in the explanation of this theory. Its fundamental aspect is the simultaneous presence, in all phases of being, of contradictory elements—"thesis" and "antithesis." The interaction of the contradictory elements leads to change—the formation of a new state ("synthesis"), which, however, also contains contradictory elements that will eventually result in change. Marx wisely refrained from applying this recondite concept to the world of nature. His disciple Engels was less cautious; for example, he maintained that the change of water when heat is withdrawn represented a dialectic transformation to—ice! Lenin and subsequent Soviet Marxists have followed this interpretation, which to most outside observers appears to be a meaningless and absurd play on words. For example, Soviet theorists assert that major advances like determination of the structural variability of chromosomes were guided by Soviet scientists' understanding of dialectics. Probably, however, a German biologist who has closely followed Soviet scientific developments is right in concluding that "today as in earlier periods there is a dialectic-materialist interpretation of the results of natural scientific research; but this interpretation is *retrospective*, after the research has been accomplished, and no longer has any influence on the question of what direction research may take or how it may be carried out." * Even in Stalin's last years ideological interference with serious research in the physical sciences declined, although the biological sciences were affected somewhat longer. Stalin, in fact, tended to detach whole fields of knowledge, like linguistics and formal logic, from the schematic division between "base" and "superstructure." In some respects, the return to Leninism after his death meant more ideological content in these fields, but considerable variation continues to exist, especially in the approach to logic. In what are sometimes called the "hard sciences," therefore, Soviet scholars proceed on much the same basis as their Western counterparts.

A major aspect of the dialectic transformation is the "transformation of quantity to quality." According to this principle, minor, imperceptible changes (in "quantity") occur in a substance or state without altering its nature, or "quality." When the accumulation of minor changes reaches a certain point, however, the change of "quality" occurs all at once—the "dialectic leap." This "leap," according to all the "classics," up to and including Lenin, is always sudden—as the example of

* Arnold Buchholz, "Wissenschaftlich-technische Revolution," in *Osteuropa*, XXII (1972), 355. Emphasis in original.

change of water to ice was intended to demonstrate. This explanation probably contains a clue to why Communist theorists are attracted to the dialectic explanation, for it provides a ready justification for revolution. Therefore, Stalin, who was bent upon the consolidation of his dictatorship, feared the "explosive" leap and revised Marxism-Leninism to maintain that dialectic change under some conditions was gradual.

Historical Materialism

The practical importance of the dialectic to Soviet Communism has, however, lain in its relation to the historical development of society rather than in its questionable philosophical validity or in its dubious application to the natural sciences. "Historical materialism," that is, the application of the dialectic to history, supposedly offers the only valid explanation of social development. However doubtful this assertion may be, Marx's original stress upon dialectic development did have the virtue of focusing attention on those elements of change and interrelation of social phenomena that many of his contemporaries and immediate predecessors had neglected. As noted in the discussion of materialism, Marx contended that every stage of history has been marked by divisions of human society corresponding to man's relationship to tools. As the tools change, the relationships change; hence the existing social order becomes unstable as the contradictory elements within it emerge. More specifically, a new dominant class rises to replace the old; at the appropriate time, the new class seizes power by revolution, usually violent. Thus, the feudal nobility replaced the slaveowners of antiquity, and "capitalist" entrepreneurs (the "bourgeoisie") replaced the nobility.

Obviously, the Marxist was really interested in the next stage—the replacement of the bourgeoisie by the industrial workers, or "proletariat," for this final change would usher in the era of the "classless" society, in which man would move toward perfection without further recourse to violent revolutions. From the philosophical standpoint, the insistence on the motivating force of class conflict throughout all previous human history, to be superseded at an arbitrary time by harmonious progress, seems untenable. Psychologically, however, the explanation has its appeal. It accepts, in part, the hard-headed skepticism of the cyclical theories of history—each stage of human society develops, unfolds its maximum possibilities, and then declines, to be replaced by a new cycle of human development. The Marxist type of cyclical development, however, avoids ultimate pessimism by the reassurance that, in terms of human progress, each cycle is higher than the preceding one. Moreover, each cycle constitutes a prerequisite for a still more progressive cycle. Finally, a stage (close at hand) is reached in which the necessity of the violent replacement of an outworn social structure ends, and the type of unilateral progress espoused by the eighteenth-century utopians appears. In considerable measure, then, Marxism-Leninism has appealed to both optimists and skeptics; its avowed contempt for "utopias" is coupled to a promise of perfection in this world.

Imperialism

Still, the emphasis of the ideology is upon the transformation from "capitalism" to "socialism." Prior to Lenin, this transformation was predicted for an advanced industrial country in which the workers constitute the overwhelming majority of the population. Marx developed immensely elaborate arguments to show that all value was produced by the workers, but that the capitalists systematically appropriated the "surplus value," i.e., all above that which the workers need to reproduce their kind. The argument appears to have little factual validity or even systematic relation to the rest of historical materialism, but its appeal for workers who are really destitute has been enormous. In the early part of this century, however, Lenin was confronted with the necessity of explaining why workers in many West European countries were not becoming progressively more impoverished, but, on the contrary were making economic strides. His answer was the theory of "imperialism, the highest stage of capitalism." The essence of his argument was that the immensely concentrated capitalist monopolies in advanced industrial countries could afford to bribe their proletariats to assist the capitalists in "exporting exploitation" to less developed areas where (one could deduce from Marxist theory) capital returns would be higher. Thus, improvement of the condition of a minority of the workers (West European whites) was achieved at the expense of a huge majority of workers and peasants (largely colored) in colonial and semi-colonial countries.

The Weakest Link

In retrospect, Lenin appears to have been uncannily foresighted in advancing a theory of imperialism so well adapted to present Communist appeals to the underdeveloped nations. At the time, however, he was more concerned with the course to be taken by the proletariat of Western Europe and, above all, with the immediate future of revolution in Russia. It is true that Lenin hesitated for a long time before definitely asserting that a "socialist" revolution could occur in so backward a country as Russia, but he maintained, at an early date, that a "bourgeois" revolution in Russia could ignite "proletarian" revolutions throughout Europe. According to Lenin's theory of the "weakest link," revolution would not occur first in the more advanced industrial countries, where the workers were temporarily bought off by minor concessions, but in a country that was in the initial and more painful stages of industrialization. Such a country's capitalists, though in an early stage of development, had to compete with those of more advanced countries in securing colonies and spheres of influence. To do so, the capitalists (like those in heavily industrialized countries) used the state machinery, the government of their country, as an instrument. As the competition among the capitalist-controlled governments became more severe, it was attended by international friction, armaments races, and, eventually, war—World War I. These developments imposed terrible burdens upon the working classes of all the competing and warring nations. These burdens were most severe, to the point of being unendurable, upon the small, weak proletariat and the larger, inarticulate peasantry of the country that was only in the initial stage of industrialization, but that was fully engaged in the unequal imperialist contest. This country was, of course, Russia; and the theory justified what Lenin was really most interested in asserting—that Russia was ripe for revolution.

THE DIRECTIVES

Russia was ripe for *a* revolution, but not yet inevitably drawn to *proletarian* revolution. For Lenin, as for Marx, the strongly deterministic theory of historical materialism was accompanied by an insistence (which many critics have felt to be philosophically inconsistent) upon the need for conscious, deliberate human action to speed and smooth the course of social development. Both Marx and Lenin maintained that theory and action are inseparable, but Lenin's emphasis on organizing a revolution was much stronger than Marx's. Indeed, many students of Lenin's work have felt that he was primarily interested in social engineering rather than in social theory.

The Party

To carry out the proletarian revolution, according to Lenin, a highly organized party was necessary. Without the leadership of this "vanguard of the proletariat," the working class, he said, lacked consciousness of its own true interests, to say nothing of the ability to implement them. This party (which of course turned out to be the Bolsheviks, Lenin's own faction of the Russian Social Democratic Workers Party) should embrace all the "conscious" elements of the proletariat and persons of other classes (like Lenin himself) who adhered to the proletarian cause. All members, Lenin held, must actively participate in the party's work, which, under the conditions of the Czarist regime, had to be illegal, therefore conspiratorial. But even where the party was legal (as was briefly the case in Russia), it must retain a conspiratorial substratum. In order to bring about the revolution, all means are legitimate: "Morality is that which serves to destroy the old exploiting society and to unite all toilers around the proletariat." * As recently as November, 1970, Brezhnev quoted this dictum of Lenin's as a guideline for all Communists.†

Democratic Centralism

The guiding organizational principle of the party was "democratic centralism." According to Lenin, this concept meant choosing leaders (in a pyramidal system of indirect election) by the rank and file, followed by binding decisions from above. Between elections, the party leaders were supreme, and any effort to agitate or combine against their decisions was treason to the party. Similarly, party policies might be debated openly (in the appropriate party meetings or committees) before decisions were made; after that no opposition was permitted. How "democratic centralism," still nominally the guiding organizational principle of the Communist Party of the Soviet Union, works in practice we shall consider in the next chapter. Let us simply note here that, in pre-Revolutionary times,

---

* *Sochineniya* (Leningrad: Partizdat, 1935), XXV, 392.
† *Pravda*, November 25, 1970.

debates and elections could not take place with any regularity in the underground party. Hence, democratic centralism meant, in practice, Lenin's continued domination. Even after the Revolution, however, he usually avoided the naked application of force within the party to accomplish his purposes.

Revolution

In his last years, Marx had considered the possibility of a peaceful victory of the proletariat. He held that in countries where elections and representative government had some meaning (specifically in Great Britain and the United States) the workers' parties might secure power by winning control of the legislative bodies. Ultimately, Lenin rejected this possibility:

> It [the capitalist state] cannot be replaced by the proletarian State (the dictatorship of the proletariat) through mere "withering away," but, in accordance with the general rule, can only be brought about by a violent revolution.*

Lenin did, however, envisage one exception:

> One cannot deny that in individual cases, as exceptions, for example in some small state, it is *possible* that after the victory of the social revolution in a large neighboring state the bourgeoisie would peacefully give up its power if it became convinced of the hopelessness of resistance and preferred to save their heads.†

For decades, Lenin's dicta on the necessity of violent revolution were not questioned by Soviet leaders (though often tacitly ignored, for diplomatic reasons). In 1956, however, Nikita Khrushchev and other Soviet spokesmen referred to the possibility of a "parliamentary path to socialism." They denied that this constituted a contradiction of Lenin, and referred somewhat vaguely to exceptions he had envisaged. Apparently,

---

* *State and Revolution* (New York: Vanguard Press, 1929), p. 128.
† *Sochineniya* (4th ed.; Moscow: Gosudarstvennoe Izdatelstvo Politicheskoi Literatury, 1949), XXIII, 57.

the exception the latter-day Soviet leaders really had in mind was the "small country" Lenin referred to (again with considerable prescience) in the passage just quoted. Specifically, Soviet spokesmen alluded to the "peaceful" Communist takeover in Czechoslovakia, in 1948. This coup had indeed been accomplished without much bloodshed; but it was brought off by mass demonstrations, hoodlumism, the threat of unchecked violence by Communists within the country, and the veiled hint of intervention by overwhelming Soviet forces strategically deployed on almost all of the Czechoslovak frontiers.

In contrast to the monolithic rigidity demanded by Stalin, recent Soviet practice has granted the satellite regimes (some Communist regimes like Yugoslavia, are *not* Soviet satellites) a certain degree of flexibility in conduct of local affairs. But all orthodox Communists agree that, however the "workers' party" comes to power, it must establish a "dictatorship of the proletariat." The purpose of the dictatorship is to suppress the exploiting classes (bourgeoisie and remnants of the nobility) and prepare the way for "socialism." Socialism, in its turn, is (according to Marx, Lenin, and their Soviet successors) a necessary transitional stage to true "Communism." Under socialism, the means of production are placed in the hands of the workers' state; private enterprise in commerce, manufacturing, or farming is eliminated as quickly as feasible. Legal and social controls remain necessary, however, not only to suppress remnants of the exploiting classes, but to ensure proper work and social behavior on the part of workers and peasants who still are influenced by "remnants of bourgeois mentality." The principle of socialism must be "from each according to his ability, to each according to his work."

Socialism in One Country

Both Marx and Lenin had thought that the stage at which compulsion is still necessary would be brief. To Marx, the great economic machine built by capitalism, once in the hands of the workers, would be almost able to furnish the abundance of goods required by the formula of true Communism—"from each according to his ability, to each according to his needs." Lenin realized that such abundance would not be achieved for many years by the backward Russian economy, but he believed that the revolution, once started, would, via chain reaction (to use an anachronistic analogy), spread to the more industrialized countries. Then the workers' governments of these countries, coming to the rescue of the Russian socialist state, which had shown them the way, would aid Russia to build up its economy rapidly. Lenin never gave up this hope, but, being practical, he concentrated in his last years upon strengthening the proletarian dictatorship achieved in Russia. This was the beginning of the practice of "socialism in one country," which Stalin elevated to the level of theory. To develop the Russian economy rapidly without outside aid, a Spartan regime of material privation was required, resembling the early period of capitalism with its harsh conditions of labor, long hours, and bare subsistence wages. Indeed, one Bolshevik economist explicitly avowed the necessity of a period of "the primitive accumulation of capital under socialism" at the expense of the mass of the population. Though Stalin never officially accepted the theory of "primitive accumulation," it seems to have been his real guide in the frightful deprivations occasioned by the collectivization of agriculture and the industrialization of the early Five-Year Plans (1928–41). Soviet leaders assert today that the U.S.S.R. has reached a stage where economic progress is compatible with the provision of considerable consumers' goods. But the "primitive accumulation" theory in fact, though not in name, is still the Communist prescription for underdeveloped countries.

The Omnipotent State

Many Marxists (even in the U.S.S.R.) had anticipated that, as socialism developed, the state and its repressive organs

would gradually diminish in scope. Stalin, however, sharply
denied this contention:

> We stand for the withering away of the state. At the same time
> we stand for strengthening of the dictatorship of the proletariat,
> which is the mightiest and strongest state power that has ever
> existed. The highest development of state power with the object
> of preparing the conditions *for* the withering away of state power
> —that is the Marxist formula. Is it contradictory? Yes, it is "con-
> tradictory." But this contradiction is bound up with life, and it
> fully reflects Marx's dialectics.*

This passage suggests the psychological utility of the concept of the dialectic, however dubious its theoretical relevance
may have been. In practice, the emphasis on the increased
power of the state meant not only forced industrialization and
collectivization, but the maintenance of a vast military establishment and a ubiquitous police. In fact, Stalin, in the 1930's,
placed greater stress upon the need for defending the Soviet
Union (increasingly identified in his speeches with the Russian nation) than upon preparing the economic basis for Communism. After 1933, the rise of Nazi power in Germany
provided more than adequate reason for this emphasis. The
view of the Soviet state as the "fortress of revolution" in a hostile "capitalist encirclement" long predated any major threat
from what the Communists described generically as "fascist"
regimes, however. Even in Lenin's day, foreign Communist
parties had been obliged to subordinate their immediate interests to the aim of building up Soviet strength. Under Stalin,
this process was carried to extreme lengths. At the same time,
he contended that the successes of socialism in the U.S.S.R.
made both its foreign and domestic enemies (the "remnants of
the exploiting classes" and those controlled by "bourgeois
mentality") more desperate in their efforts to overthrow the

* Joseph V. Stalin, *Works* (Moscow: Foreign Languages Publishing
House, 1955), XII, 381.

Soviet regime. This theory was the doctrinal justification for the Great Purge of the 1930's and the maintenance of arbitrary and ruthless police controls. After Stalin's death, the theory of the increasing antagonism of internal enemies was officially repudiated, doubtless because it was recognized as a weapon more readily turned against the Communist Party itself than against the Party's real enemies.

Transition to Communism

The role of the state is very intimately related to the transition to full Communism, the ultimate goal of all Marxists. While stressing this goal, Marx himself was wise enough to avoid setting a precise schedule for its attainment or defining its characteristics. Both Lenin and Stalin were equally cautious. In 1961, however, when Khrushchev was at the height of his power, the Soviet Communist Party adopted a new program declaring that the U.S.S.R. was making the transition toward full Communism. The "material and technical basis," the program declared, would be completed by 1980. By that time, two basic prerequisites were to "come close" to being attained: the provision of goods "to each according to his needs"; and the establishment of a single system of public ownership of the means of production in contrast to the present division between "socialist" (state-owned) and "cooperative" property.

To Each According to His Needs—or Work?

Neither the 1961 program nor earlier Communist writings ever implied that the formula "to each according to his needs" could mean satisfaction of unlimited desires. Instead, material production would be fully adequate to supply real necessities. Once abundance was assured, concern for material things would diminish, so that "normal" persons would be wholly satisfied with a moderate quantity of goods. Each would work according to his ability without concern for material reward. The rules of "Communist conduct" would become "an organic need and habit." Anything short of this kind of abundance, however, would not be full Communism, for it would not permit the psychological transformation that would liberate the "new man" from inordinate material concerns; hence Soviet spokesmen derided what they called Chinese attempts to attain a "Communism of paupers." Discussion immediately following the 1961 program envisaged a gradual transition to the principles of full Communism through the replacement of the money-exchange system with free distribution. Medical services and education were already identified as free items. By 1980, noon lunches, local transportation, and housing (including heat and utilities) would, Soviet writers speculated, also be free to all.

Since Khrushchev's ouster a gradual, subtle shift in this projection has occurred. The relatively minor trend toward salary equalization has ended. There has been little if any increase in "public consumption funds" (i.e., the proportion of personal income, about one-fourth, derived from benefits distributed outside the money wage system). More important it is recognized that even in areas like medical care, which have been supposed to be free for decades, individuals may supplement their benefits by private payment. One article even suggested that children might pay for nursing-home care for aged parents. Still more important, there has been a growing trend to relate individuals' benefits from public-consumption funds to their contribution. Recently, this principle has been advocated even for scholarships in higher education: "The stipend, as one form of conferring material goods at the expense of public funds, should share with, say, old-age pensions and temporary disability allowances the property of being directly related in size to the amount and quality of work done previously by the member of society in question. This corresponds completely with the present-day nature of public funds, a large portion of which is distributed according to just such a principle." *

Personal vs. Private Property

Under full Communism, some forms of personal property (a small collection of favorite books is sometimes mentioned as an example) would be legitimate. But—to cite another Soviet example—why should anyone want several suits of clothes, when he could select a free suit from the rack whenever he needed it? For the time being, such relatively minor items of property were tolerated, but more valuable types of property were under attack in the early 1960's. Construction (by individuals or cooperatives) of private dwellings was particularly suspect. An important novel by a regime spokesman, Vsevolod Kochetov, portrays the Party pressures on a veteran Communist to surrender the house he has built for public use as a day nursery. His Party superiors admit that he is lawfully entitled to his house but contend that a man with his attachment to private property cannot remain a Communist in good standing. By the late 1960's, a significantly different official attitude prevailed. Construction through private means—with resulting differences in standards of living—was hailed as a major method of overcoming the housing shortage. A 1969 article advocating real communal living arrangements denounced the "bourgeois" attitude "my home is my castle," but the author was obliged to emphasize that joining a commune was strictly a matter of individual preference. The reversal in attitudes toward private transportation has been even more sweeping. Khrushchev firmly rejected mass production of private automobiles, experimenting instead with a kind of car-rental service (which under full Communism

* *Izvestia*, October 22, 1970, as translated in *Current Digest of the Soviet Press*, XXII, No. 42, 22.

would, of course, have been simply a "car-borrow" service).
By the end of the 1960's, the hopeless inadequacies of this
experiment were publicly admitted. A large-scale program
envisaged an annual auto production of about 1,500,000 by
1975. Even if this goal is attained, Soviet citizens will have far
fewer wheels than West Europeans—let alone Americans. As
late as 1970 even Moscow had only one auto per hundred
inhabitants. But increased private ownership is now officially
regarded (possibly because Brezhnev himself is an avid
motorist) as a benefit, not a curse.

There are several ways in which the developments just
described can be viewed. One aspect, certainly, is the enormous
claim on resources and output that a trend like private auto-
mobile ownership places upon a society. Other aspects (considered in Chapter 6) are the effects on industrial and agricultural organization of developments like renewed reliance on
material rewards and their implications for continuing social
inequality. To a considerable degree renewed concessions to
private ownership constitute part of the regime's efforts to
stimulate lagging production by making material rewards
more attractive. At this point in our treatment, the principal
concern is the implications for the basic ideology. The essence
of Marxism-Leninism, as noted earlier, is the fundamental
importance of the base, i.e. relationships of production. According to the orthodox viewpoint, the basic change from
capitalist to socialist ownership of the means of production is
the fundamental way by which the "new man," with his
changed attitudes toward work and consumption, is created.
The Soviet ideology continues to stress absolute control of
major production means by the central authority. One article
indeed went so far as to say that "workers' collectives" (i.e.,
control of each plant by its own labor force, as practiced in
Yugoslavia and briefly in Czechoslovakia) would be more
regressive than "monopoly capitalism" itself, which at least
concentrates management.

Increasingly Soviet authors have asked how it is possible for bourgeois, individualistic attitudes to persist after a half-century of socialism. One answer is that they creep into the U.S.S.R. from capitalist countries—but this scarcely explains why these influences find such ready acceptance.

All of this ["petty bourgeois love of abundance in material goods and pleasure"] has already become the scourge of capitalist society in the West, and from there the tendencies reach us. The power of things will doubtless become a serious problem in the raising of new generations.*

Another answer is the inadequacy of indoctrination. In spite of the enormous indoctrination apparatus discussed in Chapter 4, earlier Soviet leaders did not place prime reliance on re-education as a device for constituting the "new man." Stalin was probably too preoccupied with more immediate problems, but, as noted above, he was strictly orthodox in assuming that the transformation of the economy he directed would in itself entail a transformation of attitudes. Khrushchev was generally optimistic about the imminence of a fundamental alteration of personality. His more pessimistic successors appear to be toying, at the least, with the notion of education as the main means for preparing for full Communism, not merely an auxiliary to the change in production relationships. As early as 1967 a professor wrote in *Pravda* that Communism could not be achieved until the "upbringing of the people in accordance with the special features and principles of a Communist society" was completed. He added, significantly, that this meant that the state and its authoritative regulation could not wither away until it had completed supervising this upbringing. As will be discussed in Chapter 5, this view is in line with the increasing reliance upon legal regulation in the U.S.S.R.

* I. Yefremov in *Komsomolskaya Pravda*, January 28, 1966, as translated in *Current Digest of the Soviet Press*, XVIII, No. 6, 17.

But the development poses problems for the Soviet system in two respects. Although the concept of a schoolmaster-state has had currency from time to time in Western societies, it is fundamentally contrary to Marxist-Leninist ideology. Furthermore, even the most sanguine educationalists recognize that major changes in social attitudes are matters of generations. Consequently, primary reliance on indoctrination must mean a very long postponement of the kind of social relations which accompany full Communism. In November 1967 another leading academic figure pointed out in *Pravda* that "The period of the evolution of socialism into Communism will no doubt take a rather long time, considering the scale of the tasks that must be solved." Just three weeks earlier Brezhnev himself had strongly implied that the "rather long time" would be more than half a century. These hints have been accompanied by a tacit neglect of the 1961 program (although officially it is still valid) in favor of less pretentious proclamations made at subsequent Party congresses in 1966 and 1971. To a skeptical outside observer, this change in emphasis seeems only prudent. As will appear in Chapter 8, the Soviet Union has faced numerous reversals in foreign policy since the period when Khrushchev could see "the shining image of a [Communist] Party that is marching forward victoriously throughout the whole world" toward the 1961 program's achievement of "the final settlement of the contradictions between capitalism and Communism in the world arena in favor of Communism." Moreover, the dissensions within the "socialist camp" make attainment of a favorable international milieu for full Communism highly problematic. Khrushchev's promise of a material base for Communism was explicitly based on overtaking the United States in most branches of material production by 1970. In fact, the most careful analyses indicate that the absolute production gap between the United States and the U.S.S.R. may even have widened, while the relative position of the American gross national product remains in the neighborhood of twice the Soviet Union's.

Marxism-Leninism—A Science?

The prudential considerations just examined explain the post-Khrushchev leadership's retreat from the emphasis on full Communism, but they cannot relieve its ideological discomfort. Obviously, the Soviet citizens who suffered terribly for decades and, more recently, endured considerable deprivation in order to move toward Communism will be disheartened if the regime reneges on the definite promise of the 1961 program: "The Party solemnly proclaims: The present generation of Soviet people shall live under Communism."

But eliminating the timetable for attaining Communism would not merely cost the regime popularity. Communist ideology has always insisted that Communism is not just a highly desirable goal that one should strive to attain but a historical development that can be scientifically predicted. According to the ideology, Marxism-Leninism is just as scientific in its analysis of social development as are the natural sciences. Again, to the outside observer, historical materialism exhibits little if any ability to predict—a major attribute of true science. Marx predicted the increasing impoverishment of the proletariat in the industrialized countries; the opposite came to pass. Lenin adapted the original theory by adding the new concept of imperialism. Lenin himself, regarding imperialism as the last stage of capitalism, predicted imminent world revolution. When, instead, dictatorships like Nazism arose, Communist ideologues declared that these "fascist" regimes represented capitalism's final attempt to stave off revolution. Obviously, any theory can be "preserved" if it is altered whenever factual developments contradict it. But such a theory has neither predictive utility nor scientific value.

Occasionally, the spokesmen of Soviet Communism admit

past ideological errors. Stalin, in 1941, "corrected" Engels's derogatory evaluation of the role of the Russian commander Mikhail I. Kutuzov in the Napoleonic wars. Two decades later, Khrushchev told a Romanian audience that Lenin's views on the inevitability of war were subject to revision. The reversal of a tenet advanced by Stalin (who has, in fact, been dropped as a "classic") was noted above. Ordinarily, however, Soviet Communist statements stress the continuity and consistency of Marxist-Leninist doctrine. As a recent theoretical article put it, "a particular statement" of Lenin's might be "out of date," or conceivably a new "law" might be discovered; but Marxism-Leninism as a theory is irreplaceable. This emphasis, instilled by an unchallenged system of indoctrination, has tended to strengthen the Soviet citizens' belief that Marxism-Leninism provides not only a sure guide to social development but an absolute assurance of eventual human perfection.

Until recently, the association of the claims of the ideology with the manifest advances of natural science and technology lent powerful support to this belief. The attainment of Communism, however, is by far the most important development the ideology envisages. Therefore, once a prediction of the time for attaining Communism has been publicly incorporated into the body of the ideology, indefinitely postponing the time is tantamount to renouncing the predictive power of the ideology. The problem, then, goes beyond mere disappointment of the citizenry; Soviet citizens could actually lose faith in Communist ideology.

Thus far, the regime appears to be temporizing, tacitly dropping the emphasis on attaining Communism, but avoiding a public revision of the timetable. Earlier faulty predictions could be explained away, since either they were made by theoreticians (like Marx and Lenin) who had not yet attained power, or (as in the case of Stalin's errors) they were not so intimately related to the sacrifices and aspirations of the Soviet people. The 1961 predictions are painfully contemporary; in view of the enormous publicity given to the program before 1965, it is hard to see how the present generation can be induced to forget these predictions. Moreover, since the regime that made them had enjoyed power for forty-four years, the Soviet population is not likely to forgive it its manifest inability to predict. Nevertheless, Marxism-Leninism has shown itself to be a remarkably persistent and flexible doctrine. Its skilled ideologues may yet find a way to restore its credibility.

Marxism-Leninism—A Dogma?

There is, however, another side to the unavowed flexibility of Marxist-Leninist doctrine. Because the basic tenets are actually subject to revision, there is no dogma in the true sense of the word. The dominant element in the Communist Party determines what is orthodox; those who cling to another interpretation, even one undisputed in earlier years, become heretics, and no exegetical appeal to the "classics" can save them. Obviously, this aspect of the ideology strengthens the absolutist claims of the current leadership. By opening up a broad area of ideological uncertainty, it also promotes a high degree of dynamism in the system. The Soviet Communist knows that he cannot justify himself by ideological orthodoxy; consequently, he tries to assure his position by maximum practical service to the regime and by anticipation of its shifting theoretical requirements. For the hard core of the regime's supporters, therefore, faith in the ideology as a consistent belief system is not the only basis for loyalty.

SUGGESTED READING • CHAPTER 2

The "classics" of Soviet ideology, according to the official definition, embrace the works of Karl Marx, Friedrich Engels, V. I. Lenin, and—until the mid-1950's—Joseph Stalin. Most are available in English, but many of them are of interest mainly to specialists in social thought. The few listed below are among the most important for an understanding of the U.S.S.R. and are most readily comprehensible to the nonspecialist.

LENIN, VLADIMIR I. *Imperialism* and *State and Revolution*. New York: The Vanguard Press, 1929, and many other editions. Two of the basic political works of the founder of Bolshevism. *Imperialism* tries to show that capitalism is to blame for colonialism and war, and that revolution will occur in the "weakest link," while *State and Revolution* sets forth Lenin's concept of the Party and the revolution it is to accomplish.

STALIN, JOSEPH V. *The History of the Communist Party of the Soviet Union (Bolsheviks)*. New York: International Publishers, 1939, and many later editions also published by Communist agencies. A completely distorted history, but important as the book of indoctrination under Stalin. The section on "Dialectical and Historical Materialism" is a summary of Stalin's version of Marxism.

STALIN, JOSEPH V. *Problems of Leninism*. New York: International Publishers, 1942. An earlier and more extensive ideological work. Since Stalin's death, a new *History of the Communist Party of the Soviet Union* (Moscow: Foreign Languages Publishing House, 1960) has superseded Stalin's version. While not yet a "classic," the new book (which is scarcely less distorted) plays an important part in current Soviet indoctrination.

Critical works by non-Soviet writers:

DE GEORGE, RICHARD. *Soviet Ethics and Morality*. Ann Arbor: University of Michigan Press, 1969. A balanced analysis of an increasingly important aspect of the ideology.

HISTORICUS. "Stalin on Revolution," *Foreign Affairs,* January, 1949. A brief but revealing discussion of Stalin's real consistency in advocating world revolution.

HUNT, ROBERT N. C. *The Theory and Practice of Communism*. New York: The Macmillan Company, 1954; Baltimore: Pelican paperback, 1964. The best survey of the development of Communist ideas from Marx through Stalin.

MADISON, BERNICE Q. *Social Welfare in the Soviet Union*. Stanford: Stanford University Press, 1968. The history and present organization of family and child welfare activities, based on several visits to the U.S.S.R. and careful, unbiased examination of printed materials.

MARCUSE, HERBERT. *Soviet Marxism.* New York: Columbia University Press, paperback, 1958. A personal but stimulating interpretation by a professor who has since become a guiding figure among the "New Left" in Germany and the United States.

MESZÁROS, ISTVÁN. *Marx's Theory of Alienation.* London: Merlin, 1970. An unorthodox Hungarian Communist's attempt—with critical reference to Soviet experience—to make Marxism-Leninism relevant to modern conditions.

MEYER, ALFRED G. *Leninism.* Cambridge, Mass.: Harvard University Press, 1957; New York: Praeger paperback, 1962. A comprehensive and objective analysis of Lenin's theories. related to his personality and political objectives.

MOORE, BARRINGTON. *Soviet Politics: The Dilemma of Power.* Cambridge, Mass.: Harvard University Press, 1950. A brilliant attempt to show how Bolshevik ideas changed when the Communists were confronted with the problems of running a great country.

OSBORNE, ROBERT J. *Soviet Social Policies: Welfare, Equality, and Community.* Homewood, Ill.: Dorsey paperback, 1970. An excellent survey, with much statistical data, of recent Soviet welfare policy and its relation to ideology.

WETTER, GUSTAV A. *Dialectical Materialism: A Historical Survey of Philosophy in the Soviet Union.* New York: Praeger, 1958. A thorough examination of the development of Soviet philosophical concepts (especially the philosophy of science) by a Jesuit priest who formerly directed the Vatican's Collegium Russicum.

3

THE PARTY

The Communist Party is the core institution of the Soviet
political system. Much confusion results, however, from identification of this "party" with the familiar parties of pluralist
political systems. In a pluralist system, there are almost always
two or more parties. The leaders of each party assume the continued existence of at least one opposing party, though they
devoutly hope to keep their opponents out of power, in the
role of "loyal opposition." Each party acts as a legitimate institution for articulating the political demands of a number of
groups in the society. In a multiparty system, the range of demands articulated by each such party is comparatively narrow,
for every set of interests tends to be represented by a different
party. In a two-party system, each party not only articulates a
wide range of interests but also serves to "aggregate" these interests—that is, to combine and compromise them in a way
that usually promotes the smooth functioning of the pluralist
political system as a whole.

In its conception, the Soviet Communist Party was an entirely different phenomenon. As indicated in Chapter 2, Lenin
regarded the Party as the indispensable instrument by which
the Marxist vision of a perfect society was to be attained. From
the outset, the Party was a conspiratorial instrument for over-
throwing the existing Czarist political system rather than a
legitimate instrument for articulating demands within the system; the compromises that inevitably attach to legitimacy were
rejected by Lenin, who saw them as tantamount to "reform-
ism." Following the Revolution, the Party was the essence of
the "dictatorship of the proletariat," a role it held for four

decades. In this capacity, the Party (which became officially known as the "Communist Party" in 1918, though the term "Bolshevik" was retained until 1952) was explicitly given the monopoly of political articulation; all other parties were suppressed. At the same time, Lenin and his followers rejected the concept of the single party as an overarching institution of interest aggregation, for they regarded the Party as a force to transform, rather than to mediate, the interests and the political culture of the existing society. The Communist Party became the institutional guardian and interpreter of the ideology and was charged with indoctrinating the population with the ideas and values that would make them psychologically capable of living under full Communism. All of these functions of the Party are avowed by the Soviet regime today.

The 1961 Party program implied that the Party will continue even after full Communism is attained. In 1968, faced with the liberalization tendencies in Czechoslovakia, Soviet spokesmen drastically re-emphasized the monopoly of the Party in political affairs and ideological interpretation.

In view of the enormous importance that Lenin ascribed to the Party, it is hard to imagine that it could ever have been eclipsed. Yet many observers have viewed Stalin's career as a victory over the Communist Party itself. There is much to recommend this view. Because of his bitter animosity toward the Old Bolsheviks, Lenin's companions, Stalin evidently distrusted the Party, which they symbolized. As an absolute dictator, he distrusted any institutional locus of power. Consequently, he limited the sway of the Party, devolving many functions in the execution of his will upon state organs, particularly (as will appear in Chapter 5) the police. It took, however, all of the power of an absolute ruler to reduce the scope of the Party. Even then, Stalin never tried to reduce the theoretical significance of the Party. Every Communist was taught that the Party was the only infallible guide to the course of history and that its command was beyond question. For the most part, the indoctrinating agencies of the Party (or agencies intimately associated with the Party indoctrination machine) transmitted the teachings of Marx, Engels, and Lenin, even though they were partially distorted by Stalin's reinterpretations. From his adolescence on, the Communist therefore is taught to accept the Party as the essential institution of the Soviet system.

As a result, it is scarcely surprising that the Party regained complete ascendancy soon after Stalin's death. This re-emergence of the Party as the dominant institutional force in the U.S.S.R. is very closely associated with the rise of Nikita Khrushchev. Even in Stalin's lifetime, Khrushchev had insisted on the paramount position of the Party: "The Party is responsible for everything. Whether it is Army work, Chekist [police] work, economic work, Soviet work—all is subordinate to the Party leadership, and if anyone thinks otherwise, that means he is no Bolshevik." Shortly after Stalin's death, Georgi Malenkov, who appeared to lead the field of possible successors, resigned as a member of the Party Secretariat while retaining the position of head of the Soviet Government. Khrushchev, on the other hand, became the highest Party officer. In retrospect, it is clear that the prestige and the power levers concentrated in the Party were major factors in enabling Khrushchev to win in the struggle for supreme authority in the U.S.S.R. Regardless of their rank in government agencies, other Soviet leaders were also Party members formally bound to obey orders issued in the name of the Party. Recent directives formally reiterate the rule that Communists who are members of governmental or quasi-governmental bodies have an absolute duty, regardless of their personal views, to vote for nominees advanced by the Party. Moreover, within each branch of the Soviet bureaucracy, many officials were tied to power alignments that led them to follow the Party leadership rather than their nominal superiors. Thus, in June, 1953, when the head of the police apparatus, Lavrenti Beria, sought to counter Party dominance, he was abandoned by many of the high-ranking police officers. A year and a half later (January, 1955), a Party meeting ordered Malenkov to resign as head of the government. He complied the following month. In 1957, the central economic directorates were fully subordinated to Party control. Later that year, the Party (vigorously supported by many high military officers) successfully demanded the removal of Marshal Georgi Zhukov, head of the Defense Ministry. Khrushchev's words were prophetic: "Army work, Chekist work, economic work, Soviet work—all is subordinate to the Party leadership."

The nature of collective leadership since Khrushchev's ouster (October, 1964) has led to a modest recovery of power by central governmental officials headed by the premier, Aleksei N. Kosygin. In contrast to Stalin and Khrushchev, Party leader Brezhnev has not assumed formal direction of the government. Nevertheless, Brezhnev's public stature has grown slowly but steadily. In certain areas like foreign policy, formally reserved for government officials, Brezhnev's increasing prominence inevitably implies diminution of figures outside the Party apparatus. During the 1970's Brezhnev, rather than formal government officials, has dominated Soviet negotiations both with other Communist states and with the U.S.S.R.'s principal "capitalist" rivals, including the United States. As an institution, though, the Communist Party remains pre-eminent since fundamental decisions of the "collective leadership" are made by its directing bodies. Even though these include officials of other bureaucracies, Party officials predominate. The mere fact that Khrushchev's removal was carried out by one of these bodies (the Party Central Committee) indicates this pre-eminence. During the following decade, the dominant role of the Party has been strongly reaffirmed. What has become clear during these ten years, as noted in Chapter 1, is that the Party's institutional pre-eminence does not depend on the existence of personal rule.

MEMBERSHIP: STATUS ASPECTS

The preceding discussion suggests that the significance of the Party as an institution resides in its leadership. To a considerable extent, as will appear in Chapter 4, this is true. The role of the Party as a membership organization requires careful examination, however. In sheer size, the Soviet Communist Party resembles the mass membership parties of pluralist societies. The Soviet Party membership now includes approximately 14,000,000 full members and 650,000 probationary (candidate) members, constituting about 9 per cent of the adult population of the U.S.S.R. Nevertheless, Soviet writers have always explicitly rejected the term "mass organization" for the Party. Instead, they follow Lenin's prescription that selection of members be made with great care, so that the Party may act as a leaven within the whole social structure rather than become submerged in it. In sharp contrast to pluralist parties, the Communist Party does not solicit volunteer adherents, but chooses its members. The mere fact of enrollment of nearly all eminent Soviet citizens provides a propaganda advantage. The regime constantly boasts that the outstanding citizens are Communists and uses this assertion as proof that the Party embodies the best of Soviet society. Consequently, the prize-winning physicist, the record-breaking milkmaid, the popular novelist, the renowned Arctic explorer are all prime targets for recruitment into the Party. In crisis situations such as war, extraordinary effort (to the point of complete neglect of the ideological background or intellectual capacity of the candidates) is devoted to bring all "heroic" figures into the Party to serve as examples to their fellows. Ordinarily, however, prospective members are carefully screened. Each must be recommended by three persons who have already been Party members for at least five years. In accordance with the principle that a prime duty of each Communist is to "safeguard the Party against the infiltration of persons unworthy of the lofty title of Communist," sponsors are held responsible for a new member's derelictions.

Despite the care exercised in selection, the sense in which rank-and-file Communists constitute the "elite" of Soviet society is limited. Membership is, of course, a requisite for selection as a Party official, and it is useful, if not always essential, for advancement in the state bureaucracy. At times, Party membership helps in a professional or intellectual career, but the need to utilize all highly qualified persons in such work limits the degree to which political preference is feasible. Rank-and-file membership by no means connotes membership in the ruling circles of the Soviet Union; as will be shown below, such circles are confined to a much more select group. In effect, therefore, ordinary Party membership is more an honor than a privilege, and one that carries with it the onerous burdens of constant study, indoctrinating tasks, and occasional assignment to unattractive posts. For example, while Soviet law ordinarily permits a worker to leave a job after two weeks' notice, a Party member must ask his primary organization for permission, because "he has consciously and voluntarily subordinated himself to another law—the CPSU Statutes." Members must carry these burdens diligently if not cheerfully, or face expulsion. It is far worse to be an ex-Party member than a person who has never joined the Party, for the former are pariahs in Soviet society. The annual rate of expulsions is about 50,000, or .04 per cent of the total membership, but (at least in Moscow) is apparently much higher (about 1.5 per cent annually) among recent entrants. What is very clear is that a person who views Party duties as distasteful is shrewder if he never becomes a member; in fact, many talented Soviet citizens do evade joining.

About one-fifth of the Party members have higher educations, and another third have completed secondary education. In each case the proportion is much higher than among the general adult population (in 1970, 7 per cent twenty years of age or older had some higher education, 25 per cent more had finished secondary schools). However, over one-fifth of the Party members have only elementary educations. This is an additional indication that membership in the Party, while selective, is not confined to those holding high-status jobs. During the 1960's special efforts were made to enlist ordinary factory workers and farmers, who constituted 62 per cent of admittees between 1962 and 1966. White-collar workers have declined slightly (to 45 per cent of the total 1971 membership), but they have always constituted the largest component. Proportionately, the rural areas have fewer Party members than the cities: 35 per cent of the Party as contrasted to 43 per cent of the population. Nominally collective farm peasants constitute 15 per cent of the Party, although they are 20 per cent of the general population; real "dirt farmers," as contrasted to rural officials, constitute a considerably smaller proportion of the Party membership. On the other hand, physicians and teachers are about three times as heavily represented in the Party as in the general population, while such favored—and strategic—groups as engineers and military officers are six or seven times as strongly represented as ordinary occupations. Officials (both of the state and the Party bureaucracies) are of course even more heavily represented. Women constitute only 22 per cent, although they are well over half of the adult population. As indicated in Chapter 7 and its accompanying table, some nationality groups, such as Russians and Transcaucasians, are much more heavily represented than such nationalities as Central Asians.

MEMBERSHIP: FUNCTIONS

The symbolic function of Party membership has already been noted: Enrollment of the "best" citizens demonstrates that the Party comprises the best of Soviet society. The general Party membership is also highly important to the regime as a reservoir of disposable manpower. As noted earlier, every Communist must accept assignments made by the leadership. In a crisis, therefore, the leadership can freely command millions of the most energetic and talented Soviet citizens. For example, every few years tens of thousands of urban Communists have been sent out to the villages to stimulate lagging agricultural production and to perfect political organization.

The principal activity of the Party member as a stimulator of production is carried out, however, within his primary Party organization. The Party has always maintained that these basic units should be formed in places of work; today, this principle is generally applied. Of about 370,000 primary organizations, one-fourth are in factories, transportation, and the like, while one-seventh are on farms. Today the average number of members (in the neighborhood of forty) in Party organizations in all of these types of economic activity does not vary greatly. The general average of primary organization membership is somewhat reduced, however, by the large number of units in various institutions, administrative offices, and military formations. The last kind of primary organizations are especially important, for, together with the deputy commander for political affairs (a military officer dependent upon the Party), the Party organization provides the regime with a pervasive curb upon the military. Whatever the agency of the Soviet system, the primary organization is charged with general supervision of activities. Ordinarily the primary organization may not command an agricultural agency to take specific action, but its advice is often compelling. In a military unit, on the other hand, the Party organization may not even discuss a purely military decision. Most primary organization policy actions have an effect somewhat in between these extremes and are consequently difficult to define; but there appears to have been a recent tendency for the authority of primary organizations in administrative institutions to expand. The design of the relationship in all institutions, however, is to expose officials to a constant flow of pressure and criticism from Party members who are most familiar with the officials' operations. At the same time, the primary organization is designed to stimulate its own membership (which almost always includes the officials concerned) to more strenuous efforts to further the regime's objectives.

The primary Party organization's significance is enhanced by its power to make the initial decision on the admission and expulsion of members. Admission or expulsion must be confirmed by the next higher Party echelon, however, and an expelled member may appeal to the Party Control Committee attached to the Central Committee of the Communist Party of the Soviet Union. In 1967, for example, 9,700 persons appealed to this highest level, but fewer than one-third had their expulsions reversed.

THE INDOCTRINATION FUNCTION

A third most important function of the general membership is indoctrination. The Party is the basic institution for manipulating the political culture both of its own members and of Soviet society in general. Every member has the duty to "master Marxist-Leninist theory, raise his ideological level, and contribute to the molding and rearing of the man of Communist society." The most systematic and concentrated indoctrination program is directed at the Communists themselves. Elementary and intermediate political education (frequently provided in short-term evening courses) is designed to convey a minimal knowledge of Marxism-Leninism. These levels are centered upon study of Lenin's life, CPSU history, and political and economic affairs. A somewhat higher level—but still part-time study, usually for two years—is provided by the Evening Universities of Marxism-Leninism. For the "executive cadres" of Party and state officials, on the other hand, full-time courses lasting as long as four years are provided. The most important full-time courses are at the Higher Party Schools in principal regional centers, as well as in Moscow, and the Academy of Social Sciences. Here officials obtain practical training in administration as well as instruction in ideological and academic subjects. Between 1946 and 1971, the latter institution graduated 3,400 Soviet Communist officials, as well as 400 foreign Communists. The importance which the CPSU attaches to such intensive reindoctrination is indicated by the fact that at least fifty of the Academy graduates held top posts in 1971. In recent years these men have usually obtained their full-time Party schooling (the normal age limit for admissions is 35) before being advanced to major posts. In the immediate postwar years, however, it was common for a middle-aged official holding responsibilities as great as those of an American state governor to be detached for several years' retraining.

All levels of Party indoctrination are designed not only to indoctrinate the Party member but to prepare him to indoctrinate others with the current policy "line" and with the concepts and values the regime believes to be essential attributes of members of the future Communist society. At an early date, the Soviet leadership intuitively grasped the sociological principle that transmission of ideas is most effectively accomplished by "opinion leaders" who are in face-to-face contact with small groups. Communist Party members constitute the backbone of the huge force of "agitators" who implement this principle. Agitation is officially defined as the presentation of a few ideas to the mass of the population, as contrasted to the more complicated "propaganda" directed toward groups like Party members. During a rest period in a factory workshop, for example, a Communist agitator will read an editorial from the Party newspaper, *Pravda*, embodying the current "line," to his fellow workers, lest they idle away their time. While there is evidence that such emphasis on indoctrination often irritates the average Soviet citizen, the constant reiteration of the regime's viewpoint, unchallenged by any public opposition, is bound to induce a considerable measure of acceptance. Undoubtedly, the "oral agitation" program vastly increases the impact of printed indoctrinating material.

THE MASS MEDIA

Despite the emphasis on face-to-face indoctrination, the Soviet Communist Party has always had great respect for the printed word. Some publications (e.g., *Pravda*) are directly issued by the Party, others are issued by agencies that the Party closely supervises. Reproduction of materials for public distribution—even by mimeograph—is strictly forbidden, as is importation of such items as Bibles from abroad. Undoubtedly this monopoly, reinforced by the agitators' explanations, is effective. Since the mid-1960's, however, dissident elements have become bolder in circulating *"samizdat"* (self-published) literature—some of which is discussed in Chapter 5—criticizing regime policies. Since this material is usually handwritten or typewritten and is clandestinely circulated at considerable risk, the audience for any particular item is very limited. When one considers, however, that an average of about one new *samizdat* writing reaches Western Europe every day, it is easy to see that the cumulative impact of opposition views is great. This is particularly true since circulation is mainly among young intellectuals, who spread by word of mouth the views they have picked up from *samizdat*.

Even official Soviet publications provide indications that their audience receptivity is diminishing. Recent surveys conducted by *Izvestia*, the second most important newspaper, indicate that a small proportion of readers (except older ones) read editorial matter at all. By far the most popular items are those dealing with personal conflict situations, "astonishing" stories and questions of morality, with sports, foreign affairs, and literary items following in popularity along with editorials; accounts of government activities and discussions of economic policies—major topics of the current "line"—receive *least* reader attention. The significance of these findings is enhanced by the fact that *Izvestia* readers are far better educated and more urban than the average Soviet citizen. Moreover, readers of literary magazines, who are younger and still better educated, appear to be even less attracted by political and economic topics. In the bookstores, new fictional and essay material sells out quickly, while most Party and economic publications remain readily available, because demand for them is minimal.

Most readers of the major newspapers and magazines also have access to the electronic media—for example, as early as 1967 three-fourths of *Izvestia* readers had radio or television sets. There are 50 million ordinary radio sets in the U.S.S.R., and another 50 million "wired" sets, which can only receive one local channel. Two-thirds of the population is within TV reception range (only black-and-white is available for public broadcasting); within that range it is claimed that there are nine sets for every ten families. Consequently, messages on electronic media can provide fairly complete coverage of the population. The Soviet regime has never used these media as intensively for indoctrination as it has the printed word, however, or as much, for example, as the Nazis used radio or American candidates use television. One reason, no doubt, is the prestige that Lenin's personal editorship of *Pravda* and its predecessors lent to the newspaper. Another reason, occasionally admitted, is the difficulty of controlling what goes out on the air waves, as compared to the careful scrutiny that can be devoted to every word on a printed page. Then, too, a population that has recently become literate—as is the case with older Soviet citizens—tends to have more respect for the "magic" of printed statements. As the above data show, however, young people tend to be less impressed; perhaps, therefore, the regime will turn more to electronic indoctrination activities in the future.

THE SCHOOLS AND THE MILITARY

Part of the effort to reach the younger generation with indoctrination materials is carried out by the educational system. Textbooks in courses like history and literature are designed to stress Soviet achievements and inculcate principles advanced by the ideology. Despite the relatively strong position of the Party among teachers, it would appear that relatively little emphasis on current Party policies is attempted. On the other hand, psychologists like Urie Bronfenbrenner have found that the schools do play an important part in inculcating basic attitudes like team spirit ("concern for the collective") and emphasis on group approval as contrasted to personal material rewards. At times, also, there has been extreme emphasis on status achievement, fostered by such devices as posting course grades. How much these values will be carried over to adult life—where, as noted in Chapter 2, individual material rewards are acknowledged to be very important—is questionable. It appears to be very significant that both the teachers (71 per cent women in the primary grades, and predominantly women, except for principals and coaches, in high school) and the peer-group leaders are usually female. Quite possibly, as in other cultures, Soviet women have become the bearers of certain fundamental cultural values, which they try to transmit to children. One may speculate that in the U.S.S.R., as elsewhere, this effort will be more effective with girls than boys, who, Soviet writers recognize, turn more strongly to male behavioral models.

A powerful indoctrination reinforcement for young males is military service, especially in the ground forces. Brezhnev, who was once a major figure in the military indoctrination system, stressed this point:

> In fulfilling military obligations, almost the entire male population of the country serves for some period in the Armed Forces. And this takes place during the youthful years, when the personality is taking shape and a world view and a politically conscious attitude toward life are being molded. The army thereby becomes an important school of life for our young people and a component part of the whole system of Soviet upbringing.*

While active service is becoming somewhat less nearly universal, part-time military instruction has been widely introduced in the secondary schools. Both types of training are, of course, designed to strengthen the country's military power, but the opportunity to indoctrinate the young men is not neglected. Since about one-fourth of the military personnel (mainly officers and noncommissioned cadres) are Party members, adequate personnel is available to reach all recruits. A very important aspect of military indoctrination is the opportunity it affords to reach rural youths, who previously have had little contact with the indoctrination media. For many youths from more remote regions, political indoctrination goes hand in hand with introduction to modern technology and the minimal amenities of urban society. For many non-Russians, the army is also where they acquire a minimum facility in Russian, the sole language of command. To use a sociological term, these young men are socially "mobilized" at the same time that they are made aware of political affairs—i.e., politically "mobilized." Probably their awareness of how much they have to learn makes them receptive to indoctrination as well as instruction in instrumental skills. In this way compulsory military service acts as an institution for inculcating loyalty at least to the symbols of systemwide Communist au-

---

* *Pravda,* July 9, 1968, trans. in *Current Digest of the Soviet Press,* XX, No. 28, p. 10.

thority at the same time that it makes a large proportion of the young male population more versatile and capable in jobs requiring a familiarity with modern technology. It is significant, therefore, that from the standpoint of the Soviet regime maintenance of a large military force—although it unquestionably ties up scarce manpower—has positive political and economic aspects.

THE PARTY'S AUXILIARY ORGANIZATIONS

As noted at the beginning of this chapter, the Party itself is not regarded as a mass organization. Consequently, several organizations with still larger membership were established at an early date to supplement the Party's activities by enrolling members on a less discriminating basis. These "mass organizations" are very closely supervised by the Communist Party. As the regime's emphasis has shifted, since 1964, toward long-range indoctrination programs as a principal means for preparing the "new man" able to live in a fully Communist society, the significance of the mass organizations has increased.

From the indoctrination standpoint, much the most important mass organization is the Communist Youth League, or Komsomol. The Party itself is definitely an adult organization. In 1967 only 5 per cent of the Party members were under twenty-six, as compared to 23 per cent over fifty. In view of the lengthening of the life span in peacetime conditions, the proportion in the older group has probably increased slightly since then. There is a small but growing group of elderly retired members. It is true that one may secure admission to the Party at the early age of eighteen, but all who are admitted under the age of twenty-three must have been members of the Komsomol. That organization serves, therefore, as a screening agency in which prospective Party members are indoctrinated and observed before the crucial step of admission to the Party. But the Komsomol is far more comprehensive in membership than the Party. Between 1917 and 1968, 100 million persons entered the Komsomol. A great many of these are now, of course, dead; but nearly all of the 30 million who entered the Komsomol between 1953 and 1963 are still alive. During the following decade, still larger numbers of young people passed through the Komsomol. Its present enrollment is in excess of 27 million. This constitutes nearly 80 per cent of the most relevant age groups (sixteen to twenty-four) and is perhaps about as close to saturation coverage as can reasonably be attained. Failure to cover the more remote rural regions is indicated by the fact that only 30 per cent of the membership is in rural areas (as contrasted to 44 per cent of the population); but in cities the high school age group is virtually universally enrolled in the Komsomol.

Insofar as its indoctrination proves to be a lasting influence, the Komsomol has, therefore, a place of immense importance in the Soviet system. But Soviet sources express concern over the fact that the all-Komsomol secondary school graduate contingents produce only a minority who become activists after they enter production work. Only one-tenth (2.6 million) of the huge number who passed through the Komsomol during 1953–61 actually went on to join the Communist Party; this proportion is only a trifle above the 9 per cent of the general adult population in the Party. It would appear, therefore, that the Komsomol is no more effective than less specialized social mechanisms in inducing young people to make a permanent commitment to enlist as the "best" and most active members of the Soviet political system.

Komsomol members are expected to have an acquaintance with all major ideological documents, from Marx's *Communist Manifesto* to resolutions of the latest Party congress. To a considerable extent, however, more vivid works, such as Lenin's biography and the memoirs of war heroes, provide implicit models for the younger readers.

The organizational structure of the Komsomol is modeled on that of the Party. Top officers are Party members, for a young person who enters the Party can retain Komsomol membership until twenty-eight if he is elected to office. At lower levels, few Party members do remain active in the Komsomol; only 2 per cent of its primary organizations are headed by Party members. In spite of the regime's efforts, there appears to be an increasing tendency to regard the Komsomol as a boring and restrictive institution. Precisely because it includes such a large proportion of the relevant age groups, Komsomol membership does not have the honorific significance of Party membership. Yet membership entails almost as many burdens as Party membership. Komsomol youths constituted a high proportion of those sent to farm the "virgin lands" in the 1950's. Members are frequently called for short-term work details as well as for agitation tasks. The Komsomol tries to become popular by organizing recreational activities like open-air dances, but even these are often injected with an element of propaganda. Still more objectionable to many youths is the role of the Komsomol as a guardian of morals, manners, and, of course, political fidelity. In the past fifteen years Komsomol patrols have been assigned auxiliary police power to control youths in the streets and in places of amusement. At first these patrols tried to enforce all sorts of restrictions, such as banning "loud" sport shirts. Even today excesses like illegal detention and beating of suspects are occasionally officially charged against the Komsomol patrols, although Soviet sources warn that such abuses "should not compromise the noble idea of active participation by the public and the Komsomol in the struggle against those who violate public order."

The Komsomol also exercises tutelage over the Pioneers, the organization for children of primary school age—which in turn supervises the Little Octobrists (ages seven to eleven). The latter hardly has any significance for indoctrination (the organization was allowed to dissolve for several years), but the

Pioneers are an element of some importance in the indoctrination chain. The 23 million members comprise, like the Komsomol, about 80 per cent of the relevant (ten to fifteen) age group. Many of their activities (games, camping, and the like) resemble those of Western youth groups like the Boy Scouts and the Campfire Girls. Perhaps overorganization of these nonpolitical activities as much as indoctrination has often led (according to Soviet reports) children to be bored with the Pioneers, as are their elders with other Soviet organizations.

Numerically, the Soviet trade unions, with 93 million members, are even more obviously mass organizations than the Komsomol. The immense size of the trade unions has been useful to the Soviet regime in its foreign policy—their correspondingly large representation in the World Federation of Trade Unions enabled Communists to gain control over this international organization soon after World War II. Soviet trade unions also have important domestic functions. The usual units of trade-union organization are factories, with factory unions grouped by both industry and region. But practically the entire white-collar labor force is enrolled (27 million) as well as industrial workers. Like other mass organizations, the trade unions are relatively weak in rural areas, however, with only 6 per cent of the members there—including only a few million actually working on collective farms.

Like other Soviet organizations manipulated by the Party, trade unions cannot engage in conflict behavior like strikes. In recent years their role in the managerial process, though distinctly subordinate, has been slightly increased, however. Although the trade unions have little practical effect on economic policy, they do play a restricted part in setting wage scales and in allocation of incentive funds between objectives like individual bonuses, housing construction, and amenities in the factory. Trade unions inspect sanitary and safety provisions. Perhaps their most influential role is in reviewing dismissals and (in collaboration with management) distributing coveted passes to vacation resorts and rest homes. From the regime's standpoint, however, the trade unions' role in stimulating production and promoting "socialist emulation" is most significant. Through their factory clubs and frequent meetings, the unions also have a direct role in the indoctrination process, though apparently a much more restricted one than that assigned to the Komsomol. Soviet sources admit that only a minority of trade union members are "activists," although the regime regards "public work in the trade unions [as] a good school for working people, fostering their Communist education and strengthening their concern for the interests of state and society."

A more important agency for indoctrination (not officially classed as a mass organization) is the Society for Knowledge. With a membership of 2,300,000, the Society formally resembles an adult-education organization. The bulk of its work is carried on by a body of part-time lecturers. The lectures, which are often delivered at factories and on farms, cover a wide spectrum of subjects: Communist Party policies, peace, space exploration, and technological advances. Many lectures are undoubtedly designed to impart practical knowledge as well as indoctrination. Probably the most important theme, however, is "debunking" religion.

Finally, one should mention DOSAAF—the conventional abbreviation of the organization now entitled the Volunteer Society for Cooperation with the Army, Air Force, and Navy. DOSAAF has performed a variety of tasks, including civil defense functions, entertainment of servicemen, and cooperation in the indoctrination of military personnel. Its role in fostering military-type sports for schoolchildren is especially important.

ORGANIZATIONAL PRINCIPLES

In theory, the organization of the Communist Party is based on Lenin's principle of "democratic centralism." At the

Twenty-third Party Congress (1966), Brezhnev defined democratic centralism as "free opinion in deciding questions and iron discipline after a decision is taken." Two years later, faced with the liberalizing tendencies in Czechoslovakia, Soviet writers emphasized stern central direction still more:

> Indeed, an important law of Party development is that the greater the scope achieved by inner-Party democracy and the broader the rights of Communists, the greater their sense of responsibility will be for the common cause and for implementing Party policies and the more the work of each Party organization and each Communist will be notable for its organization and discipline. . . . But is the CPSU's experience in this case perhaps of limited significance? Are the principle of democratic centralism and the requirements stemming from it, including the inadmissibility of groupings, perhaps applicable only to the specific conditions in which our party has functioned? By no means. . . . Indeed, experience teaches that lack of unity of actions in carrying out a political line and commonly adopted decisions, when some actions pull in one direction and others in the opposite direction, when everyone is free to do anything he wants—in such a situation the Party is unable to perform a guiding role. And from legalization of fractions and groupings it is but a short way to the complete disintegration of the Party.*

Each echelon of the Party is supposed to be free to discuss a matter until a final decision has been reached by a higher echelon. The present statutes allow "broad" Party discussion only if the need is recognized by several high-level Party organizations or by the Central Committee itself. In practice, as will be discussed in greater detail, this means the central authorities are free to permit or forbid discussion on any matters that impinge on general policy. On the other hand, lower Party organizations are permitted, and indeed bound, to discuss implementation of policy at their own level and below.

---

* P. Rodionov, "The Immutable Principle of the Marxist-Leninist Party," *Pravda*, August 9, 1968, translated in *Current Digest of the Soviet Press*, II, No. 32, 8–9.

"Criticism" and "self-criticism" are characteristic features of this discussion, through which inefficient or delinquent members are brought to confess their sins and, presumably, mend their ways.

In a very similar fashion, the nominally free elections in the Party organizations (and organizations which the Party supervises) are guided from above. Ostensibly, the primary Party organization, for example, annually elects a directing bureau and a secretary (usually not a full-time official), who serve as its chief officers. Every two years, the primary organization also elects delegates to a conference at the next-higher level, the rayon, or district. Our information about the actual conduct of these elections is far from complete. It is clear, however, that the *nomenklatura* system applies to elected as well as to appointed officials in the Party organization. Under this system, higher officials make personnel assignments for a designated group of lower Party organizations. In making these assignments, the personnel officials not only take into account individual qualifications of Party members, but "balance" such factors as age levels of a class of lower officials to give each age group the impression that it is adequately represented (this does not, however, apply to education levels, for an overwhelming majority of primary organization secretaries have some higher education). Obviously the *nomenklatura* system would not work if the choice of important categories of officials were left to an entirely free elective process. Apparently, the procedure actually used is to "suggest" to the Party body that it elect a specific slate—sometimes including persons who are unknown to the Party members participating in the elections. Before many important local elections, Party officials from Moscow arrive as visitors; they deliver speeches to the Party meetings and, either openly or covertly, pass on the wishes of the central authorities concerning the slate to be elected. Obviously, these "suggestions" deprive democratic centralism of significance in many circumstances, although blatant manipulation of elections is occasionally criticized by the Party press, and lower Party meetings apparently do reject obnoxious candidates from time to time.

The level of Party organization just above the primary organization is a geographical subdivision, the rayon, or district. There are more than 3,000 districts, approximately 2,750 in rural areas and 400 that are wards of cities. In each district, a conference of delegates from the dozens of primary Party organizations takes place twice every five years. The conference formally elects a committee, which, in turn, elects a bureau and three secretaries. The latter are full-time officials of the Party apparatus. The district conference also elects delegates to the next-higher level, the oblast, or province (in some cases a large city or a special nationality unit). There are more than 150 such territorial units throughout the U.S.S.R. The provincial conference elects a committee, which, in turn, elects its bureau and secretaries (three to five in number) twice every five years. Every five years, the provincial conference continues the pyramidal process of indirect election by choosing delegates to a Union Republic Party congress.* The republic congresses elect central committees, which, in turn, elect bureaus and secretaries. In addition, every five years conferences in the provinces (or in the smaller republics, the congresses) elect delegates to the "All-Union" Congress of the Communist Party of the Soviet Union itself. The Congress elects the Central Committee and the Central Inspection Commission. The Central Committee then elects the General Secretary, several other secretaries, the Politburo, and the Party Control Committee.

One may well ask at this point whether the purpose of this

* The largest republic, the Russian Soviet Federated Socialist Republic (R.S.F.S.R.) has no congress; on the other hand, the ten smallest republics have no provinces between the district and the republic levels.

VERTICAL ORGANIZATION AND SUPERVISORY FUNCTIONS IN THE CPSU

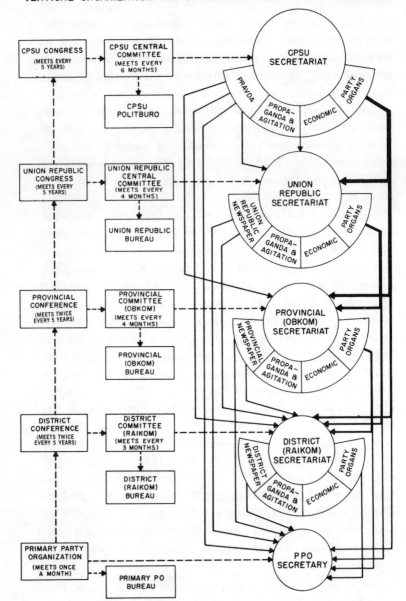

elaborate system of elections is merely to preserve the appearance of democratic centralism, a purpose that may well be achieved as far as the feelings of the ordinary Party member are concerned. As noted in Chapter 2, the concept of democratic centralism had little meaning even in Lenin's time, for the conspiratorial nature of the pre-Revolutionary Bolshevik Party prevented regular elections. Never having known anything resembling the hotly contested free elections that characterize Western political parties, it is likely that many Soviet Communists do not realize how hollow their "inner-Party democracy" is.

There are other purposes, however. The considerable investment of man-hours of important officials (for the congress and conference delegations embrace nearly all major Party and state officials in the U.S.S.R.) is justified by the experience these officials get in discussing problems with their peers and superiors, for higher officials obtain some idea of "grass-roots" feeling by talking with provincial officials. Doubtless for this reason and to preserve an impression of "inner-Party democracy," higher authorities have recently criticized meetings in which all speeches are prearranged. Through personal contact —especially if it retains a measure of spontaneity—top officials have a chance to evaluate the loyalty and ability of promising subordinates. But spontaneity cannot go too far, especially at the top of the Party pyramid. The major assemblies, especially the All-Union Congress, provide a superb forum for setting forth and publicizing the Party line of the moment. Nearly 5,000 Congress delegates, meeting for only ten or twelve days, could not (even in the absence of manipulation) debate and reach decisions on complex issues. But they provide an impressive backdrop for the speeches of the major leaders of the Soviet regime and an appearance of "monolithic" support for the regime's policies. The occasion is, in fact, so useful that All-Union congresses in recent years have several times been the scene of proclamations of major policy.

SUGGESTED READING • CHAPTER 3

Most general histories of Russia (such as those listed in Chapter 1) discuss the Communist Party; so do the specialized works listed in the following chapters. The books listed below are mainly general works on the Soviet system that stress the role of the Party.

FAINSOD, MERLE. *How Russia Is Ruled.* Rev. ed. Cambridge, Mass.: Harvard University Press, 1963. Although now rather out of date, this book was the first serious effort to relate institutions to the reality of the political process in the Soviet Union, and in some ways it is still the best work on the operation of the Soviet system.

——. *Smolensk Under Soviet Rule.* Cambridge, Mass.: Harvard University Press, 1958; Vintage paperback, 1960. Although limited to a single province, this is one of the most important books ever written about the U.S.S.R., because it is based on an extensive file of secret Communist documents originally captured by the German army and in turn seized by U.S. forces. All aspects of Soviet life in the 1920's and 1930's are covered, but the revelations on Party operations are especially important.

HAZARD, JOHN N. *The Soviet System of Government.* Chicago: University of Chicago Press, 1964. Concise, authoritative, and highly readable, this is an outstanding general survey.

LANE, DAVID. *Politics and Society in the U.S.S.R.* New York: Random House, 1971. An expert English analysis of the sociology of Soviet politics; weak on the struggle for power and on nationalities, but in many respects the best general treatment to appear in recent years.

McCLOSKY, HERBERT, and TURNER, JOHN E. *The Soviet Dictatorship.* New York: McGraw-Hill Book Company, 1966. A massive treatment of Soviet political institutions.

MEYER, ALFRED G. *The Soviet Political System: An Interpretation.* New York: Random House, 1965. An analytic approach comparing Soviet politics to those of a large corporation.

The following books are somewhat more specialized in character:

ARMSTRONG, JOHN A. *The Politics of Totalitarianism.* New York: Random House, 1961. A detailed examination of the Party and Soviet politics between 1934 and 1960.

BRONFENBRENNER, URIE. *Two Worlds of Childhood: U.S. and U.S.S.R.* New York: Russell Sage Foundation, 1970. A psychologist's analysis of early socialization patterns, particularly in the schools.

FISHER, RALPH. *Pattern for Soviet Youth*. New York: Columbia University Press, 1959. A detailed history of the Communist Youth League (Komsomol).

HOLLANDER, GAYLE D. *Soviet Political Indoctrination: Developments in Mass Media and Propaganda Since Stalin*. New York: Praeger Publishers, 1972. A comprehensive discussion of all media and their audiences.

HOPKINS, MARK. *Mass Media in the Soviet Union*. New York: Praeger Publishers, 1970. Comprehensive, up-to-date coverage by a working reporter who studied for a year in the U.S.S.R. and subsequently traveled widely in the country.

INKELES, ALEX. *Public Opinion in Soviet Russia*. Cambridge, Mass.: Harvard University Press, 1950. The only comprehensive treatment in English of the Party mechanisms for indoctrination, though very old now.

KASSOF, ALLEN. *The Soviet Youth Program: Regimentation and Rebellion*. Cambridge, Mass.: Harvard University Press, 1965. A sociological study of the Communist Youth League and related activities.

MICKIEWICZ, ELLEN P. *Soviet Political Schools*. New Haven: Yale University Press, 1967. A good treatment of the Party indoctrination system, focusing on the part-time courses.

RESHETAR, JOHN S. *A Concise History of the Communist Party of the Soviet Union*. New York: Frederick A. Praeger, 1960. A much briefer survey than Schapiro's (below), but very useful.

RIGBY, THOMAS H. *Communist Party Membership, 1917–67*. Princeton, N.J.: Princeton University Press, 1967. A complete and penetrating analysis of the evolution of membership principles and practice, together with a detailed discussion of sociological categories in the mid-1960's.

SCHAPIRO, LEONARD. *The Communist Party of the Soviet Union*. New York: Vintage paperback, 1971. A thorough and penetrating history of the Party from its beginnings to the Khrushchev era.

CENTRAL ORGANIZATION OF THE SOVIET COMMUNIST PARTY

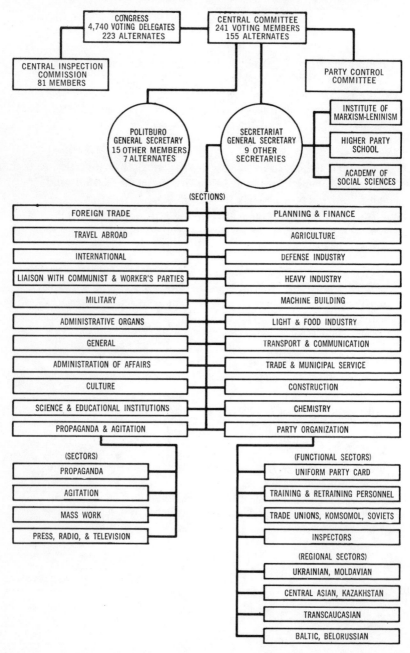

4

THE APPARATUS

In Communist theory, the Soviet political system is a mono-
lith. The Party is the infallible interpreter of the historical
process and, consequently, the irrefutable guide to action. The
doctrine does not recognize the existence of conflicting interests that the political system must adjust and compromise.
Operating under the principle of democratic centralism,
the Party leadership acts as the supreme decision-making
body, with other Soviet institutions faithfully executing Party
policies.

In fact, as we have already seen, the Soviet political system
has been frequently racked by severe conflicts. These conflicts
have involved prominent leaders and those lower officials who,
for one reason or another, have been their adherents, but, in
all cases, the divergent groups were centered around segments
of the Soviet structure of formal, large-scale institutions. In
other words, the conflicts were forms of bureaucratic politics.
What Communist ideology, as an element of political culture,
accomplished was to keep the resolution of these conflicts
largely within the institutional framework of the Communist
Party. Other institutions may serve as power bases or develop
divergent interests, but rivalries among them are formally resolved by Party bodies. Despite the monolithic nature Lenin
ascribed to it, one may view the Party as the legitimate institution for aggregating interests and demands in the Soviet system. These interests are distinguished from those of a pluralist
society in that they derive from segments of a formally unified
bureaucracy rather than from formally independent groups.
Consequently, the interests acquire legitimacy only insofar as

they are expressed in terms (usually implicit) which stress the values of the system as a whole and deny distinctive interest positions. Furthermore, because of Lenin's extreme aversion to factionalism (or, as he put it, "fractionalism"), no bureaucratic group may openly constitute an alignment even if its avowed purpose is to promote the general welfare of the system rather than some particular interest. In spite of the manifest existence of divergent positions and bitter conflict throughout the history of the Soviet system, the official doctrine still condemns factionalists in the sharpest terms. The core of the charge against the "anti-Party" group of 1957 was that its members had met secretly (in the office of the head of the Soviet Government) to concert a program and a plan for implementing it. At lower levels, officials have taken action against Party members for merely failing to report casual discussions of concerted protests to the authorities. A crucial question, therefore, is: How can decision-making involving divergent viewpoints take place in the Soviet system?

As was described in Chapter 3, the Congress is the formal supreme body; but its brief sessions and infrequent meetings would, aside from all other factors, disqualify it from making basic decisions. Consequently, one must look elsewhere for the real locus of Soviet power. During nearly all of the period between the Revolution and 1964, most observers found no difficulty in identifying the decision-maker with the personal dictator: Lenin, Stalin, Khrushchev. In retrospect, at least, it seems clear that decision-making was a much more complex affair during Lenin's and Khrushchev's ascendancy and that, even under Stalin, decision-making was less centralized than was imagined. Nevertheless, the concentration of power in the hands of these men was enormous. Some observers have superficially concluded that this concentration is sanctioned or even demanded by Communist ideology, which, until 1961, called for a "dictatorship of the proletariat." In fact, this formula never implied that an *individual* was to be dictator.

While some observers have contended that Lenin envisaged the necessity of one-man rule, probably most students of his writings agree that this was not the case. *In practice,* however, Lenin did make most of the basic decisions of the Soviet regime during his time. Stalin ruled (at least after 1937) as an absolute despot. As far as he was able, he made all important (and many trivial) decisions himself. He clothed his rule in secrecy, often avoiding the discussion of pending matters even with his own hand-picked circle of high officials. He instigated a campaign of adulation for his person that has rarely been exceeded in a modern country. Stalin was slavishly acclaimed as the greatest genius of mankind, omniscient and infallible. At the same time, he sedulously undermined any force, institutional or personal, that could possibly compete with him for power. He humiliated his associates in numerous ways, and in hundreds of cases had them executed without even publishing accusations against them. This was personal dictatorship in the most absolute sense of the term. Yet even Stalin was unable to direct all aspects of the vastly complex technological society the U.S.S.R. had become by 1953. Consequently, he had to rely on lieutenants to make countless minor decisions as well as to execute his own commands.

As indicated in the preceding chapter, none of Stalin's lieutenants was immediately able to assume full control of the Soviet system. Between March, 1953, and January, 1955 (and, to a lesser extent, until June, 1957), a real "collective leadership," based on the Politburo,* made many basic decisions. This was, in some respects, a return to the pre-1937 situation. In Lenin's later years, and during the first decade of Stalin's predominance, the Politburo met very frequently and considered a wide range of questions. In Stalin's later years, however, it almost

---

* Officially designated the Party Presidium between 1952 and 1966.

ceased to function. For a time after his death, it seemed that the Politburo was to be the select committee ruling the Soviet Union.

CONTRASTING FATES OF COLLECTIVE LEADERSHIP

One of the most difficult puzzles of Soviet politics is why, in spite of its seemingly strong start, collective leadership collapsed within two years after Stalin's death yet has prevailed for ten years in the post-Khrushchev period. Although a complete solution can not be provided, a comparison of the two periods (1953–55 and 1964–74) throws much light on the operations of the Soviet system. A major difference was the immediate influence of Stalin's heritage on the collective leaders of 1953. Beria, one of the four most powerful figures after Stalin's demise, had such an unsavory reputation as police chief that he could not trust the other leaders not to put all the blame for Stalinist excesses on him; conversely, the other leaders had good reason to suspect that Beria would resort, if he could, to a *coup d'état* to oust them. In the upshot Malenkov, Molotov, and Khrushchev joined to destroy Beria and to conduct a purge of his lieutenants. This action, understandable though it was, had devastating implications for collective leadership. First, it was necessary to take over Beria's sphere of control by promoting numerous officials and by institutional reorganization. These drastic changes threatened the balance of power among the remaining top leaders and greatly increased the influence of the appointive authority—the Secretariat under Khrushchev. In contrast, the post-Khrushchev period has been one of remarkably stable organizational structure and personnel assignments. This stability facilitates equilibrium among top leaders and minimizes the top Party secretary's temptation to assume supreme power.

Secondly, the bloodletting entailed by the execution of

Beria and his followers reinforced the profound fear engendered by Stalin's tactics that defeat in a political controversy meant utter disgrace if not physical extermination. With these lessons so close at hand, Khrushchev and his rivals perceived the stakes of rivalry to be so high that any risk was justified to attain complete victory. That such considerations were really in the minds of the contestants is demonstrated by the fact that Lazar Kaganovich (and probably others) begged Khrushchev not to treat them as Stalin had treated his enemies. In fact, Khrushchev brought such serious charges against his opponents that disgrace was inevitable and execution a credible threat. All "anti-Party" figures were charged with violating the Leninist proscription of factional activity. Several, notably Malenkov, were accused (not untruthfully) of complicity in Beria's most heinous crimes—offenses that might entail extreme penalties in any society. Significantly, however, the most severe physical retribution actually ordered (if rumors coming from Moscow at the time were true) was directed against Dmitri Shepilov, an official relatively innocent of complicity in Stalin's crimes who had, however, committed the unpardonable offense of deserting Khrushchev's personal following. Shepilov, a sick man in his fifties, was (according to the rumors) ordered to become a sheep-herder in the frigid Altai Mountains—but was lucky enough to be able to evade the assignment until Khrushchev's overthrow.

The mere fact that during a decade (1955–64) Khrushchev did not execute his defeated rivals went a long way toward establishing a new perception of the stakes of the game of Soviet politics. Since his overthrow one of the deepest resolves of the collective leadership appears to be to maintain the ban (which Lenin advocated and even Stalin respected until 1930) against internecine conflict. Khrushchev himself was allowed to live out his life in peaceful obscurity, without even explicit public criticism. Prominent figures in his entou-

rage, like his son-in-law Aleksei I. Adzhubei, although demoted
are apparently unmolested. Some of Khrushchev's disgraced
rivals have received slightly improved treatment under his successors—Kliment Y. Voroshilov, for example, was honored at
his death, and Malenkov has been seen privately in Moscow.
For nearly nine years none of the new collective leadership was
demoted, although several (notably Aleksandr N. Shelepin)
were apparently rebuffed on policy matters. In April, 1973,
Pyotr Y. Shelest and G. I. Voronov were officially expelled from
the Politburo in terms that suggested disgrace for policy failures. At the same time, heads of the principal *non-Party*
bureaucracies (Marshal Andrei A. Grechko of the military, Andrei A. Gromyko of the diplomatic service, and Yuri V. Andropov of the police) were admitted to the Politburo. But a
large majority of Politburo members who overthrew Khrushchev, including the top four (Brezhnev, Kosygin, Podgorny,
and Suslov), retain their positions. Evidently a reinforcing
process is involved: the stabler the collective leadership, the
less need to resort to extreme measures against dissidents; and
the longer the latter are treated with consideration, the more
likely they are to accept collective decisions without violent
opposition. In other words, in contrast to the Stalin period,
which eroded "collective leadership" until it became a hollow
phrase, the concept has gradually become a significant legitimizing principle of Soviet policy formation.

A third, closely related factor is the difference between the
images of personal leadership in the periods 1953–55 and
1964–74. In every modern political system there is probably a
tendency to have one man, whether he be an American President or a British Prime Minister, symbolize authority. In the
Soviet system, after Stalin's death the absence of legitimate institutional mechanisms for articulating and resolving differences vastly enhanced this tendency. As was discussed in Chap-

ter 3, the formal Party election procedures and discusssions are manipulated in the name of monolithism and to secure "balanced" virtual representation. Given this covert but continuous deviation from avowed principles of democratic centralism, it is easy for rival groups to go a step further and manipulate the Party operations for their own purposes. Furthermore, Lenin's pre-eminence and Stalin's quarter-century of dictatorship had so accustomed most Party officials to direction from above that in 1953 they probably regarded one-man dictatorship as inevitable. That did not mean, however, that they wanted a return to the Stalin type of dictatorship, which had made the member of the Party apparatus as insecure as the average citizen. It is highly significant that Khrushchev was able to undermine Malenkov, particularly, by stressing his involvement (with Beria) in the destruction of major Party officials (the "Leningrad affair"). In effect, Khrushchev was offering himself as an alternative on the "platform" of security for the apparatus. This assurance was credible for several reasons. Khrushchev had, in fact, been less involved in Party repression than the other principal leaders. During his long tenure as head of the Ukrainian Party organization, he had fostered more regular functioning of Party bodies like the Union Republic central committee and the oblast committees. While Khrushchev directed Ukrainian affairs firmly, he involved himself intimately with lower apparatus members and their bread-and-butter concerns instead of carrying out covert manipulation from the remote recesses of the Kremlin, as did Stalin and his principal lieutenants. Finally, and perhaps most significant, Khrushchev (fifty-nine in 1953) was eight years older than Malenkov, his most formidable rival, and nearly fifteen years older than Stalin was when Lenin died. Apparatus members who feared a reversion to Stalin's terror may well have considered that Khrushchev was the safer al-

ternative for top leader because his age did not permit him
time enough to repeat Stalin's crafty, step-by-step elimination
of the Party leadership.

In the upshot, such a calculation may well have been sound,
for it is quite possible that a younger Khrushchev would have
outwitted the leaders who ousted him in 1964. Through a
series of complicated organizational maneuvers (creation of
the Party bureau for the R.S.F.S.R., consolidation of the sov-
narkhozes—the provincial economic councils discussed in
Chapter 6—and the bifurcation of the apparatus between industrial and agricultural direction), Khrushchev seemed to be
preparing to replace many of his old apparatus adherents with
younger, more amenable figures. Quite possibly Khrushchev
even intended to reduce the power of the Party apparatus in
general. In the end, this slow, roundabout maneuvering was
probably too difficult for a septuagenarian (Khrushchev was
six months past seventy when ousted) to control.

On ousting Khrushchev, his principal successors could take
some comfort in the consideration that if a man as energetic
as Khrushchev had been too old to become complete dictator,
none of them was likely to possess the ability to do so. Brezhnev
was then already fifty-eight, almost as old as Khrushchev at
Stalin's death; the others (premier Aleksei N. Kosygin, sixty;
indoctrination secretary Mikhail A. Suslov, sixty-two; future
titular president Nikolai V. Podgorny, sixty-one) were still
older. It seems more than a coincidence that the "young" member of the original top five collective leaders, Shelepin (forty-six
in 1964), is the only one who has been demoted from this inside
circle. Today, with the top leaders ten years older, the prospects that any one of them will believe it possible, let alone
worth while, to exert himself to become absolute dictator appears remote.

Given these circumstances Brezhnev's unquestionable rise
in prominence during the late 1960's was a much more com-

plicated phenomenon than Stalin's or Khrushchev's movement toward pre-eminence. Like those of the earlier leaders,
Brezhnev's biography, depicting him in suitably heroic proportions, has gradually assumed a significant place in Soviet
accounts. His wartime exploits—in fact he was a moderately
important political officer at the front—are played up in discussions of World War II. Quite possibly concern for his
image (in 1945 he did play a significant part in annexing a
portion of Czechoslovakia to the U.S.S.R.) was a factor in
Soviet decisions like the 1968 suppression of Czechoslovak liberalization. But it would be most unwise to exaggerate the
import of Brezhnev's domestic prominence. Not only has he
coupled no official government title with his Party post, but
no major policy innovation has been attributed to him personally. In the foreign policy field, the situation is quite
different. In negotiations with Communist states, with Soviet
clients like India and Egypt, and more recently in high-level
conferences with the United States, Brezhnev has clearly played
the leading role, in spite of the fact that diplomacy is formally
the prerogative of government officials. But here the realities
of international relations constitute a major pressure for a single leader to symbolize Soviet power. It would be physically
difficult for the U.S.S.R. constantly to confront prominent individual heads of government like Nixon, Sadat, Tito, or
Indira Gandhi with a collective of four or five leaders. Psychologically, the Soviet Union derives some advantage abroad
by appearing to have a decisive spokesman. The most that
can be concluded, therefore, is that *when* one Soviet leader
must stand forth, Brezhnev clearly has had the advantage.

POLITBURO AND CENTRAL COMMITTEE

As has already been noted, the formal institutional expression of the collective leadership is the Politburo, but outside

observers generally agree that the inner core of four leaders is decisive. While there have been few shifts in the voting membership (now sixteen), the relative influence of individuals below the top four appears to have changed drastically, with men like V. V. Shcherbitsky (now head of the Ukrainian Party organization) and A. P. Kirilenko rising as Shelepin and Shelest declined. Most of these other members appear to be allies or protégés of one or another of the "big four," as do the more frequently replaced or promoted alternate members. The real significance of the Politburo is that it brings together most of the men with great personal influence in the Soviet elite, including the heads of major sections of the apparatus. Since a large majority reside in Moscow, the Politburo can and does function as a day-to-day decision-making body. The very fact that no major policies, at least in the domestic field, have been publicly identified with individual leaders suggests that all major domestic policy innovations receive the stamp of approval of the Politburo. It seems fair to assume that Politburo members jealously maintain their right to scrutinize every proposal. As long as this situation prevails, jockeying for advantage by promoting new policies is minimized. Thus stability is promoted, but, as discussed below, policy adaptivity is threatened.

In terms of continuity of action, the Politburo is poles apart from the other officially recognized agency of collective leadership, the Central Committee. While (according to Brezhnev) the Politburo meets every Thursday and sometimes oftener, the Central Committee averages about three meetings a year (two are required by the statutes). Usually its members are scattered over the U.S.S.R. Even when they come together, the two- to four-day sessions are too brief to permit the large membership to engage in full discussion of policies, much less to suggest and elaborate innovations. Ordinarily the timing, the agenda, and the course of discussion in Central Committee meetings have been set in advance by the Politburo. According to the principles of democratic centralism, no group of Central Committee members can suggest alternatives. Yet in several crisis situations since Stalin's death the Central Committee has assumed a position of commanding importance. Perhaps the first was the secret directive of January, 1955, which ordered Malenkov to resign as prime minister. All available evidence suggests that on this occasion the Central Committee, the Politburo, and the Party First Secretary (Khrushchev) were in full accord. Hence no question of Central Committee leadership's violating democratic centralist principles could arise. Nevertheless, the acclaim devoted to the Central Committee as the repository of Leninist collective leadership provided a tentative legitimization for its future initiative. In June, 1957, the legitimating potential of the Central Committee was greatly enhanced. There is no doubt that Khrushchev lost control of the Politburo majority, yet he refused its directive to resign. He justified what might have been considered a violation of democratic centralism by arguing that only the Central Committee, which had elected him (simultaneously with, but separate from, the Politburo), could dismiss him. That Khrushchev used formal Party provisions, which permit one-third of the Central Committee members to call for a special session, appears doubtful. In any case, the Central Committee did convene and proceeded to discuss the "anti-Party" affair on its own or Khrushchev's formal motion (thus bypassing Politburo confirmation of the agenda). At that time, the Central Committee condemned Khrushchev's rivals; but the precedent for its defiance of the Politburo majority was evidently good enough to justify, in October, 1964, a Politburo majority and a Central Committee majority to combine in defying and ousting the First Secretary, Khrushchev himself.

So far, four patterns of subordination among the top

agencies of the Party have occurred.* During his last years, Stalin, as General Secretary, virtually ignored both Politburo and Central Committee. Earlier, in the 1930's, he utilized a docile Politburo to destroy most Central Committee members. Under Khrushchev, Party chief, Politburo, and Central Committee were usually in harmony, but once Khrushchev used the Central Committee against the Politburo. Finally, the present Politburo sided with the Central Committee to remove Khrushchev. Two more patterns are analytically possible: The Politburo may dominate the General Secretary and at the same time relegate the Central Committee to impotence by preventing its meeting; or the Central Committee may seize the initiative to replace both the General Secretary and the Politburo or, conceivably, even to begin policy innovation. For the present, neither eventuality appears imminent. A moderate degree of prominence for the General Secretary appears to be fairly well assured. In the ordinary course of affairs, the Politburo, as long as it is united, has vast advantages. In a crisis, when the Politburo is divided, however, the Central Committee may take charge in line with its precedents of 1957 and 1964. The broader way in which the Central Committee represents the bureaucracies that constitute the Soviet elite and the grass-roots contacts that Central Committee members retain would then be powerful factors in its favor.

THE SECRETARIAT

Before examining the social characteristics of the Soviet elite, however, it is important to look at the organization of the

---

* There are, of course, two patterns of interrelation which do not entail subordination of any of the three Party agencies to the others: the common pattern of mutual harmony; and a hypothetical pattern in which none of the three were influential. The latter pattern, if persistent, would entail the end of the Soviet system, as we have known it, although for a transitory period in 1941–42 Party authority was replaced, to a considerable degree, by military.

Party's apparatus. The key organ is the Secretariat. Unquestionably it was Stalin's position as head of the Secretariat (General Secretary) and Khrushchev's acquisition of this post in 1953 (First Secretary) that made it possible for them to acquire commanding positions in the Soviet political system. Reasons why Brezhnev seems unlikely to repeat this process have been suggested above. Nevertheless, it is almost certain that he owes his position as "first among equals" in the Politburo to his direction of the Secretariat. The precedent is firmly set that, whatever the actual extent of his authority may be, the General Secretary occupies the highest place in the Soviet power structure.

Part of the importance of the Secretariat derives from its large representation in the Politburo itself. One-fourth of the full members and a majority of the alternates are also Secretaries. With the exception of Brezhnev, each Secretary exercises supervision over a specific sphere of operations, although until recently these spheres of activity have not been permanent; shifts and recombinations of spheres have been frequent. Below this level, the divisions of the Secretariat, although occasionally formally redesignated, are relatively stable. Two sections appear to perform routine internal tasks for the Secretariat. The remaining sections are organized according to specific areas of activity and are designed to perform broad, general functions for the Soviet system and to supervise limited areas of Soviet society and foreign affairs.

The Administrative Organs Section supervises the general state bureaucracy. There are eleven sections for economic activities. The International Section supervises relations with Communist parties in countries not dominated by Communist regimes; the Section for Liaison with Communist and Worker's Parties of Socialist Countries, as its title indicates, deals with the Communist-bloc countries. The Military Section (identical with the Main Political Administration of the Defense Ministry) supervises political officers in the armed forces. The director of the Military Section is not only a Party official but a general officer in the armed forces. Through him, the network of political officers in the armed forces is subordinated to the Secretariat as well as to the line military officers—a powerful device for securing military subordination to the regime.

As is the case with the primary Party organizations and intermediate Party levels, Secretariat sections are not supposed to direct economic activity or the state bureaucracy. They are to oversee, stimulate, and check the other bureaucracies; these, in turn, supposedly are free to administer their own areas of competence. Obviously, the line between interfering in administrative decisions and merely prodding administrators to take action is a thin one. Much depends on the balance of forces between state and Party officials. If the state economic directors have powerful friends among top members of the regime, Party influence is limited; if a segment of the economy is lagging and its formal directors are under severe criticism, the corresponding Party officials may assume practical direction. In the past ten years, state economic directors appear to have regained a considerable measure of independence. Under these circumstances, direct intervention in industry by the Secretariat economic sections and lower Party levels is largely confined to peripheral matters such as indoctrination programs for workers, expediting of shipments, and smoothing over frictions between economic agencies. In agriculture, on the other hand, Party intervention has always been more direct and important. But with both agriculture and industry, each Secretariat section (assisted by lower levels of the Party apparatus) continues to perform for its corresponding economic sphere the *nomenklatura* function—the assignment of Party members to positions. Since the overwhelming majority of administrative personnel belongs to the Party, this function is crucial.

THE INDOCTRINATION MACHINERY

Important as the sections just described are, those dealing with indoctrination and ideology are clearly closer to the heart of Party operations. In Chapter 2 the increasing importance of indoctrination as a means for approaching complete Communism was analyzed, while Chapter 3 examined the vast complex of indoctrinational activities. All of these are directed, ultimately, by the Propaganda and Agitation Section of the Secretariat. Its propaganda subsection ("sector") is officially charged with the presentation of a complex theme to a limited group and is therefore especially concerned with the supervision of the training courses described earlier. The sector for agitation (officially described as the presentation of a few ideas to the mass of the population) supervises the enormous body of Party agitators. The sector on mass work is apparently concerned with indoctrination activities in the Komsomol, trade unions, and special-purpose organizations.

The work of the Propaganda and Agitation Section is also directly connected, through the sectors on central journals, publishing, and criticism, with indoctrination through the printed word and mass media. Most newspapers are directly operated by the Party. Newspapers are important not only as vehicles for indoctrination but also as a major means for enforcing central Party standards on lower organizations. Reporters from high-level papers have the right of access to all lower-level offices and economic agencies; they may inspect the premises, examine records, and question employees. Consequently, they constitute a permanent body of roving inspectors who may drop in entirely unexpectedly upon a complacent lower official. Often these visits are prompted by letters to the editor from politically zealous or personally dissatisfied employees or clients of the agency concerned. If the reporter finds an unsatisfactory situation, he may not order corrective measures. But, after the approval of his editor (often in consultation with the Secretariat), the reporter may write a scathing article. Few officials can withstand an attack of this nature in, let us say, *Pravda*.

Pravda and the other central newspapers are by no means alone in performing this inspectional function. Each level of Party organization down through the district has its own newspaper. Moreover, since a newspaper is not confined to criticizing agencies on or immediately below its own level, but may range down the organizational scale, agencies at the lower levels may be subject to unexpected visits and attacks by representatives of several newspapers.

The Propaganda and Agitation Section of the central Secretariat has inspectors of its own; their work is largely confined to the supervision of indoctrination, but within this sphere they, too, "jump" over the chain of command by making critical visits not only to the next lower level of Party organization, but to all those below it.

In addition to the Propaganda and Agitation Section, the indoctrination sphere includes the Culture Section, the Science and Educational Institutions Section, and quite possibly the Section for Travel Abroad. All aspects of cultural activity (theaters, radio, television, literature, etc.), science, and education are, in the totalitarian view, closely linked to indoctrination. As will be described in Chapter 5, the aim of the Party is not only to exclude divergent views in all of these intellectual activities, but also to make sure that every medium for the conveyance of ideas is positively attuned to the objectives of the regime. The operational responsibility for attaining this coordination of public expression is assigned to a closely knit body of officials. In the course of his career, an official in this group may occupy such seemingly varied positions as director of a propaganda and agitation section, political adviser to a poetry review, newspaper editor, chairman of a state-television-network committee, and president of a society for the dissemination of atheism. But whatever his job, he is primarily concerned with positive indoctrination. Because of its care in selecting, training, and supervising such officials, the Party can avoid much of the obtrusive and irritating effect of direct censorship, although censorship is always available as a reserve weapon. Instead, the appropriate indoctrination official sees that the Party line is followed by the medium of expression he supervises.

Except during brief periods of intra-Party conflict when publications occasionally reflect factional positions, Party supervision of the media is highly effective.

THE PARTY ORGANS SECTION

If any part of the Party apparatus has the potential of acting as the nerve center of the control system, it is the complex known in Western administrative terminology as the "staff agencies." This potential has at times been realized, especially in the period immediately following the Great Purge of 1936–38. At that time, the Cadres Section, charged with the supervision and distribution of personnel, and an Organization-Inspection Section worked closely with the police to maintain the iron, terroristic control of the Party that Stalin required. Malenkov's unpopularity with the Party elite was apparently due in large part to his association with the staff agencies during and after the Great Purge. Since the beginning of World War II, the staff agencies have been reorganized and have somewhat declined in importance. The task of assigning Party personnel to economic fields has been transferred to the various economic ("production-branch") sections of the Secretariat, and to the corresponding sections at lower levels of Party organization. The central Party Organs Section retains the extremely important power of assignment of high- and medium-level personnel to Party and Komsomol organizations as well as to state and trade-union administrative agencies.

The Party Organs sections also play a key role in inspecting the lower Party organizations. As in the case of newspaper "inspection," the chain-of-command concept familiar in Western bureaucracies is frequently disregarded by the Party Organs sections. The central Party Organs Section retains the power of appointment (*nomenklatura*) of some key officials at much lower levels. Similarly, a Party Organs Section inspector from the central Secretariat may unexpectedly visit a district Party organization. As was discussed earlier, assignment of higher Party personnel is a key power at the disposal of the General Secretary. In the 1920's, Stalin ruthlessly utilized the assignment power to reward his adherents and to punish tacitly any official who did not support him: Since all Party members were bound to accept assignments given them by the Secretariat, a recalcitrant official in a key post could be silenced by dispatch on a mission abroad, or tormented by appointment to a post in a remote, undesirable region. Khrushchev used the assignment power much more sparingly, though he did promote a disproportionate number of his followers, especially between 1953 and 1956. It is evident, however, that, in contrast to Stalin, he was unable to "pack" the Central Committee sufficiently to make it his instrument. Having rebuffed Khrushchev's attempt to reorganize the apparatus and replace its older members, the present Central Committee seems to have concluded a "social compact" providing that members in good standing and physically capable will not be replaced. At the same time, successive Congresses since Khrushchev have enlarged the Central Committee to allow some scope for promotion of new elite members.

The effect of these two processes can be examined by determining a promotion rate and an attrition rate for the full, voting membership of the Central Committee.* Following this procedure, one can calculate that the promotion rate (in absolute numbers of individuals promoted) between 1966 and 1971 was 18 per annum, as compared to 13 during the period of Khrushchev's overthrow. Because the Central Committee was much smaller under Khrushchev, these promotion rates appear to be very similar to those prevailing when he controlled the Secretariat: 16 per annum during 1952–56 and 19 during 1956–61. If one compares attrition rates, i.e., the proportions of members dropped per year (exclusive of those who died natural deaths), however, quite a different picture emerges. During 1952–56 the attrition rate was 13 per annum, and it was 11 during 1956–61. After Khrushchev's dominance, on the other hand, the attrition rate dropped to under 7 per annum (1961–66) and barely rose to 7.6 during 1966–71. What these data appear to indicate is that, while the power of the senior members of the Central Committee which ousted Khrushchev is being diluted by the addition of new members at the customary post-Stalin rate, the senior members have a much stronger statistical probability of retaining their posts than under Khrushchev. Scrutiny of individual cases of removals of 1961 members bears out the significance of this generalization. A majority of those dropped in 1971 were, in fact, either those who appear to have been especially close adherents of Khrushchev or members from non-Slavic nationalities and

* All promotions and removals are formally made at All-Union Party Congresses, but since the intervals between congresses have varied, it seems appropriate to impute an annual rate for both promotion and attrition.

remote regions who may not be considered full participants in the "social compact."

Retention of a majority of the Central Committee members elected in 1961 or earlier is a stabilizing influence on the regime. As long as these men feel secure, they are likely to act as an additional force to prevent rivalries within the Politburo from becoming as desperate as they were under Stalin and Khrushchev. From other points of view, however, the Soviet system pays a high price for stability of elite membership. Since Central Committee members comprise most of the high officials who run all of the U.S.S.R.'s bureaucracies, the low rate of removal means that aging men are in charge at the intermediate levels as well as in the inner core of the Politburo. Today only 10 per cent of the Central Committee voting members are under fifty years old; 35 per cent are in their fifties, 47 per cent in their sixties, and nearly 9 per cent in their seventies. Moreover, the age level of the elite has been increasing rapidly. A 1968 analysis that dealt with a somewhat lower-level group (it included alternate as well as voting members of the Central Committee) indicated that only 4 per cent were seventy or over, 30 per cent in their sixties, 50 per cent in their fifties, and 16 per cent under fifty.* In other words, as recently as six years ago the center of gravity was an elite group in its fifties; now the median group is past sixty.

ELITE SOCIAL CHARACTERISTICS

Several important, though partially speculative, inferences can be drawn from the Central Committee's present age distribution. One type of inference is obtained by relating *age cohorts* (groups born in specific periods) to critical events of Soviet history. Only the cohort born before 1904 had even an

---

* Based on an analysis by Albert Boiter, Director of Research, Radio Liberty (Radio Liberty Research, CDR 200/68, mimeographed).

adolescent experience with pre-Revolutionary society or played any part in the Revolutionary upheaval. On the other hand, the majority of the Central Committee born before 1914 had a number of experiences that are alien to present Soviet conditions: as youths they became acquainted with the considerable range of private enterprise permitted in the 1920's, including predominantly private peasant farming; in the 1930's they frequently participated in the brutal suppression accompanying collectivization and experienced the shock of Stalin's purge. The latter experience probably had a dual effect: on the one hand, it instilled a deep feeling of insecurity in those who observed the apparent arbitrariness of despotic repression; on the other hand, the Great Purge opened prospects for rapid advancement for young men just entering apparatus careers—if they could stifle guilt about profiting from the execution of their mentors and comrades. It seems very likely that a deep-seated desire to avoid a repetition of the Great Purge (with the present leadership as the destined victims) lies behind the "social compact" hypothesized above and makes the present Central Committee membership inordinately fearful of drastic initiatives entailing unforeseeable consequences. On the other hand—despite the nineteen years that have passed without a "blood purge" of defeated rivals—lingering memories of the Great Purge probably imbue the present leadership with a kind of cynical opportunism regarding the "rules of the game" of politics. Finally, it is important to point out that all members over fifty (i.e., practically the entire Central Committee) served in World War II, which had become their "heroic age." This catastrophic experience probably instilled strong senses of (1) Russian or East Slavic patriotism; (2) the delicate balance of strengths and weaknesses in the Soviet system; and (3) the expendability of human life (over 20 million Soviet citizens died) in a cause of extreme importance. Certainly the impact of all of these experiences distinguishes the

dominant Central Committee cohorts from younger elements
in the Soviet population, as well as many foreign elites.

A second line of analysis considers the dominant Central
Committee age groups as generations, i.e., analysis focuses on
their present age levels. From this standpoint, they (and the
Politburo) appear as a group of elderly men, most over sixty,
stubbornly hanging on to their power. Such an age stratification is likely to give rise to feelings of a "generation gap" for
two reasons. Younger apparatus officials find their promotion
to major positions blocked, even when they have reached their
late forties or early fifties. Their resentment may be enhanced
by the fact that they know it was common after the Great
Purge for men in their middle thirties—including some of
those who still cling to power—to attain posts at the Central
Committee level. A second reason is the great perceived difference in outlook of the elite on the one hand, and the lower
officials, the Party membership, and the general population on
the other. Data on Party age distribution is released infre-
quently, but according to 1967 figures more than half were
under forty-one, and only 23 per cent in the fifty-plus age
group, which includes nearly all Central Committee members.
Apart from the vast gap in life experiences noted above, advanced age would normally lead the elite to be far more concerned with stability, caution, and maintenance of the status
quo than the younger mass elements.

Finally, a major factor is related to both cohort and generation factors—the kind of preparation that members of the
present elite have received for their posts. A considerable proportion of the elite in the sixty-and-over age group received
no regular education beyond elementary schooling (except
perhaps a certain amount of vocational training at the secondary level) until they went to the full-time Party schools discussed in Chapter 3. Since officials of this type were already
launched on successful apparatus careers before receiving this

additional training, they tended to concentrate on tasks like personnel direction and agricultural supervision, which do not require a high degree of technical expertise. Many of the older age group and most of those under sixty, on the other hand, were able (sometimes rather belatedly) either to secure regular higher educations or to acquire experience in a profession before entering the apparatus. Today men of this type clearly predominate in the Soviet elite, as well as in lower ranks of the Party apparatus. Some have higher education in social sciences, education, or journalism. Like Suslov, originally trained as an economist, they tend to specialize in indoctrination. Most, however, have technical training. Brezhnev (a metallurgical engineer), Kosygin (a textile factory director), and Podgorny (a factory engineer) typify this group. These men are much better equipped to cope with the advanced technology of the modern Soviet economy than were their predecessors. But the narrowness of their professional training limits their horizons. Few have experience in travel abroad or considerable contact with groups concerned with humanistic culture. This elite segment, therefore, tends to stress material, tangible considerations in solving problems to the neglect of the psychological aspects. It not only is increasingly separated from the intellectual segment of Soviet society but is beginning to recognize that even administrative problems call for broader training.

ELITE ATTITUDES

So much space has been devoted to uncertain, though probable, inferences about attitudes of the present Soviet elite because one has few other methods to determine these attitudes. Direct interrogation is nearly always impossible; Soviet leaders do not submit to searching questioning even by Communist journalists and social investigators. One supplementary source consists of descriptions of leaders used as models for emulation by younger Party or Komsomol members. Unfortunately for our purposes, few of these idealized biographies or autobiographies deal with personalities of contemporary officials. World War II accounts were useful for analyzing the attitudes of the older, generally uneducated group of officials who obtained top posts immediately after the Great Purge, but they are not very helpful in considering the technically trained officials who now predominate. The best substitute for actual biographical material consists of synthetic fictional portraits like Vsevolod Kochetov's *Secretary of the Obkom,* published by the Komsomol Press. Although both his rigid orthodoxy and his limited literary talents make other Soviet novelists contemptuous of Kochetov, the very fact that his work reflects official values makes it more useful to us.

In 1961, Kochetov's hero, Vasily Antonovich Denisov, had for a short time occupied the post of obkom first secretary in the fictional city of Stargorod ("Old City") in the northwestern R.S.F.S.R. Denisov was born about 1912 (i.e., a year before the median birth year for the present elite), in a poor peasant family of what became Leningrad province. Nevertheless, thanks to the opportunities provided by the Soviet system he had been able to get a good engineering education in Leningrad and then to move from technical to minor administrative to Party posts. Each of his personal successes is identified with an arduous but triumphant stage of Soviet progress:

> Life moved on, on, on. . . . The years flew by. He became an engineer, a shop director. After some time he became secretary of the shop Party organization, then secretary of the factory primary party organization. He went to war in a militia division, was wounded in battle of Gatchina, recovered, returned to the division; was wounded a second time in the Nevsky salient, again recovered and again returned to the division. Wounded a third time, severely, near Poznan, when he was already commander of an artillery regiment, he spent a long time recovering. Eventually recovered he was once more in the factory, again in the Party com-

mittee. Sofia Pavlovna [Denisov's wife] worked in her school all these years, teaching children history and working on her higher degree. Eight years ago, by decision of the Central Committee, both arrived in this city. Vasily Antonovich was [at first] Central Committee Party organizer for machinery manufacturing. She entered the regional history museum, where, under Chernogus's direction, she headed one of the sections.*

It is clear that Denisov and his colleagues enjoy larger-than-average apartments, trips to Moscow and Leningrad, the use of large, chauffeured automobiles, and a special vacation house for obkom personnel. But the novel mentions these perquisites only in passing. Like earlier models, Denisov is pictured as a faithful husband and father, but one who does not allow affection to become so intense as to interfere with his overriding duty to the Party. "The young couple twice brought this little son, who had become Vasily Antonovich's grandson, from Leningrad to visit his grandpa. The grandpa hadn't been extraordinarily affectionate even toward his own children, he didn't belong to that category of parents who lose their heads if one of their offspring sneezes or falls on the ground, leaves a button unbuttoned, or scratches a finger." † At one point Denisov replies sententiously to a subordinate who points out that their overtime work is keeping Sofia Pavlovna waiting, "Such is the fate of your wife and mine, Roman Prokofyevich. To wait and wait." ‡ Denisov takes great pains not to afford even the appearance of favoritism in dealing with the rather muddled affairs of his wife's relatives and his own son. Characteristically, the one time he lets personal feelings interfere with his duty is in retaining a war comrade, whom age and vanity have made incompetent, as director of a major factory. When Denisov finally does decide to retire him, the old buddy says

* *Sekretar Obkoma* (Moscow: "Molodaya Gvardiya," 1962), p. 16.
† *Ibid.*, p. 11.
‡ *Ibid.*, p. 8.

reproachfully, "No, Vasily, you're no Bolshevik, you're a Party hack. For you people are nothing, friendship is nothing . . ." But Denisov sternly replies, "The Bolsheviks above all remembered and upheld the interests of the Party." * One wonders how the present over-age war buddies who make up the Central Committee read these lines ten years after they were published. But the present leadership would agree entirely with Denisov's wholehearted, almost fanatical devotion to his work:

> The obkom secretary's day was spent at work—in telephone calls, in discussions, in negotiations, in preparing documents, in signing papers. Such days were unavoidable and necessary. Vasily Antonovich went out into the oblast, to rayon centers, to villages, to enterprises, he remembered that such "apparatus" days couldn't be avoided. Perhaps it would not be so in the future. But, obviously, that would be in the far distant future, when full and complete Communism had been attained. In the meantime, whether you wanted to or not, whether you enjoyed it or not— meetings, preparation of paperwork, signatures, discussions and persuasions, pressure and still more pressure, which one could still not do without.†

Because he stood at the head of the Party apparatus, Denisov was obliged to concern himself with all aspects of life in the oblast:

> He made the rounds of the factories, he drove by the fields. Plan fulfillment was not always going well in the factories, sometimes rain interfered with work in the fields. Somewhere someone was turning aside from the Party path; somewhere, despite its director's second unsuccessful appeal, insufficient construction materials were emasculating the work of a scientific institute. With each year more children were being born in the oblast, but there were not enough places for them in the day nurseries and the kindergartens, and the mothers complained, demanded, protested. Some foreign tourists were arrested on the territory of a military installation—what were they doing there with their inevitable

* *Ibid.*, p. 206.
† *Ibid.*, p. 98.

cameras? Borkov and Drozdov reported that for several days the stores had had no sugar to sell, and the people were grumbling.*

DISTRIBUTION OF THE APPARATUS

Because the obkom first secretaries occupy a crucial place in the elite, it is particularly important to gain some insight into their attitudes. But, as noted earlier, a major value of examining the Central Committee membership is that it contains the top personnel of *all* major bureaucracies, Party and state, military and civil. More than two-fifths of the full members are officials of the Party apparatus itself. More than three-fourths of the one hundred Party officials have posts in the field, usually as obkom first secretaries. Exactly the reverse is true of the almost equal contingent of state bureaucracy officials: nearly three-fourths have posts in Moscow ministries, as compared to only fifteen in provincial assignments. Approximately one-tenth of the voting members are from various special bureaucracies like the police; are famous artists or scientists; or, in a very few cases, are simply "figureheads" like record-breaking milkmaids and coal miners chosen to give a slight populist flavor to the Central Committee. Finally, slightly under 10 per cent are high-ranking officers of the armed forces; their significance will be treated in the next chapter.

SUGGESTED READING · CHAPTER 4

Nearly all the books on the Soviet system and the Communist Party listed in the preceding chapter deal with the apparatus. The following titles deal with particular aspects of the apparatus rather than Party affairs in general.

ARMSTRONG, JOHN A. *The Soviet Bureaucratic Elite: A Case Study of the Ukrainian Apparatus.* New York: Praeger, 1959. A case

* *Ibid.*, p. 14.

study of the backgrounds, turnover, and attitudes of Party officials in the Ukraine.

CONQUEST, ROBERT. *Power and Policy in the U.S.S.R.: The Struggle for Stalin's Succession, 1945–1960.* New York: Harper Torchbooks paperback, 1967. An ingenious and fascinating reconstruction of the power struggle in the apparatus.

——. *Russia After Khrushchev.* New York: Praeger, 1965. An examination of rivalries during Khrushchev's last years in power and an analysis of future prospects.

FISCHER, GEORGE. *The Soviet System and Modern Society.* New York: Atherton Press, 1968. A complex statistical analysis of the social characteristics of the Soviet elite, particularly its changing education and occupational experience.

FYODOROV, ALEKSEI. *The Underground R.C. Carries On.* Moscow: Foreign Languages Publishing House, 1952. Almost the only book of an autobiographical nature by a recent high official, this work deals primarily with partisan operations in World War II but in doing so reveals much concerning the organization and psychology of Party operations.

HOUGH, JERRY. *The Soviet Prefects: The Local Party Organs in Industrial Decision-making.* Cambridge, Mass.: Harvard University Press, 1969. A detailed examination of the relations between Party and state bureaucracies at the oblast level.

JUVILER, PETER H., and MORTON, HENRY W. (eds.). *Soviet Policy-Making: Studies of Communism in Transition.* New York: Praeger, 1967. A series of case studies on policy formation in family welfare, economic activity, literature, science, and foreign policy.

Khrushchev Remembers (Trans. and ed. STROBE TALBOTT). Boston: Little, Brown, 1970. This large book appears to contain some new material written by Khrushchev or based on conversations with him; unfortunately, it is virtually useless as a source of reliable information because there is no way to separate Khrushchev's revelations from others' insertions.

LINDEN, CARL A. *Khrushchev and the Soviet Leadership, 1957–1964.* The best detailed analysis of the period between the "anti-Party" affair and Khrushchev's own ouster.

MEDVEDEV, ZHORES. *Let History Judge: The Origins and Consequences of Stalinism.* (Trans. COLLEEN TAYLOR; ed. DAVID JORAVSKY and GEORGES HAUPT). New York: Knopf, 1971. Massive coverage of the intrigues of the Stalin period, with few new revelations but remarkable for having been composed by dissidents within the U.S.S.R.

PLOSS, SIDNEY I. (ed.). *The Soviet Political Process: Aims, Techniques, and Examples of Analysis.* Waltham, Mass.: Ginn, 1971. A symposium devoted mainly to the post-Khrushchev period, consequently providing numerous speculative but interesting analyses.

RUSH, MYRON. *Political Succession in the U.S.S.R.* New York: Columbia University Press, 1965. A study of the way top leaders have been replaced.

———. *The Rise of Khrushchev.* Washington, D. C.: Public Affairs Press, 1958. A detailed description of Khrushchev's attainment of power after Stalin's death.

SKILLING, N. GORDON (ed.). *Interest Groups in Soviet Politics.* Princeton, N. J.: Princeton University Press, 1971. A symposium discussing the extent to which specific Soviet bureaucracies and less institutionalized groups resemble groups in pluralist societies.

TATU, MICHEL. *Power in the Kremlin: From Khrushchev to Kosygin.* New York: Viking Compass Paperback, 1970. The best interpretation of post-Khrushchev power alignments, by the Moscow correspondent of *Le Monde.*

5

INSTRUMENTS OF COERCION

At the beginning of this book, we noted that though political power requires the monopoly of force, force alone is an inadequate basis for a political system. The four chapters that followed showed that the Soviet system is not, in fact, based on force alone. A political culture, the result of a blend of traditional Russian attitudes and totalitarian Communist ideology, is of critical importance. Additionally, the institutional framework of the Communist Party enables a self-chosen and self-perpetuating elite to maintain a monopoly over decision-making. Indoctrination stressing the unique legitimacy of the Party's decisions, inculcation of belief in the inevitability of a perfect Communist social order, almost exclusive control over career advancement, pervasive control of communication channels, are among the powerful factors that maintain this monopoly. Party-elite dominance was not, however, established by these devices. During the first decades of Soviet rule, Lenin and his successors tried to establish total dominance over a society that in large part did not accept the Communist claim to legitimacy. When large elements of a population do not accept a regime's claim to legitimacy, it must either coerce or retreat.

Apart from transient tactical maneuvers, Lenin and all his successors chose to employ force. From the start, the Communists had a strong base of sympathizers in the strategically located urban centers. The regime never neglected persuasion and indoctrination. There is no doubt, however, that without the extensive employment of force, the Soviet regime could not have been stabilized. By the early 1920's, the regime had achieved a quasi-monopoly of internal force, the usual criterion of an established political system. Until the late 1940's, however, the Soviet system was subject to more sporadic outbreaks of armed opposition than are usual in advanced societies. Some, though not all, of these rebellions were encouraged by the fact that the U.S.S.R. had powerful enemies abroad. Under these circumstances, the Soviet regime relied in part on military instruments for maintaining a monopoly of force.

Given the strategic situation of the U.S.S.R., the most important military element has been the ground forces, known until 1946 as the Red Army and, since then, as the Soviet Army. The navy has always been distinctly secondary and, until recent decades, so were the air forces. The army has been essential in defending the U.S.S.R. in its encounters with great powers—during the Civil War of 1918–20, in the limited wars with Japan in 1938–39, and during World War II. The army has also been the principal means by which the Soviet regime imposed Communist governments on peripheral areas of Europe and Asia. Since 1945, the Soviet ground forces have been the most powerful in the world.

The strength of the Soviet Army and its indispensable services in preserving the Soviet regime have led some observers to infer that the commanding officers of the military forces can also dominate the political system. Military commanders can dominate any society *if* they are determined, as a group, to do so; if they command the obedience of their troops; and if they can secure at least passive acquiescence from essential elements of the civilian population. In other words, the military commanders must establish a considerable measure of legitimacy in order to govern. At least until very recently, a number of factors have made attainment of such military legitimacy highly unlikely in the U.S.S.R.

Communist ideology, with its emphasis on the Party leadership as the sole custodian of doctrinal orthodoxy, is completely opposed to military rule. It is true that Lenin admired military writers, used military metaphors, and relied on armed force, but he always insisted on complete subordination of the army command. So did his successors, even when, like Stalin, they sought additional prestige by assuming military ranks and uniforms. All Soviet elites, including the military commanders, are composed of Party members indoctrinated in this principle. The other element of the political-cultural amalgam, Russian tradition, also contains no warrant for military rule. Like Stalin, the Czars utilized a military style and military symbols. But, apart from some doubtful cases in early Russian history, no military usurper ever ruled Russia.

This bias against military rule is reinforced by institutional arrangements. During the Civil War, and for two decades afterward, military commanders were required to obtain the countersignature of political officers (commissars) for every order. Since then, the political officers (known at the regimental and divisional levels as deputy directors for political affairs, or *zampolits*) have been more restricted, but they still supervise indoctrination in military units. Political officers have a wide range of personal contacts with rank-and-file soldiers; it is uncertain whether the rank and file would, in case of conflict, obey the military commander or the *zampolit*. The latter is subordinate in strictly military matters to military commanders. At the same time, the *zampolit* has a separate chain of command and reports to the Main Political Administration of the Soviet High Command, which, as noted earlier, is also a section of the Central Committee Secretariat. The head of the MPA, Aleksei A. Yepishev, is an elderly (66) associate of Brezhnev and Podgorny from the Ukrainian Party apparatus. With his key role in watching the military, Yepishev is probably more influential than many Politburo members.

The Party leadership has conducted recurrent campaigns against alleged dangers from military coups, opprobriously designated "Bonapartism." The reference is, of course, to Napoleon Bonaparte, who ended the political feuds of the French Revolution by establishing a military dictatorship. In Soviet terminology, the first Bonapartist was Trotsky. Trotsky was, however, no career military officer, though as a Party leader he had been delegated to head the commissar system. Moreover, Trotsky went down to defeat without even trying to use his military connections. In 1937, Stalin accused a group of high military commanders, headed by Marshal Mikhail N. Tukhachevsky, of plotting a coup. In recent years, official Soviet sources have revealed what outside observers long suspected: The "plot" was a frame-up concocted by Stalin. During the early months of the German invasion (1941–42), the Party organization was so demoralized that the military command was compelled to assume many important tasks, but it never tried to seize political power. In 1957, Khrushchev accused the foremost war hero, Marshal Georgi Zhukov, of Bonapartist tendencies and removed him as Minister of Defense. It is true that Zhukov, like many military men, was irritated by tight Party control of the military indoctrination system. It is also true that the military command under his direction had a role, though probably a minor one, in suppressing Beria and the "anti-Party" group. In October, 1957, however, other high officers—among them, Marshal Ivan S. Konev—fiercely criticized Zhukov. Their antagonism indicates that there was never a chance of a united military effort to gain power.

As suggested at the beginning of this chapter, however, the Party is not really a monolithic structure either. When it has been rent by factional strife in the past, military influence has somewhat increased. The stable present leadership has kept the military thoroughly subordinated. But this stability has three major potential weaknesses. The most obvious is the advanced age of the collective leadership. One or more of the four core leaders will almost certainly die or become incapacitated within a very few years. His removal will tend to upset the delicate balance, with reshuffling of personnel and organizational arrangements offering temptations to others to gain pre-eminence. Even if these elderly chieftains do not give way to such temptation, all of them, and indeed a majority of the Central Committee, will almost surely pass from active political life during the 1970's. It is extremely difficult to predict what course newer men, who have been jealously excluded from major posts for so many years, will take. Possibly a whole generation will be skipped, with men now in their thirties coming to the fore who do not have the solidarity, the training in caution, and the fear of innovation that the present oligarchy exhibits. In such a situation, military officers, with their relatively homogeneous background and corps solidarity, might gain an advantage. At present the top military commanders, even older than their Party counterparts, are rapidly departing; possibly a new generation of military men will gain top posts slightly before the Party realignment becomes unavoidable.

A second way in which the military might assume power would be through a failure of the present regime or its successor to cope with pressing problems. In the preceding discussion, the antipathy of the elderly oligarchs to innovative policies has been analyzed. In many areas (dealt with in the following chapters), the need for bold policies is apparent. At some point, if civilian authority does not advance them, the Soviet regime may be so threatened that the military may feel obliged to take over. Something of the sort happened in the autumn of 1941, as the Germans were approaching Moscow; confronted with Stalin's despair and disorganization of the Party and police bureaucracies, military commanders in the field assumed a major role in operating the Soviet political system. They meekly surrendered this position to Stalin the following spring, but a force like Stalin may not be present in the future.

The third factor which makes military rule seem less than incredible in the proximate future of the U.S.S.R. is the growing stress on Russian or East Slavic nationalism. As discussed in Chapter 7, there are special reasons why the Soviet Army is the most Russian of the great Soviet institutions. In modern times military rule has commonly been more compatible with nationalism than with other ideologies. Hence decline in ideological fervor heightens the chance for military dictatorship; such a dictatorship would, in turn, almost inevitably reduce Leninism to lip service, for, as noted above, Lenin's teachings would be a standing reproach to the military dictators. Such a development would mean, of course, a fundamental transformation of the Soviet system.

THE SECURITY POLICE

The army was, of course, indispensable to a Soviet victory in the Civil War. Since then, it has rarely been utilized for internal control. Instead, the regime has relied on entirely separate police agencies.* Under Stalin, the police was designed to act as an ultimate safeguard against a military coup as well as against other internal threats. Several divisions,

---

* The titles of these agencies have changed frequently. At first, the Cheka (Extraordinary Commission) was the core of the police. It was followed by the GPU (State Political Administration), renamed OGPU (Unified State Political Administration) after a few months. Still later, the NKVD (People's Commissariat of Internal Affairs) and the NKGB (People's Commissariat of State Security), at times combined, were the most important police agencies. After 1946, the redesignation of the commissariats as ministries meant that the police agencies' abbreviations became MVD and MGB, respectively. In 1954, the principal central agency became the KGB (Committee on State Security). For a few years in the 1960's, Union republic MVD's were redesignated Ministries for Protection of Public Order.

trained and equipped as military formations but completely under police control, were stationed at strategic points such as the environs of Moscow. Soon after Stalin's death and Beria's arrest, these divisions were disbanded. The police organization continues to control sizable military-type formations charged with sealing the Soviet borders against unauthorized passage. These frontier troops formed a special branch of the police organization for decades. In June, 1953, their officers' disaffection for Beria and his security police staff was a prominent factor in the Party leadership's ability to remove Beria.

Under Stalin and Beria, the security police constituted the principal instrument of force for maintaining internal control. The fact that opposition to Stalin's dictatorship could rarely attain the level of armed resistance was largely due to the security police. So pervasive and frightening was its activity that many observers identified terror as an essential characteristic of the Soviet political system. Today, terror can hardly be called a permanent characteristic of the system, but it is probable that terror was a necessary means for establishing the system. The principal methods of security-police terror were (1) pervasive clandestine surveillance; (2) secret arbitrary arrest and condemnation; and (3) confinement to concentration camps. By considering each of these methods and its relation to the current Soviet system, one can estimate the extent to which police terror has become obsolete.

Concentration camps have been largely eliminated. At the height of Stalin's dictatorship, fantastic numbers—estimates range from 5 to 20 million—were incarcerated in camps in remote areas of Siberia, Central Asia, and the European Arctic. While systematic brutality seems to have been rare, living conditions in the concentration camps were terrible. Common criminals received better treatment than "politicals." Most prisoners performed arduous physical labor. Clothing and housing were utterly inadequate for the extremely severe climate and hard working conditions. Especially in the years of scarcity during and following World War II, food rations generally were below subsistence levels except for favored categories of prisoners. Even from the purely material standpoint, waste of manpower through the high death rate and through the inherent inefficiency of forced labor was enormous. Almost as soon as Stalin died, the regime began to empty the concentration camps. Apparently, some 80 per cent of the inmates were released by 1956. As described below, there are still corrective labor camps for those who do not adjust to the work requirements of the system. Political prisoners—members of nationalist undergrounds, religious leaders, and dissident intellectuals—still exist. But these categories contain far fewer persons than in 1953.

The present status of security-police surveillance is more obscure. Under Stalin, the aim was to enfold all of Soviet society in a web of surveillance. For the most part, the professional police director of the "special section" in a military unit, factory, farm, or other element of the Soviet organizational structure relied upon informants outside the police corps. Occasionally these informers were real volunteers, motivated by ideological zeal, patriotic fervor, or personal malice. Soviet indoctrination stressed—and still stresses—the need for universal vigilance against foreign and domestic enemies of the regime. The average citizen, and especially the Party member, is obliged to report suspicious circumstances to the police. There is considerable evidence, however, that many Soviet citizens abhorred the role of informer. In any case, the "special section" directors felt it necessary to recruit a special network of informers bound by formal, though secret, contracts with the police. Many if not most of these contracts were signed under duress. A man accused of crimes was allowed to remain free as long as he informed on his neighbors or fellow-work-

ers; a woman whose husband or father had been sentenced
was allowed to send him food parcels as long as she acted as
a spy or *agent provocateur*. By one means or another, the
police rarely failed to find a professional informer in each
critical sector of public life.

The fact that the surveillance network extended even to the
Politburo was one reason why the Party elite was eager to
curb the security police after Stalin's death. It seems unlikely
today that the police dares to maintain regular informers in
high Party and government bodies. Soviet sources indicate,
however, that the security police still maintains informers
among ordinary citizens (such as unauthorized student discussion groups) it suspects. Defectors from the Soviet police and
other agencies report that surveillance networks are especially
active in aspects of Soviet society related to foreign affairs.

Sweeping personnel changes followed Beria's elimination.
Many of his henchmen were executed; other police leaders
were retired within a few years. In 1958, Aleksandr Shelepin,
First Secretary of the Communist Youth League, was placed in
charge of the KGB. Between 1961 and 1967, another Komsomol
secretary, Vladimir Semichastny, held the post; he was followed
by Yuri Andropov (who also has a lengthy early background
of Komsomol work). Stalin also utilized the device of ensuring
police loyalty by replacing its officers with Party and Komsomol members. Recent Party leaders, however, have apparently made sure that the police does not become an instrument in the hands of a single official like Shelepin.

The third aspect of police terror consisted of secret arrest
and arbitrary condemnation after a closed hearing. Arrests
were usually made late at night. Families and friends of the
arrested person frequently were not informed of his where-
abouts for months. During this time, "confessions"—often prepared by the police investigators—were extorted from the
accused, both to condemn him and to provide "evidence"

against others whom the police wished to incriminate. Interrogations took place in the small hours of the morning, when the prisoner was most susceptible to trickery, psychological pressure, and plain torture. After the confession was secured, the prisoner was brought before a police "special board" empowered to set sentences of up to five years in concentration camps. Apparently, the special boards sometimes even exceeded this legal limit, though death sentences were usually set by secret sessions of military tribunals attached to the regular court system. The special boards operated in complete secrecy. The accused was not informed of the charges until he appeared before the board and was not permitted counsel.

Arbitrary and inhumane as the Soviet security police was in its heyday, it rarely resorted to the public beatings and lynchings that marked Nazi and Fascist police measures. These limitations did not help the victims, but they did enable the Soviet regime to avoid the appearance of barbarity. It must also be recognized that the Soviet system does confront serious problems of social control arising from the recent introduction of much of the population to urban conditions; the harsh conditions of life in congested housing in an extraordinarily severe climate; and a recent history that has depreciated the value of human life. The common escape mechanism is drunkenness, which all too often leads to brutal crime. In these circumstances, it is not surprising that the police show a deep concern for law and order:

"From the streets and avenues," a member of the Collegium of the U.S.S.R. Ministry of Internal Affairs told me [a journalist], "the decline of morals is creeping into gateways, doorways, and apartments. The moans and cries emanating from these places are not heard by the public." *

* *Izvestia,* April 20, 1972, translated in *Current Digest of the Soviet Press,* XXIV, No. 16, 16.

MECHANISMS FOR LABOR DISCIPLINE

Very soon after Stalin died, the Soviet regime began to emphasize the judicial system at the expense of the police special boards, which were abolished. Both the police and the courts remained active but acted much less coercively, particularly during the period 1956–62, than the police alone had under Stalin. This tendency had important implications for the ability of the Soviet regime to maintain control over the population; the effect soon became apparent in maintaining work incentives. As noted in Chapter 1, the principal reliance has always been upon material incentives, i.e., each is rewarded according to his work. In the U.S.S.R. anyone in need is given financial assistance only if he is physically incapacitated; others seeking relief (including mothers of small children) are simply offered jobs. But the prospect of pay loss has never sufficed to keep all Soviet citizens employed at their maximum work capacity. For a large number, particularly recent immigrants from rural districts, the rhythm of industrial life has been a major difficulty. Tardiness, absence for a few days (often while sobering up), or loafing on the job have been major problems for Soviet management. Other workers, perhaps more ambitious, disrupted schedules by frequent changes of jobs. To overcome these problems, Stalin *legally* bound every worker to his job. Changes could take place only with the permission of management, and absence or even tardiness was a criminal offense. The labor laws were eased toward the end of Stalin's life and abolished in 1956. This was a major reform, for it is probable that no single aspect of the Soviet system was more bitterly resented by the common man than the labor laws.

Many formal restrictions on freedom of movement were retained. Unauthorized job changes can cost a worker his social-security benefits. Every Soviet citizen must carry a domestic passport and report every change of residence to the police. Transportation to another locality is often hard to obtain unless one has an official requisition. Twelve major cities (Moscow, Leningrad, Kiev, Baku, and eight smaller but attractive cities in the European part of the U.S.S.R.) are "restricted"; legally one may not move to them without a permit. Conversely, graduates of universities and other higher educational institutions are legally bound to work at assigned jobs for three years. Party members, as noted earlier, must accept job assignments on penalty of expulsion.

But all of these restrictions, it seems, have not been able to ensure the complete devotion to work demanded by the feverish tempo of Soviet economic development. Even with considerable increases in the availability of consumer goods, incentive pay is inadequate to induce all workers to devote their full capacities to production. Attempts to gain money by using state property or by speculating (buying and selling for a profit) have been criminal for decades. In recent years, those who resort to large-scale theft of state property or currency speculation have been condemned to death—a far harsher punishment than is meted out for property crimes in capitalist societies. By 1958, the Soviet regime evidently was also determined to punish those it suspected of living off illegal earnings—without bothering to prove that they had actually engaged in embezzlement or speculation—and to suppress loafing and other violations of work discipline even if the offender had no illegal earnings. Coupled with this immediate purpose was the regime's long-range intention, under Khrushchev, to move from legal enforcement toward "social persuasion." The 1961 Party program and the statements that preceded it regarded such a move as an essential step on the way to Communism. Social persuasion would enable the state and its instruments of law and coercion to "wither away." At the same time, social persuasion would act as an educational device to prepare Soviet citizens for the stage when each would work "according to his ability" without regard for reward or punishment.

One technique of social persuasion, the Komsomol youth

patrols, has already been mentioned. Another, also still in operation, is the "comrades' court." These bodies, set up at places of work and in residences, consist of several laymen nominally chosen by trade unions or local governmental bodies but, in all likelihood, actually appointed by the Party. They may deal with a wide range of minor offenses, whether strictly illegal or not: drunkenness, neglect of one's family, absenteeism, poor-quality work, carelessness. Acting without concern for rules of legal procedure, comrades' courts often make arbitrary judgments. This breach of the principle of "socialist legality" (which, as discussed below, was supposedly re-established after Stalin's death) is, however, insignificant, for the comrades' courts have never acquired much influence. In one urban district, only 100 of 8,000 residents attended a meeting to elect comrades' courts—with the result that half of the 100 became court members. At times during Khrushchev's ascendancy, it appeared as though similar irregular tribunals would indeed acquire major powers to deal with nonconformity. In 1958 "popular assemblies" in some smaller Union Republics were authorized to banish offenders against work discipline, and in 1961 "working people's collectives" in the R.S.F.S.R. received still broader powers.

In practice, however, the Soviet regime has used state agencies rather than "transitional," "popular" institutions to enforce conformity. As a recent article put it, "It would be naive to think that we can turn over all [law enforcement] functions to the public." The 1961 decree on banishing "parasites" has been considerably modified. In 1965 all reference to enforcement by "working people's collectives" was omitted. Under the 1970 revision, an explicit police warning must be given before legal action. An offender is then tried in a regular district court, which can only sentence him to an assigned job in his own oblast; later, if he fails to work as assigned, he may be sent to a "corrective labor camp" by administrative decision.

EXTRA-LEGAL SUPPRESSION OF DISSENT

The treatment of openly dissident citizens has paralleled the coercion of those who do not meet the regime's work standards. Under Stalin dissent was paralyzed by the sudden, unpredictable impact of the terror. Indeed, the lingering psychological effects of this terror appear to have lasted throughout most of Khrushchev's period. Khrushchev's control of dissenting opinion was also facilitated by the fact that he deliberately permitted a considerable safety valve of criticism of Stalin's "cult of the individual." Indeed, Khrushchev fostered exposés of Stalin's crimes in order, as discussed in Chapter 4, to turn public indignation against rivals more deeply implicated in these excesses. Thus Khrushchev shielded the editor Aleksandr Tvardovsky from attacks on his satiric poem criticizing Stalin's misconduct of World War II, and permitted Aleksandr Solzhenitsyn to publish a horrifying account of the concentration camps. When fundamental criticism of the regime was at issue, however, Khrushchev was no more "liberal" than his predecessors or his successors. In such cases, however, he preferred to use a variety of subterfuges rather than to condemn offenders legally. The simplest device was to utilize the regime's publishing monopoly to silence dissenters, who, in the 1950's, did not have as effective *"samizdat"* facilities as exist today. For example, Boris Pasternak's *Doctor Zhivago* could not be published in the U.S.S.R. Pasternak himself was allowed to live out his life unmolested, although after his death his close companions were sentenced on a charge—probably trumped up—of currency manipulation. More deviously, some dissident writers were convicted under the "parasite" laws. By far the most shocking subterfuge, however, was the misuse of psychiatric diagnosis. It is important to note that this abuse began under Khrushchev, although it has been vastly expanded more recently. Its victims number at least in the hundreds, perhaps the thousands. Two special prison–mental hospitals (in Leningrad and Kazan) have been set up, with real sufferers from mental illness mixed with sane persons confined for political activity—just as Stalin's concentration camps included a proportion of real criminals to make life harder for the "politicals." These conditions, often accompanied by intensive treatment by insulin shock or depressant drugs, sometimes induce real mental aberration in stubborn "oppositionists." Confinement is carried out entirely by medical boards, without any appeal to the courts, but there is little doubt that the whole procedure is directed by the KGB. A frequent formal complaint is that the "patient" shows "poor adaptation to the social environment"—i.e., that he does not accept the social norms set by the regime. But persons caught up in the process are often informed that they can escape its terrifying prospects if they simply refrain from writing or complaining, particularly about their "psychiatric treatment."

Significant as the resort to pseudo-psychiatry is, it would be wrong to conclude that it has either reached the proportions of Stalin's terror or has as paralyzing effects on opposition. Instead, there is no doubt that open dissidence, especially among intellectuals, has increased almost at an exponential rate since the early 1960's. The quantity and rapidity of circulation of *samizdat* material discussed in Chapter 3 constitute important evidence of this increase. Oppositionists protest arbitrary treatment of their sympathizers, occasionally by small public demonstrations. Many dissidents maintain regular contacts with foreigners in Moscow. The nature of the protests is changing, too. Much of the *samizdat* consists of apolitical writing, particularly poetry; such "formalist" writings are unacceptable for publication only because they do not meet the test of substantive contribution to Communist objectives, which the regime insists must be made by using the style of "socialist realism"—i.e., presenting models for general behavior. Other officially unacceptable writings criticize particular policies in the name of a return to Lenin's "real" positions. Consequently much *samizdat* (like Zhores Medvedev's book described in the readings section at the end of Chapter 4) is devoted to historical critiques that might have been legitimate under Khrushchev but now emerge as implicit attacks on the present regime, which suppresses detailed criticism of Stalin. Increasingly, however, important writings, openly identified by author, assail the bases of the Soviet system. From critiques of Stalin's specific atrocities, Solzhenitsyn has turned to a sweeping Christian criticism of the Soviet regime. Another dissident, Andrei Amalrik, has predicted that its faults and weaknesses will soon overwhelm the Soviet system. Indeed Amalrik (now re-imprisoned) appears to have been engaged for a decade in "testing" how far a clever and courageous writer can go before he is suppressed. To ensure that their views get a hearing, these and less extreme oppositionists have increasingly arranged to send their *samizdat* writings, or permitted them to be sent, to Western publishers.

THE LEGAL SYSTEM

Beginning in 1966, pressures upon the limits of its toleration led the post-Khrushchev Soviet regime to take the fateful step of trying some dissident writers. It is not altogether clear why the regime did not continue to resort to the subterfuges described above. One of the main themes of the post-Stalin reforms was restoration of "socialist legality." Legal specialists—hardly a politically powerful group, but one with some access to the decision-makers—had openly protested the irregular "popular" tribunals and probably objected privately to devious practices like psychiatric confinement. Probably the regime was persuaded that public exposure and condemnation of "flagrant" cases would deter others, and even "educate" the public on the evils of dissidence as well as "parasitism." In fact, the nature of the Soviet law facilitates these objectives. Consequently, some consideration of its procedure and substantive features is necessary. At the same time, one should always bear in mind that the vast majority of court proceedings involve cases which are not peculiar to Soviet conditions (nearly one-third are divorce hearings). Consequently, in weighing the stifling effect of the Soviet legal system on nonconformity, one must recognize that this system has certain advantages as well as disadvantages for the ordinary litigant.

The U.S.S.R. (and the Czarist government before it) has always adhered to the Continental European inquisitorial legal system. This system has many advantages for a person accused of an ordinary crime, but it is especially susceptible to abuse when an arbitrary regime considers its interests are at stake. A large part of the administration of justice is in the hands of a procurator who is supposed to carry out completely impartial investigations of crimes, report to the court all circumstances favoring or inculpating the accused, and even appeal cases in which the defendant's rights (as well as the prosecution's) were violated. The Procurator General and his subordinates are officers of a central agency, formally independent of all local judicial, police, and Party authorities. In theory, the procurator can act as a safeguard for the rights of the accused as well as a vigorous defender of the interests of society. Compared to the adversary system prevailing in English-speaking countries, the accused's case is not so heavily dependent upon his ability to engage skillful defense counsel, a condition that can often put poor or ignorant defendants at a severe disadvantage. The accused may retain a defense lawyer of his own choice or be assigned one by the court, but only after the procurator has completed his preliminary investigation. At that point, the accused has the advantage of learning what evidence the prosecution will use against him. However, prior to that point, he may have been held under arrest and interrogated for many weeks while the procurator was building his case. Naturally this case, which is presented in written form to the court, makes a strong impression. Soviet legal authorities insist that, regardless of the conclusion of guilt reached by the procurator during the preliminary investigation, which underlies any case brought to trial, the court must proceed to hear the case without a presumption of guilt. Nevertheless, procurators, and occasionally judges, often appear to be acting on this presumption in court, merely "verifying" the preliminary investigation. The investigation report may contain numerous affidavits by persons who do not appear at the trial, and the accused cannot always have adverse witnesses cross-examined. His defense counsel may be present at the trial but, when state interests appear to be at stake, must act circumspectly. This is especially true in crimes such as espionage, which are tried before the special military tribunal of the U.S.S.R. Supreme Court, where (one suspects) the overriding objective is the accused's abject confession and speedy conviction.

All judges are supposed to give priority to the interests of the state, and the law has always regarded crimes affecting the state as more serious than offenses affecting individuals alone. Nevertheless, the courts constitute a distinct part of the governmental mechanism. Most cases are tried in the "people's courts." Fairly small judicial districts are established for a people's court, but a court may have several judges, with the work being divided on a territorial basis or by types of cases. Judges are nominally chosen by popular election but, as elsewhere in the Soviet electoral system, there is only one nominee, who, in effect, is chosen by the Communist Party. Today, this means that a majority of judges are professional, for the Party has insisted on raising the level of legal preparation. We shall assume (as appears likely from available evidence) that the district court, like the school and the hospital, is an institution where women predominate. As elsewhere in Continental Europe, the judge plays an extremely important role. She may cross-examine the accused and other witnesses at length and freely express her opinion on their credibility. Politically suspect defendants' statements are treated very skeptically. Since hearsay evidence is not prohibited, admissibility of testimony is largely at the judge's discretion. In dissident and "parasite" cases, the prosecution brings forward "witnesses" who have no personal knowledge of the case in order to demonstrate "popular indignation" at the accused. There are no juries. Each case, however, is heard by two "people's assessors" "elected" for two-year terms (nearly 44 per cent are Party members), who pursue their ordinary occupations except for ten days' court service each year. Nominally, the assessors serving in a court have the same powers as the judge and can outvote her on a verdict; in practice the judge usually guides the decision. Proceedings can be very summary; one woman was sentenced to five years' banishment after a hearing lasting five minutes.

Cases are automatically reviewed by a provincial court, which has original jurisdiction in extremely serious criminal cases; such verdicts are automatically reviewed by the Union Republic Supreme Court. In addition to its original jurisdiction in certain cases such as espionage, the U.S.S.R. Supreme Court reviews some decisions of the lower courts, but (like the U.S. Supreme Court) it usually determines which cases are important enough to merit its attention. All courts include lay assessors when exercising original jurisdiction; reviews are conducted by a panel of professional judges.

Substantive Law

Though the procedures just described may impress an outside observer as inadequate to safeguard the accused's rights, they were a major aspect of the drive for "socialist legality."

Another major aspect consisted of sweeping revisions of substantive-law codes. Soviet law has always contained some moderating features, such as the unusual provision that an offender may not be punished for an offense that has ceased to be a "social danger," even if his act was illegal when committed. After Stalin's death, harsh treatment of youthful offenders (who, at the age of twelve, could be punished as adults) was greatly moderated. The step many foreign and Soviet jurists regarded as the greatest substantive achievement of the post-Stalin legal reforms related, significantly, to the definition of crime in general.

One of the most firmly established principles of modern law—older and more widespread than modern democracy—is *nulla poena sine lege:* no penalty except for violation of a specific legal provision. Until 1958, however, Soviet law codes provided that "if one or the other socially dangerous activity is not directly covered by the present Code, the ground and limits of responsibility for it are to be determined in accordance with the articles of the Code covering offenses that resemble it most closely." In 1958, this "principle of analogy" was implicitly repealed by the provision that acts were criminal only if specified by criminal law.

Unfortunately for the individual, the principle of analogy has not been the only vague and sweeping article in the penal codes. At the end of 1961, for example, neglect of farm machinery, even if due to carelessness rather than to intent, was made a crime. Though other provisions (such as the anti-sabotage statute) continue to require intent as an essential element of the crime, the danger that an individual who is merely inept or unlucky may be treated as a criminal still appears to exist. In marginal cases (under R.S.F.S.R. Criminal Code Article 190, "failure to report a crime") punishment for the acts of a relative—a clear violation of the principle of individual responsibility—appears possible, although the worst of the pre-1958 provisions for guilt by association have been dropped.

Since 1966 by far the most significant of the omnibus provisions used for legally punishing persons whom the regime dislikes has been Article 70 of the R.S.F.S.R. Criminal Code, along with corresponding provisions for other union republics. This article forbids all "agitation or propaganda conducted in order to undermine or weaken the Soviet power . . . or even distribution, preparation, or possession for the same purpose of literature of such content." Despite their eloquent pleas that they had no intention of criticizing the fundamentals of the Soviet system, or injuring it as a whole, in that year two well-known writers, Andrei Sinyavsky and Yuli Daniel, were sentenced to long prison terms for violation of Article 70. Their real offense—nowhere specified in Soviet law—had been publishing abroad under pseudonyms when their satirical works had been rejected by Soviet publishers. A year earlier, Article 70 had been utilized to condemn a British teacher whose sole offense was distributing leaflets prepared by an émigré organization; it appears likely that the provision had been applied to nationalist and religious groups still earlier. Since 1966, on the other hand, Article 70 has been used repeatedly to stifle intellectual dissent.

Religious and national dissent have always been the special targets of Soviet legal repression. The nationality question will be discussed at length in Chapter 7. As noted in Chapter 1, Communist doctrine is fundamentally atheistic. The whole force of the indoctrination machinery is directed against the remnants of religious belief. Nevertheless, religion persists in rural areas and may well be reviving in the cities. In 1970 *Pravda* made the unusual admission that one-eighth of the residents of the old Russian city of Pskov declared themselves to be believers in religion. In a Belorussian village one-third of the *non*believers considered baptism desirable for children.

In both cases just mentioned the religious influence was

probably Orthodox Christian. As discussed in Chapter 1, the Russian Orthodox Church has traditionally submitted to the secular authority. Whatever their motives, its bishops have co-operated with the regime; in 1962 the late Patriarch Aleksi was even awarded the Order of the Red Banner. Consequently, although very restricted in training priests, using church buildings and obtaining liturgical books, the Orthodox Church is allowed to function. So are major religious bodies such as Baptists, Lutherans, Catholics of the western (formerly Latin) rite, and Moslems. Ukrainian ("Greek") Catholics (see Chapter 7), on the other hand, have been suppressed, and Jews are severely harassed. So are active small Protestant denominations such as Pentecostalists, Jehovah's Witnesses, and dissident Baptists. Article 124 of the Soviet Constitution cryptically guarantees "freedom of religious worship and freedom of anti-religious propaganda." But the law (Article 227 of the R.S.F.-S.R. Criminal Code) prohibits both any attempt to persuade others to "abandon public activity" (such as Komsomol membership, where youths are exposed to atheist indoctrination) and any organized religious instruction of young persons. Severe sentences have been imposed for organizing Sunday schools. Legally, religious parents may instruct their children at home. Despite its reaffirmation by jurists, even this freedom is dubious. The 1968 Principles of Marriage and Family Law provide that a court may remove a child from parents "if the child is endangered by remaining." Still earlier, a father was convicted for "forcing" religion on his daughter, and the children of religious parents were removed to the custody of a brother who had renounced religion. Apparently the basic line was set by Komsomol first secretary Sergei P. Pavlov in a 1962 speech:

It must be an object of our special concern to protect children from the influence of believing parents and relatives. The freedom of conscience that is set down in the Constitution applies to adult

citizens who can answer for their actions. But we must not allow
anyone to cripple a child spiritually, to do violence to his im-
mature mind.*

FROM TERROR TO REPRESSION

The speech just quoted suggests how flexible legal or constitutional provisions can be when they require twisting for
the Soviet regime's purposes. The Soviet system is not only
not a liberal democracy, it is far from being even a government
of laws. In Max Heyward's phrase, it is a "pseudocracy," a
regime that cloaks its real behavior in facile phrases which are
lies because there is no intention of being bound by them. On
the other hand, the Soviet system is no longer a police state in
the usual sense of the term. High-ranking police officials do not
exert a major influence on policy decisions, and the police as
an institution is not a major factor in political struggles. Very
real terror certainly exists for the brave intellectual dissidents
who risk having their reason destroyed in pseudo-psychiatric
treatment, as well as for religious and nationalist oppositionists
who are sent to brutal corrective labor camps. But terror is no
longer wholesale, and thus cannot permeate the whole social
order. For every dissident locked up, a dozen indignant sympathizers take up the cause—or so it would appear. The old
phrase, "the blood of martyrs is the seed of the church" is
proved once again, *now that the martyrs can be identified.*
Under Stalin's terror, the victim's mysterious disappearance
aroused dread rather than emulation. Today sympathizers
make verbatim records of their friends' trials, and even the
details of psychiatric commitments become widely known. No
matter how harsh the outcome of present procedures, the fact
that they follow a protracted, fairly predictable course makes
courageous defiance possible. This knowledge has another

* *Pravda*, April 17, 1962, as translated in *Current Digest of the Soviet
Press*, XIV, No. 16, 5.

aspect: It suggests the limits to which dissent can be pushed without arousing extreme regime reaction. Instead of inducing would-be opponents to refrain even from whispered criticisms, the processes of warnings, examinations, and trials counsel them on how far they can go in their criticisms. The Soviet regime is moving from a position of securing positive compliance or overcompliance to the traditional stance of the censor who publicizes his suppression by leaving blank spaces where he has cut out offending passages. Thus every repressive act tends both to suggest how much others can get away with and to advertise the forbidden fruit of free expression. So far, this process has proceeded only a short way, for the strict Party supervision discussed earlier is still generally enforced in printed and electronic media. Already, however, the informal channels of dissident opinion have challenged the regime's monopoly of indoctrination.

SUGGESTED READING • CHAPTER 5

Many of the books listed in chapters 3 and 4 contain detailed discussions of the police system in the context of Soviet political developments. The only major works specifically devoted to the police system are *The Soviet Secret Police,* edited by SIMON WOLIN and ROBERT M. SLUSSER (New York: Praeger, 1957), based on émigré accounts and on analyses of Soviet publications, and BORIS LEVYTSKY. *The Uses of Terror: The Soviet Secret Police, 1917–1970* (New York: Coward, McCann and Geoghegan, 1972). Most of the numerous accounts by defectors from the Soviet police and intelligence networks are so lurid that they are hard for the nonspecialist to evaluate intelligently, but WALTER KRIVITSKY, *I Was Stalin's Agent* (London: Hamish Hamilton, 1939), though dated, is still remarkably good. Four books on purges and the treatment of prisoners in the Stalin era stand out:

BECK, F., and GODIN W. *Russian Purge and the Extraction of Confession.* London: Hurst and Blackett, 1951. A remarkably dispassionate analysis by two purge victims.

BRZEZINSKI, ZBIGNIEW. *The Permanent Purge.* Cambridge, Mass.: Harvard University Press, 1955. A scholarly study of the Great Purge of 1936–38 and of the general implications of the purge process.

CONQUEST, ROBERT. *The Great Terror: Stalin's Purge of the Thirties.* New York: Macmillan, 1968. A massive review of the Great Purge, based on a great mass of recent official and clandestine revelations, as well as material from the 1930's.

JELAGIN, JURI. *Taming of the Arts.* New York: Dutton & Company, 1951. Especially ineresting as an examination, by a participant, of the impact of terror on music and the theater.

Personal accounts of the post-Khrushchev repression are discussed at several points in this book, particularly in relation to the apparatus and to nationalities. Four other accounts of great general interest are:

ALLILUYEVA, SVETLANA. *Only One Year.* New York: Harper & Row, 1969. This second volume contains new facts as well as reflections provided by Madame Alliluyeva after a year in the U.S.

——. *Twenty Letters to a Friend.* New York: Harper & Row, 1967. As Stalin's daughter, Madame Alliluyeva was able to put into this book (written before her arrival in the U.S.) some very significant revelations.

AMALRIK, ANDREI. *Will the Soviet Union Survive Until 1984?* New York: Harper & Row, 1970. Amalrik answers this rhetorical but serious question by speculating that a war with China, plus internal nationality conflict, will bring about Soviet collapse.

MEDVEDEV, ZHORES, and MEDVEDEV, ROY. *A Question of Madness.* New York: Knopf, 1970. A fascinating account of the authors' personal experience with psychiatric imprisonment, and their observations of the general significance of this abuse.

For the nonspecialist, four books on law and social disorder are particularly valuable:

BERMAN, HAROLD J. *Justice in the U.S.S.R.* Rev. ed. Cambridge, Mass.: Harvard University Press; New York: Vintage paperback, 1963. A competent account by a lawyer specializing in the Soviet legal system.

CONNOR, WALTER D. *Deviance in Soviet Society: Crime, Delinquency and Alcoholism.* New York: Columbia University Press, 1972. Unlike many studies, this recent book relates Soviet social control measures to the extremely serious nature of social disorder in the U.S.S.R.

GEIGER, H. KENT. *The Family in Soviet Russia.* Cambridge, Mass.: Harvard University Press, 1968. Historical and ideological factors are considered in this comprehensive study, which focuses on the disorders created by rapid change.

HAZARD, JOHN N. *Law and Social Change in the U.S.S.R.* London: Stevens & Sons, 1953. A lawyer and political scientist who combines American and Soviet legal training, Hazard is pre-eminently qualified to analyze this topic.

A book of capital importance, but hard to place in any special category because it is essentially an analysis (based on very extensive interviewing of émigrés) of the reactions of the Soviet people to its regime, is

INKELES, ALEX, and BAUER, RAYMOND A. *The Soviet Citizen.* Cambridge, Mass.: Harvard University Press, 1959.

A recent British work, based largely on published Soviet materials, brings Inkeles's and Bauer's social data up-to-date:

MATTHEW, MERVYN. *Class and Society in Soviet Russia.* London: Allen Lane, 1972.

6

THE ADMINISTRATION AND
THE ECONOMY

For the average citizen, the crucial difference between a pluralist system and the Soviet political system is the extent to which the regime interferes with his personal conduct. As was discussed earlier, this interference is an essential corollary of the Communist belief that a "new man" can be developed. It is important to recall, however, that Marx and Lenin maintained that the decisive factor in creating the "new man" does not consist of elements of the "superstructure," such as indoctrination and police coercion, but of the "relationships of production" which are supposed to constitute society's "base." Despite its recent movement toward reliance on indoctrination, therefore, the Soviet regime still asserts that its fundamental task is the remaking of the economic environment. Recently, in attacking the Maoist "illusion" that politics is "the commanding force," Soviet ideologists have reaffirmed this position:

> In defining the role of politics, Marxism-Leninism proceeds from the fact that it is on no account the primary factor in the transformation and development of society. . . . However, it does not follow from this that the role of politics is reduced to the role of a passive reflection of economics. It acts as a very powerful tool. . . .*

* G. Glezerman, "The Leninist Principle of the Correlation Between Politics and Economics," *Pravda,* January 29, 1968, translated in *Current Digest of the Soviet Press,* XX, No. 5, p. 18.

Consequently, Soviet leaders insist that constructing the material foundations—first for socialism, later for Communism—has been the principal concern of the regime. At the same time, it is obvious that both the internal stability of the Soviet system and the influence it exerts abroad are dependent on economic success. As a result, economic matters receive a disproportionate amount of the public attention of both Party and state officials. A large majority of all questions considered at Party congresses and central committee plenums are economic in nature, and the amount of recorded discussion devoted to such questions is, relatively, even greater. The same is true of meetings of the Supreme Soviet and the lower soviets. While these superficial indicators of the relative importance attached to questions are unavailable for the Council of Ministers and the local executive committees, it seems safe to assume that these state bodies also devote most of their time to economic affairs. It is likely the Politburo is relatively more occupied with foreign affairs, personnel allocation, indoctrination, and other questions not directly economic in nature, but it also devotes much time to economic matters.

Indeed, a principal aspect of the eclipse of the Politburo under Stalin was the dominant role assumed by the principal state body, the Council of Ministers (or its committees), in directing the economy. The Council of Ministers lost most of these powers in the sovnarkhoz period (1957–64), but in recent years the Council has regained a considerable measure of importance. Compared with Stalin's time, however, the Council of Ministers remains limited by (1) the high-level decisions of the Politburo on economic as on other matters; (2) the enhanced role of lower Party organizations in agriculture; and (3) the greater leeway permitted directors of individual industrial enterprises. A thorough consideration of these developments would far transcend the scope of this book. A brief acquaintance with current developments in Soviet industrial direction is essential, however, for comprehension of the political system.

PLANNING IN THE COMMAND ECONOMY

Since its inception, the Soviet economic system has been a "command economy." In this type of system (in contrast to the "market economy" of countries like the United States), political decisions rather than "automatic" market forces are the principal method of determining what shall be produced and how it shall be allocated. At the top, decisions are made (as indicated in the preceding paragraphs) by the political bodies that exercise general control over Soviet society. They are primarily concerned with the ends for which economic production is carried on: military strength, the rate and direction of economic growth, the kinds and the levels of personal consumption. Theoretically, political decision-makers should, for the sake of efficiency, confine their directives to these economic *ends;* but in practice political bodies also interfere in the *means* by which goods are produced.

As a result, the problem of coordination of production is complicated. In principle, it has been accomplished by the somewhat rough-and-ready process known as "material balances," carried out by the State Planning Committee, or Gosplan. Briefly (if somewhat oversimplified), this means that the Soviet planners (1) determine the myriad products that they want the economy to turn out; (2) calculate the amounts of several hundred major raw materials, semifinished parts, and pieces of equipment that will be needed to make these products;* (3) calculate the interaction in time and space between the principal elements of production needed to achieve the desired output. Until very recently, no precise calculation of

* The supply of less important commodities is planned at lower levels.

these extremely intricate interactions was feasible. Instead, past experience was used as a guide, while sectors of the economy considered most important were given priority. These sectors received the best material and workmen and often overfulfilled their planned output at the expense of less favored industries. As long as the range of products was comparatively limited and the resources in raw materials and unskilled labor abundant, this system worked fairly well, as indicated by the high industrial growth rates in the U.S.S.R. during the 1930's, late 1940's, and early 1950's. As the economy became more complex and sophisticated, the "slack" was taken up. Skilled labor became relatively more important, and the reduced labor supply, due to low wartime birth rates, made careful allocation of even unskilled labor resources important. The number and complexity of products and production techniques increased, and the number of interactions (a function of the square of the number of enterprises) increased enormously. As the minimal needs of personal consumption were nearly met, individual consumers became more selective. As a result of all these developments, by the late 1950's Soviet economic planning had become seriously deficient.

Three principal avenues of improvement have been tried. In 1957 Khrushchev introduced a sovnarkhoz (council of national economy) for each major oblast. Undoubtedly political considerations played an important part in this decision, for it enhanced the influence of his backers in the Party territorial apparatus. The ostensible reason, however, was decentralization of economic decision-making to the "grass-roots" level to minimize the rigidities and complexities associated with centralized direction by the Council of Ministers. When it became evident that the sovnarkhoz system went to the opposite extreme by encouraging the development of autarchic provinces unconcerned with broad economic aims, Khrushchev engaged in further administrative experiments by reducing the number of the sovnarkhozy and by bifurcating the Party apparatus so as to have one set of territorial Party organizations for industry, another for agriculture. As noted earlier, his political objectives were involved in this reorganization, too. Khrushchev's successors hastened to abolish all types of sovnarkhoz as well as Party bifurcation. Anastas I. Mikoyan later privately contended that "Khrushchev suffered from an organizational itch. . . . In the local regions intolerable conditions were created for the population where it lived." Certainly it seemed that the more administrative reorganization was tried, the more complicated economic direction became.

The second way for improvement involves massive use of computer technology. Theoretically, advanced methods of data-processing could "save" the command system. The rapid increase in the effectiveness of computer technology may provide a method for precise calculation of the enormous number of economic interactions required. "Input-output" technique employs, in effect, an enormous number of simultaneous equations to calculate the interrelation of product requirements, thereby making it possible (in theory) to command each enterprise to produce the commodities required to make supply just equal to demand for all kinds of output. A more refined technique, linear programing, may even provide precise calculations concerning the effects of utilizing alternative methods or materials.

Many signs suggest that this technological solution is the one the Soviet leadership prefers. In principle, it would permit them to maintain, as in the past, complete control over the economy, but with far greater effectiveness. Soviet institutes have devoted great attention to what was once scorned as the "bourgeois" theory of cybernetics. A vice-chairman recently praised the work of the Gosplan's new Main Computer Center, which "drew up more than 3,500 equations with several thousand unknowns. It was not easy to solve these equations—

several electronic machines in succession worked on this task for about 100 hours!" And this was merely to answer the relatively simple question, "Where is it more advantageous to develop deposits of coal, gas and petroleum, and where should new plants be built?" The sheer fact is that Soviet computer technology is entirely inadequate for the vastly more complicated task of planning the entire economy. According to a penetrating review made in West Germany in 1970, the U.S.S.R. had only 4,200 computers, somewhat less than West Germany, Japan, Great Britain, or France, and only *6 per cent* of U.S. computer capacity. Moreover, the Soviet computers were mostly clumsy "second generation" machines, far behind the American "third" and "fourth generation" computers embodying compact, sophisticated technology. Even Kosygin's projection of 15,000 third generation computers by 1975 will leave the U.S.S.R. far behind the U.S.—which, of course, does not depend on economy-wide planning and therefore has less need for intricate economic calculation.

Apart from the technological difficulties, no computer calculation is better than the data supplied—as the saying among computer specialists goes, "Garbage in, garbage out." Not only is Soviet collection of economic data inadequate, but also (as will appear below) the impact of the present administrative system upon the individual economic enterprise tends to generate inaccurate data.

Undoubtedly awareness of the extreme difficulties in resorting to computerized planning in the proximate future played a major role in the Soviet regime's hesitant experimentation with the third alternative, modification of that nation's command economy through the adoption of features of the market economy. A relatively minor modification would be the establishment of financial criteria for the success of individual state economic enterprises. In theory, such criteria have been embodied for decades in the "economic cost accounting" (*khozraschot*) system. Each enterprise is supposed to make a monetary profit over its costs. In practice, however, volume of physical output has been a far more important criterion for judging the success of enterprises in crucial sectors like defense and machinery production. Even more important, economic cost accounting is unable to provide success indicators unless prices accurately reflect costs of production. All prices are set by the state. In consumers' goods production, the state endeavors to set these prices in accord with one principle of the market economy, the relation between supply and demand. The objective is to adjust the effective demand to the supply the regime decides should be available to consumers. For example, let us say competing priority demands for raw materials and workmen mean that only 1 million refrigerators can be manufactured. If refrigerators were to be sold at a little above production cost, potential buyers would be so numerous that the supply would soon be exhausted. The "solution" (not always successful by any means) is to set the price so high that only 1 million persons can afford refrigerators. Thus the demand is made to equal the supply. If this were the end of the matter, however, the refrigerator producer would show an enormous profit. To avoid this situation, which would reduce his incentive to operate efficiently, a "turnover tax" is placed on the item. Theoretically, the turnover tax is just large enough to cover the gap between cost of production (plus a small "planned profit") and fixed sale price. Alternatively, the turnover tax is kept low, but a large planned profit (which, of course, goes to the state just as the tax does) absorbs the difference between production cost and price to consumer. The turnover tax and the state profits on consumers' goods together are so great that they provide the Soviet state with the bulk of its revenue. At one time the turnover tax alone furnished 59 per cent of state revenue. It is now down to about 34 per cent, but profits from enterprises have risen to furnish another 36 per cent of revenue. Since these two items are both "hidden" taxes, they enable the regime to propagate the fiction that the average Soviet citizen pays less taxes than the citizen of any other major country.

The regime has no reason for imposing a turnover tax on goods like steel and cement, which are bought not by private individuals but by state enterprises. Moreover, the regime cannot set the price for these goods by assuming that demand should be restricted to an arbitrary amount, for the main problem confronting Soviet planners is precisely the amount of such factors of production that optimum economic production requires. In practice, therefore, the prices for most production goods have been set arbitrarily, occasionally at levels that appear to be well below the real cost of producing the goods. As a result, economic cost accounting is not very meaningful as a method for determining the efficiency of enterprises turning out production goods.

During the 1960's, Soviet economists—notably Yevsei Liberman—argued strongly for movement toward a market system. During 1964 and 1965, some steps were taken in this direction. Instead of having the nature of their product (total quantity, assortment, and quality specifications) entirely specified by the central officials, enterprise managers were permitted to engage in direct negotiations with the enterprises that used the product. Enterprise directors were instructed that they would be judged successful if their enterprises were financially profitable. Enterprise directors were also given more leeway in internal management of their plants, particularly in the kinds of labor employed and, to a limited degree, of labor incentives offered. In general, there has been a tendency to leave technical aspects of economic policy to the judgment of trained economists and practical administrators rather than to decide these matters on ideological or political grounds.

Nevertheless, the effect of the "reform" has so far been very limited and may even have retrogressed. In 1969 an authoritative statement warned that "those economists who try to make profit the chief criterion of the development of socialist production are wrong." Each enterprise is still given an over-all plan assignment. Prices have been revised to reflect costs somewhat more adequately. While earlier Soviet practice failed to reflect the cost of capital investment, various devices now permit planners to include this factor in cost accounting. Prices continue to be administered, however, rather than determined by market forces; consequently, the financial criteria for success are artificial. An enterprise manager can negotiate with his suppliers as well as with the enterprises that consume his product, but he cannot be sure that the former will provide him with the amount and quality of materials needed if he is to produce, or that the materials will arrive on schedule. Because of the artificial price relationships, financial sanctions, which are supposed to induce his suppliers to meet their commitments, remain only partially effective. The Soviet regime is still unwilling to permit prices to find their own level. One reason, no doubt, is that, in a simulated market system, it would be difficult to retain control over all of the ends of production. Consumers' choices could hardly be prevented from assuming a larger role as compared to the regime's present emphasis on defense and industrial investment, and the kinds of goods consumers obtain could not be manipulated as readily. Another reason is bureaucratic inertia and self-interest. We are, therefore, back to the consideration of the administrative aspects of the system.

The enterprise manager is still subject to a wide range of institutional controls and pressures. In the direct chain of command, he is under a ministry (in Moscow or in a Union republic capital) with at least one intermediate level of authority, the *glavk;* in some cases there are "production associations" as well. A major task of the ministry is to see that the plan is fulfilled. Consequently, the ministry officials are inclined to watch enterprises under their direction very closely and to interfere whenever they suspect that something may go wrong. Since most ministers (and probably their principal subordinates) have had long experience in the centralized command economy, it is not surprising that they continue to use highly detailed plans and to issue frequent direct orders to enterprise managers. As financial considerations have become more heavily emphasized, the role of the State Bank, which acts as a superauditor for enterprises, has also become more important. Available information suggests that Bank officials carry out their supervision in a rigid manner, which further hampers the enterprise manager. Since 1964, oblast Party organizations have not been as directly concerned with larger enterprises as they were during the sovnarkhoz period (even then, Party officials tended to find major industrial problems too complex to deal with). In each factory, however, the primary Party organization secretary (a full-time apparatus member in large factories) transmits central pressures that often interfere with orderly processes of production. Recently the authorized scope of this primary organization intervention has been somewhat increased.

Considering the variety of pressures he faces, it is scarcely surprising that the enterprise manager continues to resort to those irregular practices that sprang up under the unmodified command-economy system. Of these practices, one of the most important is the effort to restrict the plan assignment to a level that is below the real production capacities of his enterprise. By getting a small assignment, he is protected against failure to meet the plan and is able to show a gratifying "above-plan" output. In order to get a small assignment, he falsifies data concerning plant capacity and current output, thereby distorting the data the central planners use in their calculations. The enterprise director may also maintain an inventory of materials, in the form either of finished products or of raw materials. These inventory reserves, being unknown to the central planners, further distort their calculations. If they are not utilized, the inventories also constitute unproductive capital. However, in many cases the inventories do not remain unutilized. Because of the difficulty of enforcing the commitments of suppliers, many enterprise managers employ special expediters (*tolkachi*). The job of the *tolkachi* is to induce suppliers to meet their schedules or, if this fails, to find available supplies that the plan did not allocate to the expediters' enterprises. Obviously, the most likely source of such unplanned supplies are concealed inventories in other enterprises. If an expediter's enterprise also has a concealed inventory, a mutually beneficial barter deal may be arranged.

The practices described in the preceding paragraphs are entirely illegal and the clandestine atmosphere in which they occur facilitates chicanery for personal gain. They do, however, provide a measure of flexibility in the command economy, which is probably indispensable even after the modest "Liberman" reforms. As long as an enterprise manager is successful in meeting his planned production assignment and avoids involvement with unsuccessful political factions, his resort to these extralegal practices is apt to be overlooked. At times even Soviet writers admit that there is an unwritten law: "Victors are not judged." Soviet press accounts contain wry admissions that the *tolkachi* and the hidden inventories may serve the ends of the economic system as a whole. If, however, the manager is clearly unsuccessful or in political disfavor, his illegal practices can become the basis for serious charges. In Stalin's time, such charges resulted in death or long imprisonment. Today, such severe penalties for economic derelictions that do not involve embezzlement or speculation are uncommon, but the least a disgraced manager could expect would be reduction to a low-paying and obscure position.

On the whole, the Soviet industrial system has been successful so far. During World War II, the capacity of industry to resume production after evacuation from areas threatened by the Germans was almost miraculous. The over-all growth rate has been extremely impressive. In recent years, however, this rate has slowed considerably. Labor efficiency is low compared to that common in the United States and the quality of many manufactured goods and of much construction is shoddy. Undoubtedly, the U.S.S.R. can produce items such as rockets or jet airplanes technically equal or superior to any others in the world. Apparently, however, only a fairly narrow range of Soviet industry can attain such standards. In "normal" times, the regime uses this sector of industry for the highest-priority items. But it is still doubtful whether Soviet industry as a whole has the capacity for vast expansion of output of items requiring extremely high technical standards of production.

AGRICULTURE

In terms of over-all production, Soviet agriculture presents a picture almost opposite to Soviet industry. In contrast to the slowdown in industrial growth, recent agricultural production increases have been encouraging, but the over-all record of agriculture is greatly inferior to the industrial growth record. While countries as diverse in background as the United States and Japan increased their crop yields enormously between 1913–53, Soviet food production in the mid-1950's remained almost the same as it had been in 1913. During the late 1950's and early 1960's, various measures introduced by Khrushchev—such as the "virgin lands" program of exploitation in arid regions—led to a growth spurt, but the situation greatly worsened in 1963. In 1964, however, food production (mainly grains) exceeded all previous records, even on a per capita basis. Since 1966, growth has tended to level off, with sharp ups and downs in major crop yields.

The very mixed record of Soviet agriculture is undoubtedly due in part to adverse climatic conditions. Most of the U.S.S.R. has extremely severe winters and short growing seasons, while the southern parts of the country are largely arid. Limitations of capital and human resources are also very important; these limitations are undoubtedly dependent, at least in large part, on the regime's policies. Until very recently, the Soviet regime gave a high priority to heavy industry in terms both of capital investments and of the assignment of skilled personnel. Agriculture, like other consumers' goods sections, tended to receive only those resources left over after industry was taken care of (a notable exception was "technical-crop" farming—fibers, sugar beets, et cetera—which made rapid progress even under Stalin). Drainage of the numerous swampy areas was neglected. The infrastructure of farm-to-market roads was primitive, and chemical fertilizers and insecticides were very scarce. A considerable amount of heavy farm machinery (tread tractors, combines) was supplied, but small, flexible mechanical implements were not made available or could not be properly maintained. It appears that much of the very recent grain increase is due to drainage measures and the provision of chemical fertilizer, but the road and implement problems remain unsolved.

Probably more important than capital-equipment deficiencies are the social problems confronting Soviet agriculture. In 1929, Stalin launched a campaign for total collectivization of farming. The campaign took a heavy toll—approximately 5 million deaths. Many of these were "kulaks" (officially defined as "richer" peasants employing hired labor, but in practice taken to mean all those who resisted either passively or actively) or their families, shot or exiled to Siberia. Other peasants died in the famine that followed the disruption of agricultural operations. Loss of livestock, while less horrifying, had a profoundly depressing effect on the development of Soviet agriculture. Two-thirds of the sheep and goats, half of the swine and horses, and one-third of the cattle were lost between 1929 and 1933. The number of cattle did not reach the 1929 figure until 1958.

It appears that Stalin's principal motivation for the drastic collectivization campaign was political control of the peasantry, who up to then had been less affected by Communist indoctrination than any other major segment of the population. The regime has never relaxed its grip on the countryside, but the instrumentalities of control have varied considerably. Until 1958, major instruments were the MTS (machine tractor stations), which operated most of the heavy agricultural machinery, thereby dominating the planting and harvesting operations. The MTS were agencies of the Ministry of Agriculture, but during much of Stalin's life their key political sections were controlled by the police agencies. Even at that time, however, the local Party organizations (especially the raikoms) exercised far more control over agriculture than over industry. Khrushchev secured for the local Party an almost complete ascendancy over state organizations when it came to agricultural control. During the Khrushchev period, the MTS were abolished and their machinery "sold" to the collective farms. At the same time, consolidation of collective farms and the spread of rural Party membership made it possible to establish primary Party organizations on nearly every farm. Since 1964, the raikom and the primary Party organizations have remained the most important rural control agencies, but the Ministry of Agriculture has regained influence. Like the industrial ministries, the Ministry of Agriculture has the task of seeing that its economic branch—the collective farms and the state farms (which are especially important in the production of technical crops) —meets its quotas. As an aid in accomplishing this task, the

Ministry directly supervises a broad network of experimental stations, agricultural specialists, and veterinaries.

THE KOLKHOZ

Since 1929, the agricultural artel, known more commonly as the kolkhoz or collective farm, has been by far the most important form of agricultural organization in the U.S.S.R. Today, about 70 per cent of the peasants live in kolkhozes, although only about 60 per cent of the agricultural workers are employed there. Most of the remainder are in state farms (the sovkhozes). On the 15,000 sovkhozes, workers are paid wages like factory hands. The 33,000 kolkhozes, on the other hand, are in theory cooperatives rather than state enterprises. The average kolkhoz has some 430 families and about 8,000 acres of cultivated land. The collectivized fields include most of the cultivated areas and produce the bulk of major food crops, such as grain and potatoes. Most larger types of livestock are also raised in collective herds. Every able-bodied member of the collective farm—women and men, adolescents and adults— must work a fixed minimum of days (nearly 300 in the case of able-bodied men) in the collective "sector" of the farm.

Obviously, the success of Soviet agriculture depends to a large extent upon the efficiency attained in cultivating the collective sector. The official directly responsible is the chairman, nominally elected by the members of the farm, but actually designated by the Party. It is the chairman's job to see that the kolkhoz produces the kind and amount of products set for it in the state plan and that produce deliveries are made to the state on schedule. A major problem is stimulation of the peasants' efforts. Most industrial workers are under a piece-work system, which rewards each according to his output; it is, however, harder to evaluate the peasants' performance of agricultural tasks. The usual system was to set a fixed number of labor days (*trudodni*) for a real day spent at a given task. Thus a skilled agricultural-machine operator might receive two labor days for each day actually worked, while an elderly woman might get only one-half a labor day for a full day spent in the poultry yard. While various bonus systems were tried, all workers performing a given task on the same kolkhoz tended to receive the same labor-day credit, regardless of their efficiency. Probably even more important was the fact that the labor day did not have a fixed cash value. At the end of the crop year, the collective farm sold much of its produce to the state at fixed prices. Some of the produce was stored for seed or reserve. The remainder was sold on the free market or distributed to the collective members in proportion to their accumulation of labor days, as was any cash surplus the farm might have after paying its expenses. No one knew in advance how much these distributions in cash or kind might be, nor was there any apparent justice in the allocation. A collective farm fortunate enough to have good soil and a good location provided far higher rewards for its members than another with equally efficient farmers but less favorable conditions, and all were dependent on the whims of the weather. Consequently, personal initiative seemed to count for very little on the farm.

Khrushchev tried to stimulate the peasants' motivation by greatly reducing the financial burdens on them through lowering taxes and increasing the prices the state paid for crop deliveries. On the other hand, his programs threatened the peasants' chief economic interest, the private garden plot. On the average, the kolkhoz peasant (sovkhoz workers have less) has an acre of land near his house which he can cultivate as he wishes. Altogether, these plots constitute only one-thirtieth of the cultivated land. Nevertheless, they provide most of the peasants' fruit and vegetables and a sizable surplus for the kolkhoz market in the towns. With the help of feed grain distributed from the collectivized sector, the peasants have been able to produce an astounding proportion of the animal products consumed in the U.S.S.R. As late as 1971, one-third of the milk and meat and two-thirds of the eggs were produced on these garden plots. Because their labor on the plots produces higher and more predictable results (a recent U.S. study estimates that the average peasant still makes about 80 per cent more per hour on his plot than in the collectivized sector), peasants have tended to divert as much time as they could to the private sector. Moreover, the whole concept of individualistic farming and the animated bargaining of the kolkhoz market is contrary to the idea of rapid advance toward complete Communism. Consequently, Stalin and Khrushchev repeatedly sought to curb the garden plots, most drastically in the *agrogorod* scheme of 1950–51, which would have brought the peasants together in large "agricultural cities" and required them to sell most of their livestock to the collective farms. The scheme seemed designed to prevent the peasant from sneaking time from his collective assignments to tend his garden, which would have been situated far from his house. Moreover, peasants grouped in compact settlements could be more easily subjected to political control and indoctrination. The scheme was abandoned before Stalin died, evidently because the regime discovered that peasant resentment threatened another catastrophic disruption of agricultural production. Nevertheless, Khrushchev appears to have retained a lingering hope that some such change could be introduced; from time to time he moved cautiously to reduce privately owned livestock and to curb the kolkhoz market.

One way in which the post-Khrushchev regime has sought to invigorate agricultural production is by full recognition of the value of the garden plots. While the ultimate objective is still publicly operated farming (and therefore sovkhozes are still increasing relatively), the tacit postponement of Communism to the indefinite future makes private farming and marketing tolerable. As a result, the dispersed peasant housing, private plots, and the kolkhoz market, like the cooperative and personal apartment building in the cities, are encouraged.

A second way the post-Khrushchev leadership has sought to solve the agricultural problem is through encouragement of the initiative of small teams in the collective sector. The team ("link" or *zveno*) of a dozen members was a necessity during World War II, but during 1947–64 it was largely replaced by the large brigade for work in the collectivized fields. Each team is temporarily assigned up to two thousand acres, with machinery and supplies, and members are told to arrange their work as they see fit. The team must, however, cultivate the crops prescribed by the plan. The team's members know each other well (many are relatives), and thus can put pressure on laggards to work effectively. Consequently, various methods can be effectively employed to reward the team members in proportion to their achievements; as one Soviet journalist commented, "I think we have here the happy case where common and personal interests coincide."

The team may be productive only in favorable circumstances. Besides, some officials still fear, with some reason, that the team may be the basis for a "state within a state" in the present regime. Small work teams based on family groups make it difficult to carry on indoctrination among the peasants, the population element that is already least susceptible to Soviet influence. Moreover, relaxation of controls over their individual activity may whet the peasants' appetite for more land and more freedom to cultivate it. Consequently, though team labor still exists, after 1969 the Soviet regime turned to a third way of stimulating agricultural production. Starting as early as 1966, the *trudodni* system was replaced by piecework wages. Within any job category, pay nominally depends on individual output per day worked, at a fixed regional scale rather than as a share of kolkhoz profits. Moreover, 60 to 70 per cent of the scale is paid in advance, and is therefore guaranteed even if performance is poor. The total annual pay (in cash and kind) for the average collective farmer is only about 900 rubles, compared to 1,600 for the industrial worker (one ruble nominally equals $1.10). When this is compared to about 300 rubles (at present prices), which the kolkhoz worker received in 1953, however, the improvement is notable. Moreover, the collective farmer, unlike most urban workers, derives much of his income from his garden.

Continuing Social Division Between Town and Country

Despite all these measures, agriculture remains a problem area for Soviet planners. Much has been accomplished by providing more abundant fertilizers and better machinery. It appears, however, that whatever effect on labor efficiency the post-Khrushchev measures have had is largely offset by the constant drain of vigorous young people from the farm to the city. The farm work force includes a higher proportion of women, elderly persons, and adolescents than does the urban labor force. As a result, the level of education and technical training is low. With the best of will, these farm workers have difficulty in handling the increasingly complicated mechanical devices needed for efficient farming. For example, as late as 1962 only 25 per cent of the cows could be milked by machine, apparently because maintenance of machines was inadequate.

On the other hand, the considerable reduction (3 million between 1960 and 1970) of the farm labor force has been a major objective of the regime, both to increase the industrial labor force and because urban life is the dominant model for future Communist society. Soviet demographers recognize, however, that, unless labor productivity can be greatly improved, the rural reservoir of manpower has been about used up. Further migration from countryside to city would undermine agriculture. It would also tend to lower the birth rate, which (among European ethnic groups) is near the zero-growth rate in the cities already. The leadership on the other hand wants to raise the birth rate both because it envisages a continuing need for manpower inputs for economic growth and to maintain international political prestige.

Continued reliance on rural child-raising as a major source of population increase has, however, disturbing implications for the goals of class equality and equalized life chances for Soviet young people. A major prerequisite of complete Communism is elimination of differences in rewards and opportunities between town and country, but the Soviet ideology admits that industrial workers and collective farm peasants still constitute distinct classes, along with the "stratum" of intelligentsia or white-collar workers. Soviet sociologists increasingly admit that "intraclass" differences among both workers and peasants are significant and could be eliminated completely, at least in the proximate future, only by drastic measures like public upbringing of children, which have so far been rejected. Even in urban areas, the children of specialists (who usually have higher educations themselves) have four times as great a chance to complete high school as do children of manual workers. Rural young people suffer especially both because they lack educated family backgrounds and parental stimulation, and because the level of teaching and special educational facilities in the villages is low. A Soviet study found that only one-eighth of the students entering Moscow University came from rural high schools. Apparently this resulted partly from inferior preparation (only two-thirds as large a proportion of rural as urban applicants for the sciences passed the entrance examination), and partly because of a "psychological barrier" that made rural youths afraid to take the tests. These disparities would constitute a continuing prob-

lem for the Soviet system even if they were evenly distributed
by ethnic groups. Since, however, most of the non-Russian elements are much more rural than the Russians, the inequalities
between town and countryside constitute a major factor in the
strains discussed in Chapter 7.

SUGGESTED READING • CHAPTER 6

Many of the general works on the Soviet system listed in earlier
chapters have sections dealing with economic affairs, especially in
their administrative and political aspects. The following works are
more particularly concerned with the economy.

AZRAEL, JEREMY R. *Managerial Power and Soviet Politics*. Cambridge, Mass.: Harvard University Press, 1966. The most systematic
analysis of the relation of industrial to political decision-making.

BAYKOV, ALEXANDER. *The Development of the Soviet Economic
System*. New York: The Macmillan Company, 1947. The most
complete treatment of the development of the economy and
economic administrative institutions up to the end of World
War II.

BERLINER, JOSEPH. *Factory and Manager in the U.S.S.R.* Cambridge,
Mass.: Harvard University Press, 1957. A fascinating study (based
largely on interviews with émigrés who had once held managerial
posts in Soviet industry) of the problems and personalities of
Soviet directors.

CAMPBELL, ROBERT W. *Soviet Economic Power: Its Organization,
Growth and Challenge*. 2d ed. Boston: Houghton Mifflin Company, 1966. A very clear and readable summary, available in
paperback, of the basic economic features of the U.S.S.R.

GRANICK, DAVID. *The Red Executive*. New York: Doubleday &
Company, 1960. A very interesting study of the industrial manager based on published materials and the author's observations
in the U.S.S.R., with a wealth of comparative material from
Western Europe and the United States.

JASNY, NAUM. *The Socialized Agriculture of the U.S.S.R.* Stanford,
Calif.: Stanford University Press, 1949. A massive discussion of the
evolution of collectivized agriculture until the postwar period.

KATZ, ABRAHAM. *The Politics of Economic Reform in the Soviet*

Union. New York: Praeger, 1972. A good re-examination, mainly of the post-Stalin period.

LAIRD, ROY D. *Collective Farming in Russia: A Political Study of Soviet Kolkhozy*. Lawrence: University of Kansas Press, 1958. A comprehensive study of the political aspects of Soviet agriculture in the early Khrushchev period.

MILLAR, JAMES R. (ed.). *The Soviet Rural Community*. Urbana: University of Illinois Press, 1971. This symposium, which covers both the history and present situation of Soviet agriculture, is unusual for including the most up-to-date, detailed research as well as comprehensive analysis.

NOVE, ALEC. *The Soviet Economy: An Introduction*. Rev. ed. New York: Praeger, 1966. An excellent, concise treatment, available in paperback, by a leading British economist.

SCHWARTZ, HARRY. *Russia's Soviet Economy*. Englewood Cliffs, N. J.: Prentice-Hall, 1954. The best general survey of the Soviet economy, with special emphasis on the growth and distribution of production facilities.

U.S. Congress, Joint Economic Committee. *Comparisons of the United States and Soviet Economies*. Washington, D.C.: U.S. Government Printing Office, 1960. An extremely useful set of three pamphlets consisting of articles and statistical analyses by experts.

———. *Soviet Economic Prospects for the Seventies*. Washington, D.C.: U.S. Government Printing Office, 1973. An extensive updating of the preceding examination.

7

THE SOVIETS
AND THE NATIONALITIES

At first glance it seems anomalous that one can examine a wide range of fundamental Soviet political institutions before considering the formal constitution of the country. As has already been described, however, the real locus of power is the Party, not the formal governmental structure; and even certain crucial elements nominally within that structure, like the police, have had little relation to the constitutional prescriptions. Indeed, it is often asked why the U.S.S.R. has a constitution providing for a formal governmental system at all. One reason, certainly, is the burning nationality question, outlined later in this chapter. Another is the need to impress the outside world and the Soviet people with the claim that the Soviet state is the "most democratic in the world," although Brezhnev was careful to point out at the Twenty-fourth Congress that "there is no abstract freedom, just as there is no abstract democracy. This is a class concept." Aside from these motivations, however, Communist ideology has constantly proclaimed the necessity of distinguishing (before complete Communism is attained) between the Party, supreme though its decision-making power may be, and the detailed legislative and administrative tasks that must be performed by the state. Maintenance of a separate state structure serves the additional function of drawing large numbers of Soviet citizens into the operation of the system, without the necessity of diluting the

Party ranks with unacceptable human material. The Soviet state is indeed a façade behind which the real power of Communist control is exercised, but it is a façade that is not wholly devoid of functional significance.

THE SOVIETS

Lenin sharply criticized parliamentary government as a screen, "the most perfect shell" (because the most deceptive) for rule by the capitalists. Existing legislative bodies were "bourgeois talk shops," which could not be utilized for the "dictatorship of the proletariat" even after complete overhauling. Today, when Communist ideologues write of the "parliamentary path to socialism" (see Chapter 2), they envisage parliaments only as avenues for Communist seizure of power, not as permanent legislatures in Communist states. However, since Lenin, like his followers, insisted on a state structure apart from the revolutionary Party, he needed a new form of legislative body. He found it in the "soviets." The original soviets were merely *ad hoc* bodies ("soviet" means simply "council" in Russian) formed by worker groups to direct the general strike at the start of the unsuccessful 1905 Revolution. Lenin's Bolsheviks neither originated nor dominated these soviets, but he welcomed them as a proletarian creation that, unlike parliaments, combined execution with deliberation. Doubtless Lenin was also aware that the impetuous nature of the soviets and their lack of procedural rules and traditions would make them easier for a conspiratorial minority to manipulate. When the soviets were revived during the 1917 Revolution, the Bolsheviks, with their temporary Left Social Revolutionary allies, eventually did succeed in dominating the soviets, which were then adopted as the symbol of the Bolshevik regime.

THE CONSTITUTION

Soviets in the present-day U.S.S.R. are rather different, however, from the original bodies composed of delegates from factories, railroad lines, and military units. In 1936, a new constitution was adopted as part of Stalin's plan for strengthening and regularizing the state structure and at the same time making it superficially more attractive to world democratic opinion.* On the ground that hostile classes no longer existed in the Soviet Union (industrial workers, peasants, and "intelligentsia" all qualified as "toilers"), all citizens over eighteen not detained in concentration camps were declared entitled to equal and direct vote for members of the legislative bodies. Consequently, instead of being elected from occupational bodies, soviet deputies are elected, as in most Western countries, from territorial districts. The highest level, the Supreme Soviet of the U.S.S.R., consists of the Council of the Union, composed of over 700 members elected from single-member districts with a population of approximately 300,000 each, and the Council of Nationalities, composed of slightly fewer deputies apportioned among the nationality subdivisions outlined below, with the deputies elected at large. The Supreme Soviet is, therefore, a bicameral body. But many of its most important sessions are held jointly.

The Supreme Soviet is elected for a four-year term (in even-numbered years other than leap years—1962, 1966, etc.—since there was a hiatus during the war period). The voter turnout (about 99.9 per cent) is startling, until one notes the tremendous effort and pressure brought to bear by the regime to secure universal participation. Indeed, the principal function of a Soviet election is obviously that of a mass rally in favor of the regime rather than an exercise of popular sovereignty.

* Plans for a revised constitution have been discussed for more than a decade, but, at present, it is hard to tell whether the regime is seriously planning a change.

The ballots have never listed more than one nominee per office. Numerous accounts make it evident that the Party picks the nominees in advance. Even Article 141 of the Constitution hints at this situation by listing the Party first among "public organizations and societies of the working people" entitled to nominate, while Article 126 states that "the most active and politically conscious citizens in the ranks of the working class and other sections of the working people unite in the Communist Party . . . which . . . is the leading core of all organizations of the working people, both public and state." A recent Soviet article puts the matter bluntly:

During the nomination of candidates for Deputy many meetings name several candidates. Why does only one candidate's name remain on the ballot? Back in 1937, M. I. Kalinin, speaking at the pre-election rally in Leningrad, said: "If in our country in a number of places candidates withdraw their names in favor of a single candidate, this is the consequence of their social kinship and the community of their political goals. After thorough discussion, tens and thousands of voters have agreed on a single candidate. This is also a hallmark of socialism, a sign that there is no, and cannot be any, discord among our laboring masses, the kind of inner discord that exists within bourgeois society." . . . This is why all Soviet people have recognized the Communist Party as the guiding force of our society, the directing nucleus of all state and public organizations. This is written in Article 126 of the U.S.S.R. Constitution, the basic law of our state. This is why our Party, Y.C.L., trade union and other public organizations, all the working people come forward at elections in a single bloc— the bloc of Communists and non-Party people. This is why in our country all the voters unanimously cast their ballots for the candidates of this bloc, as the best and most worthy representatives of the people.[*]

Aside from its determination to fill the Supreme Soviet (and all other soviets) with reliable deputies, the Party maintains

[*] P. Tumanov, "Guarantees of Democratism," *Izvestia*, May 13, 1966, as translated in *Current Digest of the Soviet Press*, XVIII, No. 19, 32–33.

complete direction of nominations in order to form the Soviet version of the "balanced ticket." Supreme Soviet delegations from each major area are carefully arranged to include representatives of the nationality groups, various occupational categories, and women. In addition, persons who are celebrities —war heroes, exemplary workers, and (probably less often) cultural figures—often appear on the ballots. Such slates serve two purposes: They give each major population group a feeling that it is represented, however little the nominee may really have in common with this particular group; and they suggest that all outstanding citizens are lined up behind the regime.

Thus the Soviet electoral campaign assumes the aspect of an affirmation of solidarity in support of the Communist system. Frequently it is also the occasion for stressing some particular propaganda line of the moment. Obviously, in addition to a complete voter turnout there must be a virtually unanimous vote for the nominees, who symbolize solidarity. There is. All unmarked ballots cast are counted in favor of the uncontested nominees; consequently, there is no need for the voter to exercise his constitutional right of retiring to a private polling booth *unless he wishes to oppose the ticket.* Foreign observers report that extremely few voters are bold enough to do this. In a very small number of local elections, individual nominees have been rejected when a majority of the voters crossed out their names. Whether these instances were prearranged or whether they represented a spontaneous rejection of very unpopular persons whom the Party is willing to see discarded is not known.

LEGISLATIVE PROCEDURE

According to the Constitution, the Supreme Soviet is the primary legislative body of the U.S.S.R. But an examination of its operation indicates that the Supreme Soviet could not really consider much legislation even if its members were able and willing to make fundamental political decisions. The Constitution provides for semiannual sessions; these have in fact been held since Stalin's death. Each session is very short, however—usually it lasts less than a week. These sessions seem like mere ceremonies of ratification, characterized by set speeches rather than debate, and by unanimous acceptance of legislation introduced by government spokesmen. Since the Supreme Soviet members have regular jobs apart from their legislative duties, it is obvious that they lack both the time and the sustained familiarity with governmental business needed to exercise real influence on legislative proposals. It is true that various standing commissions (committees) of the houses of the Supreme Soviet review these proposals in advance of the sessions. Much of these commissions' operations is obscure, since their deliberations are not described in detail in the Soviet press. Recently, the commissions seem to have become somewhat more active. It appears that a proposal receives somewhat more detailed consideration in the commission than in the Supreme Soviet as a whole, but that the commission's deliberations are guided by its carefully selected Party contingent. In recent years, public discussions of specific features of a few items of proposed legislation have taken place. The reorganization of industrial direction considered in the spring of 1957 is an example of such discussion. The participation of members of the commissions considering the legislation in such press debates suggests that commission consideration may in fact proceed before the final form of the proposed law is decided. Such discussion takes place only when authorized (either because of real policy indecision or for tactical reasons) by the Party leadership. In the case of industrial reorganization, Khrushchev's report on the "theses of the Central Committee and the Council of Ministers" that preceded the press discussion was couched in language clearly designed to indicate that the details of reorganization were open to discussion. More often, however, a firm decision is made by a Party meeting (Central Committee meetings frequently take place just before the Supreme Soviet convenes) and is merely ratified by the nominal legislative body. For example, in its plenary session of January, 1955, the Central Committee secretly decided to replace Malenkov as prime minister; his resignation, presented to the Supreme Soviet session early in February, was just a formality.

In spite of its docility, the Supreme Soviet is not always permitted to exercise even the formal power of passing the legislation the Constitution assigns to its sphere. Many major laws are in fact enacted as decrees of the Presidium of the Supreme Soviet. This body of thirty-three members nominally elected by the Supreme Soviet in joint session can be manipulated more readily than the entire legislative body. Actually in session, or available, at all times, the Presidium is the formal collective head of state of the U.S.S.R. Its chairman (at present, N. V. Podgorny) acts as the formal representative of the Soviet state in dealing with foreign emissaries. Many of the laws are initially issued as decrees of the Presidium or of the Council of Ministers. Many are later perfunctorily ratified by the Supreme Soviet, but other decrees on a wide variety of subjects remain in force without even this nominal ratification.

In view of all these circumstances, it is no exaggeration to describe the Supreme Soviet not as a real legislature but as a rubber stamp. In line with Lenin's concept of the soviets as working bodies, however, Communist writers claim another substantial function for the Supreme Soviet—that of overseeing the administration of the laws. But there is no evidence that the Supreme Soviet actually performs this function. Except for the limited commission activity, there is no institutional arrangement to facilitate legislative oversight, such as the question period in the British House of Commons or the committee investigation of the American Congress. One may well ask, therefore, what the real purpose of the Supreme Soviet is. As noted above, it impresses some segments of world opinion with the "democratic content" of the Soviet system. Its elections and its sessions serve as demonstrative rallies of opinion behind the regime. In addition, Supreme Soviet sessions may be viewed as "schools" for impressing the relatively humble and provincial figures who constitute much (though by no means all) of its membership with the nature of the current Party line and the potency of the Soviet system. The deputies, in turn, transmit these concepts to their remote constituents. Deputies who learn their lesson exceptionally well may be drawn into the Party apparatus itself. Thus, Supreme Soviet sessions (and especially those of local soviets) may serve as part of the cadres screening process. Furthermore (following Lenin's view of the soviets as barometers), the Party utilizes the Supreme Soviet sessions as a device for testing public opinion. This is accomplished not through the "dangerous" procedures of uncontrolled debate and voting, but by more indirect sounding of the attitudes of deputies who, after all, have been chosen to represent to some degree the extremely varied geographical, national, and social groups of the U.S.S.R. Finally, the Supreme Soviet must necessarily exist as a cap to the whole system of state elective bodies.

LOCAL SOVIETS

Immediately below the Supreme Soviet are the supreme soviets of the Union republics; their significance is noted later in this chapter. Leaving aside other nationality divisions, the next-lower level of the administration is usually the province (oblast), of which there are approximately 120. Each province has a soviet elected from single-member territorial districts for a two-year term. In contrast to the U.S.S.R. arrangement, the

FORMAL STRUCTURE OF THE SOVIET GOVERNMENT

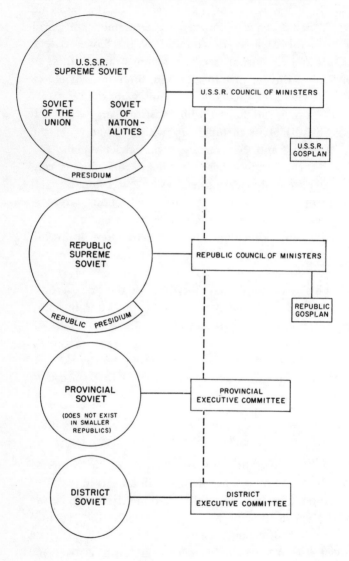

provincial soviet has no presidium or council of ministers, but an executive committee, which combines the functions of both at a lower level. Similarly, the 1,600 city and the 3,000 district (rayon) soviets (elected in the same way) have only executive committees. However, in larger local areas, the presidium of the executive committee seems to carry out most of the duties nominally assigned to the executive committee. The lowest territorial subdivision, the village (about 41,000 in number), usually has only a chairman, vice-chairman, and a secretary. Even Soviet sources admit that the practical importance of the village soviet and its officers is negligible.

Sessions of the local soviets at all levels tend to be perfunctory ceremonies. In one respect, however, especially in cities, the soviet—within its own area—may have an importance much greater than that of the Supreme Soviet. The principal distinguishing feature is the importance of the standing commissions of the soviet. Since their constituencies are small, members of local soviets (even though they owe their election to Party manipulation) are more immediately and practically concerned with the needs of the people whom they nominally represent. Assignment of deputies to local soviet commissions is usually based on practical qualifications: e.g., a teacher or a mother may be assigned to the educational commission. Here the deputy may play a role of real, if limited, importance. He cannot alter or even criticize basic policies of the regime. He can, however, serve as a channel for criticism and suggestions from constituents whose interests and background are not very different from his own, and his own special experiences qualify him to deal with considerable assurance with the problems that confront his commission. Deputies serving on a commission may be given reduced schedules in their usual jobs. The deputies are then able to devote considerable time to on-the-spot inspection of the local administrative agency with which the commission is concerned. Sometimes the deputies even provide practical assistance for the agencies. This activity tends not only to be functionally useful, but also tends to "humanize" the Soviet system at this level by bringing it in contact with ordinary people and their problems. In a sense, it may even give an impression of "grass-roots" democracy to constituents who secure practical relief as a result of their complaints to their deputies. But both constituents and deputy are aware that the range of safe complaints is limited.

THE SOVIET EXECUTIVE

Basic decisions made by the Party apply to the executive or administrative arm of the Soviet Government as well as the legislative branch, but administrative operations have considerably greater importance than legislative operations do. Under Stalin, various aspects of the government administration tended to assume positions in the power structure (under the absolute dictator) on a par with the Party. This was particularly true of the police machine and, during World War II, the military forces. But Stalin also tended to elevate the position of the directing body of the government administration, the Council of Ministers. For more than a decade prior to his death, Stalin held the position of head of government (Chairman of the Council of Ministers, generally called Premier) as well as head of the Party (General Secretary). After Stalin died, Georgi Malenkov surrendered his Party Secretaryship shortly after assuming the post of Premier; yet, for months, he seemed to be the most powerful figure in Soviet politics. Khrushchev's ascendancy meant a restoration of Party supremacy. The Council of Ministers remained somewhat important, however, as indicated by Khrushchev's assumption of the Premiership in 1958. Since Khrushchev's ouster, the Premiership has again been held by a leader (Aleksei N. Kosygin) who is not simultaneously Party chief, and the Council of Ministers has regained significance.

As was noted above, the Council of Ministers is the directing agency of the executive branch of the Soviet Government. While the Party makes the basic decisions, the Council of Ministers plays a very important role in carrying them out, issuing decrees with the force of law that in fact constitute much of the important legislation of the U.S.S.R. Just below the Chairman, or Premier, are two First Deputy Chairmen and nine Deputy Chairmen. Each of these apparently supervises a specific sphere of governmental activity. In addition, the Chairman and Deputy Chairmen constitute a kind of inner cabinet of the Council of Ministers. The Council itself includes, in addition to the chairmen just described, about sixty ministers and a dozen heads of committees and similar bodies. Chairmen of Union-Republic councils of ministers are also at least nominal members of the U.S.S.R. Council of Ministers. Among the important bodies represented there, the People's Control Committee deserves special mention because it serves as the "staff agency" for internal inspection of the government bureaucracy. The presence in the Council of Ministers of the directors of so many bodies, in addition to the heads of the other ministries, means that the Council continues to be an unwieldy body requiring direction by the smaller group of Chairman and Deputy Chairmen.

The Ministries

There are two types of central ministries: All-Union and Union-Republic. All-Union ministries direct matters exclusively in the sphere of central government; consequently, these ministries are found only in Moscow. Most of the All-Union ministries direct major branches of the economy. Union-Republic ministries, on the other hand, direct spheres of activities, that, at least nominally, are shared by the central government and the Union republics.* Consequently, in addition to the ministers in Moscow, who are members of the Council of Ministers of the U.S.S.R., there are counterpart ministers in some or all of the Republic capitals. In Soviet legal theory, the Union-Republic ministries in republic capitals are subordinate both to the corresponding Union-Republic minister in Moscow and to the council of ministers of the republic. If it were not for the peculiar nature of the Soviet system, it is hard to see how this dual subordination could operate smoothly; but in practice, both the Moscow Union-Republic minister and his counterparts in the republics must follow Party decisions. In addition, the Soviet Constitution provides that a "definite and limited number" of agencies in the sphere of a Union-Republic ministry may be directed exclusively by Moscow. In the case of the Ministry of Defense (nominally Union-Republic), apparently all activity is directed by the Minister in Moscow. For many years, as a matter of fact, the identity of none of the ministers of defense in the republic capitals has been revealed. In practice, the conduct of foreign affairs is equally centralized. It is true that the republics have counterpart ministries of foreign affairs, but these are merely propaganda agencies designed to deal with foreign visitors and send delegations to international organizations. Though nominally a Union-Republic ministry, the Ministry of Foreign Affairs in Moscow is the sole governmental authority for the conduct of diplomatic relations. The central ministries maintain a very large measure of control in other areas as well; for example, they require adherence to uniform study plans in the higher educational institutions.

As the preceding discussion indicates, each of the fifteen

---

* A few of the state committees of ministerial level are also legally organized as Union-Republic agencies.

Union republics has its own council of ministers.* Like the central Council of Ministers, each of the republic councils is headed by a chairman (at present none of these are Party secretaries), assisted by several first deputy chairmen and deputy chairmen. Each republic council of ministers also contains a number of committees and commissions, including, in particular, counterparts of the State Planning Committee and the People's Control Committee. The republic councils of ministers also comprise, of course, the republic counterparts of the Union-Republic ministries in Moscow, though some republics do not have all of these ministries. In addition, each republic has a number of ministries for which there are no Moscow counterparts. As a rule, these are ministries for motor transport and highways; municipal utilities; education; social security; construction; and local industry. In theory, these ministries operate without direct control from Moscow; in practice, their activities are closely coordinated and supervised by various central governmental and Party agencies. The activities of the republic ministries probably have some administrative advantages, inasmuch as they provide a measure of decentralization in the huge Soviet Union. The presence of the councils of ministers in the republic capitals also provides a semblance of independence for the republics. But the power to decide important matters remains firmly lodged in the central apparatus in Moscow.

LOCAL EXECUTIVE BODIES

The executive bodies in the provinces, districts, and cities are less complicated than those at the republic level.† Each of

---

* The R.S.F.S.R. has its own council of ministers (in Moscow) as well as its own supreme soviet, even though (as noted in Chapter 3) it does not have a Party organization like that of the other republics.

† The autonomous republics (A.S.S.R.'s) have councils of ministers resembling (on a smaller scale) those of the Union republics.

these levels of government generally has departments that are branches of the republic ministries and that work under ministry direction. Each local level also has an executive committee elected by the soviet of the area. The executive committee exercises general supervision of administration and at the same time functions as an interim legislative body, since the local soviets do not elect presidiums empowered to act between sessions of the soviets.

THE FUNCTIONAL POSITION OF THE NATIONALITIES IN SOVIET POLICY

A survey of the general situation of nationalities in the U.S.S.R. is hardly enough to reveal the vital role they play in the Soviet system; there is little doubt that the regime actually has quite different aims for individual national groups. Borrowing a term used in a different context to describe social organizations, we may conclude that each nationality has a special "function" from the standpoint of the regime's objectives. The regime does not openly avow these aims, but they can be deduced, with a reasonable degree of certainty, by piecing together scattered evidence. Most of this evidence is derived from examining the history of Soviet policy toward individual nationalities and from reading between the lines of Soviet policy statements. In contrast to most aspects of the Soviet political system, there is a considerable body of statistical data concerning the nationalities. Manipulation of this statistical data enables one to construct "indicators" of several crucial elements of the nationality situation, as in the Nationalities Table at the end of this chapter. Most of the indicators provided are static; i.e., they present information on aspects of the nationalities situation at a single point in time, about 1970 unless otherwise stated in the column headings. For some crucial aspects (e.g., scientific workers per one hundred thousand of each ethnic group), increasingly abundant Soviet data permit calculation of indicators which show *trends* over a decade or more of recent Soviet development.

One group of indicators provides additional though indirect evidence on Soviet aims (columns 6–10). Since Party membership is controlled by Moscow, the proportion of Party members of each nationality tends to reflect the extent to which the regime emphasizes the integration of that nationality into the dominant political element. Central Committee membership is an even stronger indication of political integration. One must be careful to note, however, that both these indicators are only suggestive of tendencies; factors other than the regime's objectives may influence the statistics. This reservation applies even more strongly to the other indicators of Soviet policy. In large measure, the proportion of Russians residing in the home territory of each nationality reflects deliberate Soviet encouragement of migration since 1917, but to some extent the migration of Russians to these areas has been voluntary or occurred before the Revolution. Similarly, the proportions of printed materials issued, while ultimately subject to the regime's control, are also influenced by popular demand in each nationality group. Consequently, only by examining a combination of these indicators, together with the historical evidence and Soviet policy statements, can one draw conclusions concerning the nature of Soviet objectives. We shall follow this procedure in discussing each nationality.

Indicators of social mobilization (columns 11–23) are somewhat less ambiguous. Social mobilization is the process by which a basically agricultural society with a traditional culture becomes "modernized," that is, comes to resemble the urban industrial societies of Western Europe and the United States. As noted in Chapter 2, a major objective of the Soviet regime has been modernization along these lines. Consequently, the functions performed for the regime by each nationality are

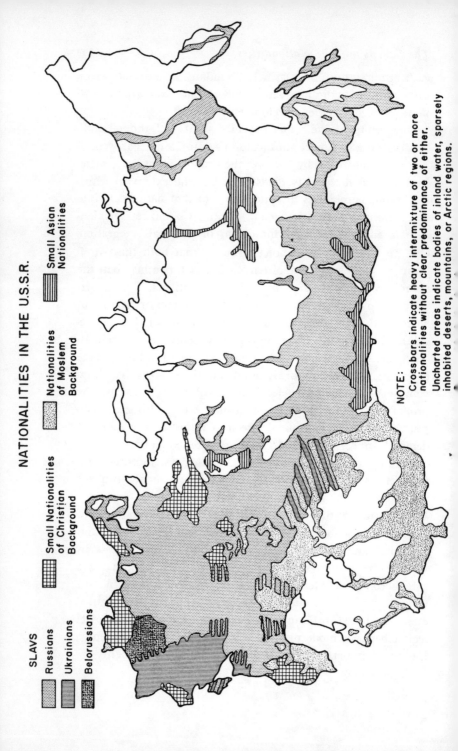

NATIONALITIES IN THE U.S.S.R.

SLAVS

Russians

Ukrainians

Belorussians

Small Nationalities of Christian Background

Nationalities of Moslem Background

Small Asian Nationalities

NOTE:

Crossbars indicate heavy intermixture of two or more nationalities without clear predominance of either.

Uncharted areas indicate bodies of inland water, sparsely inhabited deserts, mountains, or Arctic regions.

closely related to the nationality's degree of social mobilization. The proportion of urban inhabitants is, by definition, an indicator of social mobilization. Experience throughout the world indicates that the proportion of children is also very significant: It is high in traditional and transitional societies, lower in fully modernized societies. Most traditional societies place a much lower value on the education of girls than of boys; hence, the relationship between the proportions of males and females with more than the legally required elementary education is also a good indicator of social mobilization. Indeed, all indicators of relative educational achievements are also indicators of the extent of social mobilization. Since virtually all people in the U.S.S.R. receive elementary educations, simple criteria such as the extent of literacy (frequently used to compare developing nations) are worthless in comparing Soviet nationalities. Examination of higher educational achievement is meaningful, and several indicators of such achievement are given in the Nationalities Table. One must be cautious in using these indicators, however, for some (particularly current enrollments in higher education) may reflect artificial stimulation of the educational level by the regime rather than long-term educational achievement by the nationality group. Another major indicator of social mobilization is the extent to which members of a group change their place of residence, though this factor may also be influenced by the regime's decisions. Data for nationality groups as a whole are unavailable, but data on the extent to which scientists leave to work in the R.S.F.S.R. provide some basis for comparison of residential mobility. The available statistics do not enable one to determine the precise proportion (some non-Russian scientists now residing in the R.S.F.S.R. were born there) which has moved, but the data provide at least a crude indicator of residential mobility.

Social mobilization indicators relating to wages and per capita income suggest the level of economic development attained by each nationality. Since such data are available only for territories (Union republics) rather than for nationalities as such, this group of indicators may be less reliable than other social mobilization indicators presented. In many Union republics a large share of the higher-paying industrial and white-collar jobs are held by Russians and other ethnic groups such as mobilized diasporas. As column 20 indicates, the proportion of national groups engaged in higher-income nonagricultural work varies enormously. In several cases it is evident that relatively high average wage levels for a Union republic are actually the result of the presence of well-paid Slavs in nonagricultural work there rather than high earnings by the local nationality.

Finally, there are indicators (columns 24–28) of the extent to which each nationality has become Russified. In a sense, these indicators represent the "feedback" of Soviet policy, for Russification is a general objective. However, the indicators do provide evidence of Soviet policy intentions: The relative success in Russification may provide clues to the extent to which the regime really is determined to pursue the objective. For some nationalities, Russification appears to be a feasible policy goal; for others, it seems virtually unattainable. Given the general rationality of Soviet policy, one may therefore hypothesize that there is no serious, short-run concern for Russification in such cases. One of the best indicators of Russification is the extent of intermarriage. Unfortunately, Soviet sources provide few data (although the amount is increasing) on this factor. Quantitative indicators are generally limited to data on language habits: the extent to which members of a nationality group habitually speak their own language compared with the extent to which they adopt Russian for everyday use or at least as a second language. In this regard, it is important to note that rural inhabitants everywhere adhere to their own language, while significant numbers of urbanites adopt the "all-Union" language. To put the matter another way, the interrelation between social mobilization and Russification is intimate. But, as the Nationalities Table indicates, the relation varies enormously from nationality to nationality. One must, therefore, turn to a survey of each major group to assess its position in the Soviet system.

The Russians

The Russians are the dominant group in the U.S.S.R. Numerically, they constitute a slight majority. While the proportion of Russians who are Party members is not quite the highest, it is much higher than the proportion among the other *large* nationalities. Central Committee membership is overwhelmingly Russian, though the proportionate role of Ukrainians and some smaller nationalities in the Central Committee, at least during and after Khrushchev's time, has been comparably large. Per capita availability of printed material in Russian is high. These indicators suggest that the regime places extraordinary reliance on the Russians, and there is a considerable amount of additional evidence that the Russian language is favored. These generalizations are borne out by historical evidence, which indicates that the Russians have constantly formed the most reliable and strongest element supporting the regime. This was particularly true during the Civil War when, for many months, Bolshevik power was virtually restricted to the Russian core areas around Moscow and Leningrad, and during World War II when most of the non-Russian population fell under German control. While Stalin was not Russian and relied, to some extent, on non-Russians in the police and the Party apparatus, key organizations like the army officer corps have always been predominantly Russian in recruitment and tradition.

One reason that the Russians have been so useful to the regime is their high degree of social mobilization, suggested by all available quantitative indicators. In a very real sense, at least until the 1950's, the cities, which are predominantly Russian in population even in many minority-nationality republics, were fortresses from which the regime dominated the countryside. As an urban, educated group, the Russians have been the backbone of the program of forced modernization.

The "Younger Brothers"

The social mobilization of the Russians stands out strongly in comparison to the other East Slavic nationalities in the U.S.S.R. Numerically, the 50 million Ukrainians and Belorussians are, next to the Russians, by far the most important nationalities. As East Slavs, they are also closest to the Russians in language. Party membership is high among both the Ukrainians and the Belorussians; the indicators would be more striking if one took into account the *rate of increase* of Party membership among these nationalities since Stalin's death. Since very recent data on Party membership by nationality are not available, we have not tried to show statistical trends in the Nationalities Table. But some general indications are revealing. In 1952, there were approximately half as many Party members for each thousand Ukrainians and Belorussians as for each thousand Russians; today, there are about four-fifths as many. Similarly, proportional representation of both groups in the Central Committee has increased from a very low level to near parity with the Russians. These increases undoubtedly result from the regime's desire to give symbolic recognition to Ukrainians and Belorussians, to convince them that they are really "shareholders" in the Soviet system. All available evidence indicates, however, that members of these groups who enter the Party, or at least those who achieve the elite status of Central Committee membership, are highly Russified. They habitually speak Russian and accept much of the Russian historical tradition. As a result, the regime's policy implies *individual* equality of opportunity for the minority East Slavs, but does not really mean that, *as nationalities,* they are on a par with the Russians. The indicators of printed materials strongly support this view. As compared with the amount of material printed in Russian, the provision of Ukrainian-language and Belorussian-language materials is, per capita, very low. In fact, we know that huge quantities of Russian publications are printed in the Ukrainian and Belorussian republics, or imported from the R.S.F.S.R., while only half a dozen publications in Ukrainian or Belorussian are printed outside those republics. A similar asymmetry exists in the school situation: Russian-language schools educate a sixth of the children in the Ukrainian and Belorussian republics, but there are few if any native-language schools for the substantial Ukrainian and Belorussian minorities outside their republics. Even official statements refer to the Russians as the "elder brothers" of the other East Slavs. The regime's aim appears to be to draw them closer to the Russians, toward eventual assimilation.

The Belorussian group appears to present relatively slight obstacles to the "younger brother" role. The far larger Ukrainian group, on the other hand, is influenced by factors strongly impeding Russification. Historically, there has been considerable antipathy of Ukrainians toward Moscow. It is true that common adherence to the Orthodox religion led most Ukrainians to look toward the Czars in Moscow for protection. But a significant portion (now about one-seventh) of the Ukrainians, in the western region, have been Roman Catholics of the Byzantine (now Ukrainian) rite. As a distinctive religious group, the West Ukrainians opposed both the Latin-rite Catholic Poles and the Orthodox Russians. Prior to 1939, the West

Ukrainians were outside the boundaries of the U.S.S.R. Nationalist organizations were so prevalent among them and so bitterly opposed to Communism and Russian domination that guerrilla activity against the Soviet regime was strong until the late 1940's. More important, perhaps, West Ukrainian nationalists, now incorporated into the U.S.S.R., still try to spread their doctrine of national independence for the Ukraine among the large majority of East Ukrainians. The regime severely represses nationalist sympathizers, but it appears that their appeal arouses memories of independence among the East Ukrainians. During the Civil War, the East Ukrainians maintained a precarious independent republic for some months. After the Bolsheviks gained control of the Ukraine, they felt obliged not only to establish a nominally separate Ukrainian Republic but, until 1930, to encourage use of the Ukrainian language in education and publication.

Probably more important as a source for Ukrainian dissatisfaction with the Moscow regime than memories of historical friction are social differences. Indicators of social mobilization clearly demonstrate the relatively low position of the Ukrainians and Belorussians. In the Ukraine and Belorussia, even more than in most other non-Russian territories, Russians (and Russian-speaking members of other nationalities) predominated in the cities during the 1920's and 1930's. Yet, that was the period when "primitive accumulation" of capital at the expense of the peasants took place. In practice, this meant that the hardships of collectivization were largely borne, in the Ukraine and Belorussia, by the native inhabitants; urban expeditions to enforce collectivization were predominantly Russian, or at least Russian-speaking. In Belorussia, the impact was not as severe as in the Ukraine, for the impoverished peasants had less to lose. The Ukraine contained, then as now, a high proportion of the best agricultural lands in the U.S.S.R. As a result, the peasants were comparatively well off. They were also more attached to individual farming, for the *mir* had never been as strong in the Ukraine as in Russian territories. Consequently, collectivization was a greater departure from tradition; as such, it was more repugnant to Ukrainians. Peasant resistance in the Ukraine was undoubtedly stronger, on the average, than in Russian rural areas. The regime's repressive measures, including wholesale banishment to Siberia and ruthless collection of harvests, was correspondingly more severe. Mass starvation decimated the Ukrainian countryside in 1933. It is not surprising that many Ukrainian peasants identified oppression, directed from Moscow and carried out by Russian-speaking city men, with Russians in general, or that, at least during World War II, Ukrainians were receptive to arguments for national independence.

As the decades have gone by, memories of collectivization undoubtedly have become less important in the Ukraine, especially to the increasing urban element. On the other hand, West Ukrainian nationalism has had some chance to spread. The post-Stalin regime has tried to enhance Ukrainian loyalty but, apart from the impeding factors just outlined, emphasis on East Slav unity is hampered by other considerations. A unified nation of Russified East Slavs would undoubtedly be extremely powerful, for it would include nearly three-fourths of the Soviet population. The Ukraine alone provides one-fifth of the agricultural and industrial production of the Soviet Union. In terms of skills (as reflected in higher education), however, the "younger brothers" are below average. Moreover, official recognition of the dominant position of the East Slavs would have extremely serious consequences for the over-all position of the U.S.S.R. How could it continue to claim to be a multi-national state, the prototype and progenitor of a future Communist commonwealth of nations? What effect would avowed Russian domination have on Soviet claims to lead world Communism or even the Communist bloc of Eastern

Europe? How could Moscow justify its continued control of admittedly non-Slavic territories in a world where national independence is an almost universally popular slogan? A survey of the principal non-Slavic nationalities underscores the complexities involved in the Soviet position.

Mobilized Diasporas

Many societies that are in the transitional stage from traditional to modern include ethnic minorities that perform special functions in the social mobilization process. Such special-function minorities are geographically dispersed (hence, "diasporas") and, relative to other elements of the population, have attained a high degree of social mobilization (hence, "mobilized diasporas"). Frequently, because social or political pressures have prevented them from following the rural occupations typical of a traditional society, these nationalities are more urban than other population elements. Mobilized diaspora members have relatively superior educational attainments, partly because education offers one of the few channels of advancement open to their minority group. Consequently, they provide a disproportionately large share of the modernizing society's highly trained manpower (and womanpower, because mobilized diasporas are exceptionally ready to encourage the education of their women). Mobilized diasporas are also very valuable to modernizing societies because their members frequently have talents in commerce, negotiation, and administration even highly educated members of the dominant nationalities lack. These talents include a wide knowledge of languages, which is essential to members of dispersed nationalities living among populations speaking different tongues, and a sensitivity to human-relations problems, which minority members must have to survive. Because of their useful qualities, mobilized diasporas obtain a disproportionate share of the key positions in a modernizing society. As the society becomes more modernized, this apparently favored position of the minority arouses jealousy among the increasing educated stratum of other nationalities. As a result, members of the mobilized diaspora are frequently subject to discrimination and usually cease to perform specialized functions when the society approaches complete modernization.

Compared to other modernized countries, Russia has had an unusually protracted process of modernization. It began the process in the mid-nineteenth century, roughly at the same time as the United States. While the United States may be considered to have basically completed the transition by about 1920, the U.S.S.R. is still, in many ways, in the latter stages of modernization. It is not surprising, therefore, that several nationalities in succession appear to have acted as mobilized diasporas. We have already noted the place of the Germans among the nobility in the Czarist Empire. They were also very prominent in administration, diplomacy, and the professions. Since the Germans were largely displaced as a mobilized diaspora before the Revolution (though there are still nearly 2 million Germans in the U.S.S.R.), they need not be considered further. During the Czarist period, the numerous Jews of the Empire were persecuted more severely than in any other major nation. Many Jews also suffered as a result of the disorders of the Civil War. Jewish religious life was frowned on by the Bolsheviks; Jewish businessmen eventually lost their property. Individual Jews, however, especially if they were not religious, were not discriminated against. After the Revolution, several rose to prominent positions in the Party and the state. Many other Jews (who, for the most part, preferred democratic socialism to Communism) were able to get higher educations and to move freely into skilled occupations all over the Soviet Union. Among other factors, the centuries-old urban background of most Jews and their traditional emphasis on learning made it relatively easy for them to adapt to the modernization process. As a result, in the 1920's and the 1930's, the Jews assumed an important place in Soviet society as a mobilized diaspora.

Throughout the Soviet period, every Soviet citizen of Jewish parentage, regardless of his own religious attitude, has been required to carry a passport identifying him as a Jew by nationality. The regime set this requirement partly because most Jews in the U.S.S.R. did have some characteristics of a nationality, especially in the habitual use, at the time of the Revolution, of the Yiddish language. Obviously, however, compulsory identification according to parental background paved the way for treating individual Jews as members of a group rather than in accordance with their personal attitudes and merits. This ominous potential for discrimination began to be realized in the early 1940's. Reliable reports indicate that, early in World War II, quotas setting an upper limit on the number of Jews in Party and government posts, in the arts and professions, and in higher education, were secretly decreed. In 1948–49, Yiddish cultural institutions were almost totally abolished and several prominent Jewish cultural figures were secretly executed. In the notorious "Doctors' Plot," a predominantly Jewish group was falsely accused of atrocious crimes. One motive for this persecution seems to have been Stalin's personal prejudice, but, even after his death, thinly disguised accusations of Jewish corruption and the revival of old slanders against the Jewish religion suggest that anti-Semitism is widespread. While this prejudice has many sources, one (as Khrushchev once implied) is jealousy of the prominent role occupied by Jews in highly skilled occupations. But, the numerous Jewish scientists, physicians, and other highly trained personnel constitute an almost indispensable resource for the Soviet system. Moreover, the claim of the U.S.S.R. to be a society of brotherhood and equality is tarnished by evidence of discrimination. Under these circumstances, the regime has played an ambivalent game. Some indirect slurs on Jews as a group continue to appear; Judaism is discouraged as a religion. But anti-Semitism is, occasionally, officially denounced. Jews continue to occupy important positions, but their *proportion* in the highly skilled occupations and in university student bodies regularly decreases (compare columns 16 and 17). Yiddish (and Hebrew) instruction is virtually precluded; as a result, Jews have rapidly Russified linguistically. Nevertheless, a relatively low rate of intermarriage with non-Jews suggests that a large proportion of Soviet Jews cling to their ethnic identity. From the 1960's on, manifestations of Jewish ethnic consciousness (such as street gatherings on holy days) multiplied. While the Soviet regime acted harshly to discourage these manifestations, it gradually relaxed restrictions on Jewish and German emigration, perhaps hoping that departure of the most dissatisfied elements in these diasporas would make absorption of the remainder easier.

With the reduced importance of the Jews as a mobilized diaspora has come the increased importance of Armenians in this role. As the indicators (columns 12, 16, 17, 18) in the Nationalities Table show, Armenians do not reach the extremely high levels of urbanization, higher education, and skilled professional status attained by the Jews, but the Armenians equal or exceed the Russians in these indicators of social mobilization and are far ahead of most other nationalities. Curiously enough, though their women have nearly as high an indicator of educational attainment as their men (columns 14 and 15), indicators of Armenian population increase (column 11) remain very high. Armenians are less concentrated in their home territory than any major nationality other than Tatars. (Jews, Germans, and Poles, who, practically speaking, have no home territory in the U.S.S.R., are not included in this comparison). Armenians are especially important as a mobilized diaspora throughout the Transcaucasus, the North

Caucasus, and the Transcaspian regions. They also perform some specialized tasks in over-all Soviet institutions, especially in the area of domestic and foreign commerce. Compared to earlier mobilized diasporas, their importance may be slight; one reason for this reduction in importance of the mobilized diaspora is that Soviet society has become more modernized.

For the time being, the Armenian group enjoys certain privileges. Its distinctive Gregorian Church is subjected to less pressure than most other religious groups in the U.S.S.R.—partly because the regime tries to use it to influence the numerous Armenians living in other parts of the world. The proportion of Russians in the Armenian S.S.R. is unusually low. In some areas, Armenians outside their republic are provided with their own language schools. The relatively low per capita rate of publication in Armenian suggests that the regime does not encourage linguistic autonomy in all respects, however. At any rate, Armenians, as a highly dispersed nationality, tend, much more than most nationalities, to adopt Russian as their habitual speech. In the long run, the regime may hope to assimilate the Armenians; in the meantime, it apparently finds it worthwhile to encourage them to function as a mobilized diaspora.

The State Nations

A glance at the Nationalities Table shows that most indicators of social mobilization for the Georgians, the Estonians, and the Latvians are of the same order of magnitude as for the Russians and the Armenians. In contrast to the Armenians, however, the Georgians, Estonians, and Latvians are highly concentrated in their home territories. Each of these territories has, in recent times, constituted a national unit of special strength. Between 1918 and 1939, Estonia and Latvia were independent states with flourishing cultures and highly developed economies. Georgia was independent for only two

years, but its favored position under Stalin, a Georgian himself, provided a kind of substitute for the cultural development and national self-confidence that is usually an attribute
of statehood. As a result, linguistic Russification has made
remarkably little progress among these three nationalities.
Much evidence suggests that a dominant tendency among
them is the determination to maintain their national identi-
ties. Consequently, we may designate these nationalities as
"state nations."

The situation of the Lithuanians and the Moldavians is
rather different. In terms of nearly all indicators of social mobilization, both nationalities rate well below the nationalities
discussed so far. On the other hand, both have a recent memory of independence from Russia: during the interwar period,
separate statehood for the Lithuanians, and incorporation
into ethnically similar Romania for the Moldavians. Both also
show a strong resistance to Russification. Consequently, it
seems desirable to include them, too, among the state nations.

All of the state nations occupy highly strategic positions on
the frontiers of the U.S.S.R. Under Stalin, all except his fellow
Georgians were severely repressed, and a heavy immigration of
Russians into their republics was encouraged in order to establish what amounted to frontier garrisons of reliable elements.
The increasing strength of the U.S.S.R. has made such pre-
cautions less vital. At the same time, the regime seems to have
recognized that Russification of the state nations cannot be
accomplished quickly and that strong overt pressures in this
direction will increase dissatisfaction among them and disrupt
their significant, though minor, contribution to the Soviet
economy. As a result, a kind of stand-off appears to exist: The
state-nation territories are firmly incorporated into the Soviet
defensive and economic systems, but the regime permits a relatively high degree of cultural autonomy (indicated by high
per capita publication rates) and a relatively low degree of

political integration (suggested by low Party membership and fluctuating Central Committee membership indicators) for the state nations.

Colonials

The Russian Empire, in contrast to West European colonial empires, expanded into adjoining land areas inhabited by peoples representing a gradual transition of physical types. As a result, Russians commonly do not maintain notions of racial superiority. Nevertheless, as the Russian Empire expanded into the vague borderlands of Europe and, then, into the heart of Asia itself, it absorbed nationalities that differed from the dominant Russian culture as much as the typical colony of a West European country differed from the metropolis. Even today, these nationalities, in their relatively low levels of social mobilization, resemble typical colonies. The educational and skilled occupational attainments of all seven (Azerbaidzhanis, Uzbeks, Turkmens, Kazakhs, Kirgizes, Tatars, and Tadzhiks) listed in the Nationalities Table are generally, though not universally, below those of the Soviet nationalities considered earlier in this chapter. Residential mobility appears somewhat lower, on the average, for the colonials. Their most striking difference, in the indicators of social mobilization, appears in the extraordinarily high proportion under 20 years old and the great disparity between male and female educational attainment.

Both of the latter indicators reflect not only the less modernized situation of the colonials but the wide traditional cultural gap between them and other major Soviet nationalities. All of the colonial nationalities presented in the Table (as well as a number of smaller Soviet ethnic groups) were traditionally Moslem. While the Islamic faith does not require the relegation of women to agricultural and household tasks, most Moslem cultures have, in fact, put a low value on female education and discouraged women from moving into industrial and professional occupations. Even today, Soviet publications frequently complain that the persistence of these traditional attitudes associated with Islam prevent utilization of women in the work force of the once-Moslem territories.

The inferior position of women is but one of the sharply different cultural traits that persist in colonial society. The vast majority of colonials speak closely related Turkic languages. As a result, there has been considerable cultural contact and mutual cultural reinforcement among them despite the fact that the regime replaced its early efforts to set up unified Soviet Moslem republics in Central Asia and the North Caucasus with the present fragmentation along lines of minor linguistic differentiation. Today, educational indicators for Tatars do not differ much from those of other Moslem groups. Tatar educational advance, however, predates the Revolution by generations and was accompanied by a strong nationalist and religious movement. For several decades before and immediately after the Revolution, the widely scattered Tatars played a particularly important role as educators and propagators of Turkic national feeling. Dispersed as they were, the Tatars nevertheless underwent a considerable degree of Russification. All colonial groups, however, have exhibited a high degree of resistance to linguistic Russification, while intermarriage with Slavs is almost negligible. Their children usually attend native-language schools apart from Russians. However, the relatively low levels of education for these groups has meant that publication in Turkic and in other colonial languages is not extensive on a per capita basis.

The regime has pursued a consistent policy of modernizing the Moslem societies, with notable results in terms of literacy and economic progress; this has been done despite the inflexible attitudes held by some elements of the colonial culture (such as that toward women). The regime has de-empha-

TABLE OF MAJOR NATIONALITIES OF THE SOVIET UNION

NATIONALITY	1. Total number in the U.S.S.R (in thousands)	2. Percentage residing in home territory	3. Location of home territory of nationality	4. Linguistic group	5. Traditional religion	6. Central Committee members and alternates, 1966, per million nationality	7. Party members, 1967, per thousand nationality	8. Percentage of Russians in total population in home territory	9. Books (copies per capita) published annually in national language	10. Newspapers (copies per capita) published annually in national language	11. Percentage under age 20	12. Percentage of nationality residing in urban areas	13. Percentage growth of proportion of nationality residing in urban areas, 1926-70	14. Urban population (10 years and older) with more than elementary education (per thousand) Male	15. Female	16. Scientific workers (per one hundred thousand)	17. Percentage increase of scientific workers (per one hundred thousand), 1960-70	18. Students in higher education (per thousand in 20-29 age group)	19. Percentage of scientists residing in R.S.F.S.R., 1963	20. Percentage of labor force of nationality (residing in home territory) holding industrial and white collar jobs, 1959	21. Average wage in home territory (as proportion of R.S.F.S.R. average wage), 1968	22. Per capita yearly income in home territory (rubles), 1968	23. Per capita income in home territory (percentage growth), 1958-68	24. Percentage habitually speaking native language	25. Percentage increase or decrease of proportion habitually speaking native language, 1959-70	26. Percentage of urban population habitually speaking Russian	27. Percentage of urban population using Russian as a second language	28. Total percentage of urban population familiar with Russian
Russian	129,015	84	More than U.S.S.R.	East Slavic	Ortho-dox	1.5	61	—	8	190	36	68	219	613	571	475	167	160	—	76	100	1,160	174	100	−.4	100	27	100
Ukrainian	40,753	87	SW Eur.a. U.S.S.R.	East Slavic	Ortho. & Gr. Cath.	1.4	49	19	2	58	32	48	361	666	574	246	183	116	29	47	94	1,005	163	86	−2.3	24	—	81
Belorussian	9,052	81	W Cen. Euro. U.S.S.R.	East Slavic	Ortho-dox	1.3	47	10	1	27	35	44	324	658	598	209	198	112	36	43	80	837	200	81	−4.3	36	47	85
Jewish	2,151	.5	Very widely scattered	Germanic	Jew-ish	.5	—	—	.03	.05	15	98	19	843	811	2,988	92	428	6	—	—	—	—	18	−17.7	79	49	95
Armenian	3,559	62	Trans-caucasus	Separate Indo-Euro. group	Sim. to Ortho.	1.4	56	3	2	50	44	65	83	604	580	567	152	212	19	60	93	754	166	91	+1.7	11	38	49
Georgian	3,245	97	Trans-caucasus	Japhetic (obscure relationship)	Ortho-dox	.9	64	9	4	152	37	44	160	749	721	567	122	223	6	45	88	668	142	98	−.2	3	37	40
Estonian	1,007	92	NW Euro. U.S.S.R.	Finnic	Protes-tant	3.0	37	25	9	185	25	55	—	592	574	467	124	144	10	73	97	1,448	199	96	+.3	6	37	43
Latvian	1,430	94	NW Euro. U.S.S.R.	Baltic	Protes-tant	2.8	35	30	8	135	26	53	—	617	584	416	124	121	13	65	93	1,472	187	95	+.1	6	51	57
Lithuanian	2,665	94	NW Euro. U.S.S.R.	Baltic	Lat. Cath.	1.1	27	9	5	108	34	47	—	534	505	306	176	138	4	48	88	1,179	208	98	+.1	3	52	55
Moldavian	2,698	85	SW Euro. U.S.S.R.	Romance	Ortho-dox	.8	18	12	2	70	41	20	151	582	499	92	321	97	6	17	81	837	170	95	−.2	16	61	77
Azerbaidzhani	4,380	86	Trans-caucasus	Turkic	Mos-lem (Shiite)	.5	18	10	2	67	57	40	33	603	450	299	162	205	3	39	91	628	124	98	+.6	3	32	35
Uzbek	9,195	84	Central Asia	Turkic	Mos-lem (Sunni)	.5	24	13	3	54	59	25	1,967	561	426	132	224	167	3	35	86	568	134	99	+.2	2	35	37
Turkmen	1,525	93	Central Asia	Turkic	Mos-lem (Sunni)	1.3	23	15	3	57	58	31	1,114	559	408	120	158	150	2	22	101	580	114	99	0	2	32	34
Kazakh	5,299	80	Central Asia	Turkic	Mos-lem (Sunni)	.9	38	43	2	52	56	27	950	569	456	141	245	165	—	60	98	721	150	98	−.4	4	57	61
Kirgiz	1,452	88	Central Asia	Turkic	Mos-lem (Sunni)	1.4	27	29	2	65	52	15	255	653	559	131	225	202	.5	30	90	639	155	99	+.1	2	53	55
Tatar	5,931	26	NE Euro. U.S.S.R.	Turkic	Mos-lem (Sunni)	.3	—	—	.5	25	43	55	42	557	516	196	215	146	—	—	—	—	—	89	−2.1	16	72	88
Tadzhik	2,136	76	Central Asia	Iranian	Mos-lem (Sunni)	.9	22	12	2	49	59	26		546	366	110	172	133	2.5	26	93	509	147	99	+.4	2	32	34

NOTES TO NATIONALITIES TABLE

(numbers refer to table columns)

1. Based on 1970 U.S.S.R. census (*Itogi Vsesoyuznoi Perepisi Naseleniya 1970 Goda*, Vol. IV, 1972), p. 20, hereafter cited as *Itogi*, 1970. Page numbers refer to Vol. IV only, unless otherwise indicated. These 1970 census data are, unless otherwise indicated, the base for calculating per capita figures in other columns.

2. Based on *ibid.*, pp. 20, 365, 377–83.

3. For an analysis of regional divisions of the Soviet Union, see David Hooson, "The Outlook for Regional Development in the Soviet Union," *Slavic Review*, XXXI (1972), 536–54.

4. Based on Frank Lorimer, *The Population of the Soviet Union* (Geneva: League of Nations, 1946), pp. 55–61.

5. *Ibid.*

6. Based on data for 89 per cent of the universe (N = 360) presented in S. Voronitsyn, "The Present Composition of the Party Central Committee," *Bulletin of the Institute for the Study of the U.S.S.R.*, XVI, 22.

7. Based on data in *Parttinaya Zhizn*, No. 19, 1967 (*Current Digest of the Soviet Press*, XIX, No. 43, 10).

8. *Izvestia*, April 17, 1971 (*Current Digest of the Soviet Press*, XXIII, No. 16, 16–18).

9. *Narodnoe Khozyaistvo SSSR v 1970 g.* (Moscow: "Statistika," 1971), p. 679.

10. *Ibid.*, p. 685. The Russian figure is an estimate based on the assumption that nearly all newspapers published in Union republics other than the R.S.F.S.R., if not in the languages of those republics, are in Russian, and that no other language group has significant newspaper publication outside its home territory. Figures for Tatars and Jews are rougher estimates based on various sources.

11. Based on *Itogi*, 1970, pp. 360–64, 370, 373. Data for Tatars and Jews are for portions of these nationalities in the R.S.F.S.R. only.

12. Based on *ibid.*, pp. 21, 27.

13. Based on *ibid.*, and Lorimer, pp. 55–59. The vast majority of Estonians, Latvians, Lithuanians, and Moldavians were not in the U.S.S.R. in 1926.

14. Based on *Itogi*, 1970, pp. 393–450 (Tables 36 and 37). Data for Tatars and Jews are for portions of these nationalities in the R.S.F.S.R. only.

15. *Ibid.*

16. Based on *Narodnoe Khozyaistvo SSSR v 1970 g.*, p. 658.

17. *Ibid.*

18. *Ibid.*, p. 651, calculated to *base of 1959 census*; includes part-time students.

19. Based on data in *Narodnoe Khozyaistvo RSFSR v 1965 Godu* (Moscow: Tsentralnoe Statisticheskoe Upravlenie RSFSR, 1965). p. 495, calculated to *base of 1959 census*. Data for Jews, Tatars, and Kazakhs are not meaningful because of the high proportions of these nationalities native to the R.S.F.S.R.

20. Yu. V. Arutyunyan, *Sotsialnaya Struktura Selskogo Naseleniya SSSR* (Moscow: "Mysl," 1971), p. 84.

21. V. Zlatin and V. Guggaizer, "Comparison of the Levels of Economic Development of Union Republics and Large Regions," *Ekonomicheskie Nauki*, 1968, No. 8, p. 32 (trans. in *Problems of Economics*, XII, No. 69, 3–24). The Soviet authors assert that most of the wage differentials are accounted for by differences in economic structure among the Union republics, particularly higher proportions of agricultural workers in republics with relatively low wages, rather than differential pay for the same type of work. While this assertion is unquestionably accurate in the main, it leaves open the question of whether members of nationalities which have disproportionate numbers of workers in low-paid occupations perceive this disproportion as grounds for resentment against Russians in better-paid occupations.

22. Hans-Juergen Wagener, *Regional Output Levels in the Soviet Union*, Radio Liberty Research Paper No. 41, 1971, p. 14. I am indebted to Prof. Yaroslav Bilinsky for analyzing these data and bringing them to my attention. One should note that there are great discrepancies between the relative positions of Union republics according to these data and to those presented in column 21. Most of these discrepancies are accounted for by the low proportion of workers in the populations of certain Union republics, especially those of Central Asia. As a result, relatively high wages (especially in republics with a small agricultural sector) do not result in high per capita incomes. Since the figures in column 22 reflect high birth rates as well as earning capacity, they are generally more sensitive indicators than wages taken by themselves. However, in some low-birth-rate areas (the Baltic Union republics) relatively low per capita income in spite of very high wage levels may reflect voluntary withdrawal of married women and the elderly from direct economic activity—phenomena usually indicating a high level of social mobilization.

23. *Ibid.*

24. *Izvestia*, April 17, 1971 (*Current Digest of the Soviet Press*, XXIII, No. 16, 16–8).

25. *Ibid.* and *Itogi Vsesoyuznoi Perepisi Naseleniya 1959 Goda: SSSR* (Moscow: Tsentralnoe Statisticheskoe Upravlenie, 1962), p. 190.

26. Based on *Itogi*, 1970, pp. 360–64, 370, 373. Data for Tatars and for Jews are for portions of those nationalities in the R.S.F.S.R. only.

27. *Ibid.*

28. *Ibid.*

sized the unity of the colonial nationalities and particularly their ties with related nations (like the Iranians) outside the U.S.S.R. Correspondingly, the Soviet regime has emphasized equality of opportunity for capable members of the colonial groups and has even taken special measures to provide higher educational opportunities and access to higher positions for them. Indicators of Party membership and Central Committee membership, while not as high for colonials as for most other nationalities, would probably be much lower if the regime had not made concentrated efforts to recruit promising colonials. As with other groups, rapid upward mobility for a colonial means a measure of assimilation to the Russian culture. Apparently, however, the sense of national identity remains much stronger among upwardly mobile colonials than among persons rising from other non-Russian nationalities. This could hardly fail to be the case in view of the sharpness and duration of the distinction in cultural background. Furthermore, while we have little direct evidence of colonials' identification with national independence movements beyond the Soviet frontiers, it is most unlikely that educated persons of Moslem background would fail to draw a parallel between their own situation and that of closely related national groups in the Middle East, which have successfully asserted their independence of Europe. The situation has become more critical since Communist China denounced the Soviet Union's claim to be an Asian as well as a European state.

Under these circumstances, it is easy to see how risky it would be for the Soviet regime to emphasize East Slavic solidarity to the point of hegemony in the Soviet multinational political system. As long as the regime emphasizes its doctrinal basis and seems to be making significant progress toward Communist millennial goals, it can continue (though with uncertain success) to claim to represent the interests of the numerous non-Slavic nations. The day the Soviet regime admits the practical irrelevancy of these goals, it will stand revealed as the master of the last of the world's great colonial empires.

SUGGESTED READING • CHAPTER 6

Because the formal governmental system of the U.S.S.R. is of secondary importance, no major critical works have been devoted exclusively to it. However, most of the books listed at the end of Chapter 3 provide extensive information on Soviet government. On the other hand, a considerable number of books deal specifically with the important ramifications of nationality relations in the U.S.S.R.

ALLWORTH, EDWARD (ed.). *Soviet Nationality Problems.* New York: Columbia University Press, 1971. A symposium emphasizing the theoretical significance of nationality in the Soviet system rather than the situations of specific ethnic groups.

ARMSTRONG, JOHN A. *Ukrainian Nationalism.* New York: Columbia University Press, 1963. A study of recent nationalist movements among the largest non-Russian group in the U.S.S.R.

BARGHOORN, FREDERICK. *Soviet Russian Nationalism.* London and New York: Oxford University Press, 1956. The most comprehensive discussion of the relation between Russian nationalism and Communism.

BILINSKY, YAROSLAV. *The Second Soviet Republic: The Ukraine After World War II.* New Brunswick, N. J.: Rutgers University Press, 1964. A highly detailed effort analyzing Soviet policy.

BROWNE, MICHAEL (ed.). *Ferment in the Ukraine.* New York: Praeger, 1971. A carefully edited collection of the most important work of non-Russian dissidents of the 1960's.

CAROE, OLAF. *Soviet Empire: The Turks of Central Asia.* New York: St. Martin's Press, 1967. The most comprehensive work devoted specifically to the Turkic peoples of Moslem background.

CONQUEST, ROBERT (ed.). *Soviet Nationalities Policy in Practice.* New York: Praeger, 1967. More useful for the evolution of Soviet doctrine on nationalities than on practice.

CURTISS, JOHN S. *The Russian Church and the Soviet State.* Boston: Little, Brown & Company, 1953. Deals mainly with relations between the Orthodox Church and the atheism of the regime but also has important information on Russian nationalism.

DZYUBA, IVAN. *Internationalism or Russification?* New York: Humanities Press, 1968. The most systematic, documented presentation of the "Leninist" case against Russian nationalist suppression, by a Ukrainian dissenter still in the Soviet Union.

GOLDHAGEN, ERICH (ed.). *Ethnic Minorities in the Soviet Union.* New York: Praeger, 1968. A symposium that provides the most comprehensive recent treatment of all major aspects of the nationalities situation.

HODNETT, GREY, and POTICHNYJ, PETER J. *The Ukraine and the Czechoslovak Crisis.* Canberra: Australian National University, 1970. A very revealing documentation of the penetration of Czechoslovak liberalization into the Ukraine.

KOCHAN, LIONEL (ed.). *The Jews in the Soviet Union Since 1917.* London and New York: Oxford University Press, 1970. The best recent treatment of the changing position of Jews in the U.S.S.R.

MATOSSIAN, MARY A. K. *The Impact of Soviet Policies in Armenia.* Leiden: E. J. Brill, 1962. A good survey of a very complicated ethnic situation.

PIPES, RICHARD E. *The Formation of the Soviet Union.* Cambridge, Mass.: Harvard University Press, 1954. A very important treatment of the early relations of the Bolshevik to the non-Russian nationalities and of the impact of this relationship on the constitutional structure of the U.S.S.R.

RESHETAR, JOHN S. *The Ukrainian Revolution.* Princeton, N. J.: Princeton University Press, 1952. The beginnings of the modern Ukrainian nationalist movement.

SULLIVANT, ROBERT. *Soviet Politics in the Ukraine, 1917–1957.* New York: Columbia University Press, 1962. The most comprehensive discussion of the relation between Ukrainian nationalism and Communism.

8
INTERPENETRATION OF
DOMESTIC AND FOREIGN
POLICY

Soviet foreign policy is so obviously important in our times, yet so extremely complicated, that it is hard to discuss at all without using the kind of detailed treatment presented by the excellent books cited at the end of this chapter. Most of those books are, in fact, histories of Soviet foreign policy, examining the evolution of the Soviet regime's relations with other countries from the Revolution on. Since the scope of our study precludes presenting even the major internal aspects of the Soviet system in historical detail, this book obviously cannot provide such consideration of a subject like foreign policy. At a few points in the preceding chapters—notably in the discussion of ideology in Chapter 2—some glimpses of the relationship between foreign and domestic policies have appeared. In closing our consideration of the Soviet system, however, a somewhat more systematic discussion is essential.

Foreign policy is especially critical to examination of the Soviet system because, in James Rosenau's terms, the U.S.S.R. is an extraordinarily "penetrated" society. In other words, factors in the domestic and the international environment of the Soviet system are almost inextricably intertwined. In large part this complex interrelation arises from the nationality situation discussed in Chapter 7, as will be analyzed later in this chapter. In part the "penetration" derives from ideological factors. Here, however, one must be cautious. While Leninist ideology posits a continuity of foreign and domestic affairs, it would be naïve (although numerous observers have in fact taken this position) to assume that Leninism presents a set of prescriptions for action in foreign affairs which the decision-making elite follows consistently. Instead, the dynamics of actual developments in the political system—both domestic and foreign—have crucially affected the elite's perceptions of the way in which actual moves in the international arena should be adapted to ideological prescriptions. Thus, for example, Stalin's decision to build "socialism in a single country" drastically changed the relation between the ever receding goal of "world Communism" and the kind of foreign policy perceived to be necessary to preserve the Soviet socialist state. Today, the more immediate interests of the aging oligarchy, or perhaps their psychological limitations, induce a further postponement of universalistic, millennial objectives. And throughout the lifetime of the Soviet system its peculiar geographical position and ethnic composition have drastically conditioned its role in world affairs.

THE U.S.S.R. AND THE INTERNATIONAL ENVIRONMENT

Whatever alterations in foreign policy objectives a country's internal political system may induce, actual efforts to achieve these objectives are heavily conditioned by the nature of the external environment in which the system operates, i.e., by the distribution of forces in the world arena. The scope of the foreign policy of the U.S.S.R., whatever the elite's perceptions of ideological demands, is similarly conditioned by environmental constraints. The concept of the position of the U.S.S.R. in a "capitalist environment," * which greatly circumscribed Soviet actions, was a common theme of Soviet pronouncements before World War II. Between 1917 and 1940 the Soviet regime operated in an international system composed of

---

* The word *"okruzhenie"* is more frequently translated as "encirclement" but "environment" is equally valid.

seven great powers, and a considerable number of lesser states (in particular Poland) with notable military power. Apart from the remote satellite of the Mongolian People's Republic, there was no other Communist state. Under these circumstances, any imminent prospect of attaining world Communism as a direct result of Soviet foreign policy was illusory. Even if the U.S.S.R. had overcome one or two neighboring states, the operation of the international balance of power would have meant that other major powers would have joined to set limits on Soviet expansion, as did indeed occur to some degree during the Soviet invasion of Poland in 1920. In other words, in such an international system broad distribution of power tended to make any individual state's expansion self-limiting. The only short-range prospect, therefore, for fulfilling the Leninist prescription of world revolution was through revolution within other major powers, assisted perhaps to some degree by the U.S.S.R. (as the vaunted fatherland of the "world proletariat"), but overwhelmingly the result of internal developments within other countries. As a result, the foreign policy actually pursued by organs of the Soviet regime during the interwar period often appeared to be schizophrenic, combining violent verbal proclamations (usually by the Communist International headquarters in Moscow) with complicated diplomatic maneuvering by professional foreign affairs personnel. Since the other great powers usually recognized that the Soviet potential was extremely limited, Moscow's verbal "playing at revolution" did not prevent the U.S.S.R.'s participation in conventional balance-of-power politics. The Soviet regime was usually able to make covert if not overt alliances with several of the capitalist great powers. Especially after 1933 the cleavage between the expansionist Axis powers (Germany, Italy, Japan) and the status quo Western democracies (Britain, France, United States) was a far more fundamental aspect of international relations than the existence of a relatively weak Communist state. Curiously, this division corresponded at least superficially to Lenin's prediction that the major, inevitable conflicts of the "age of imperialism" would be among capitalist countries. Nevertheless, the ambiguous relationship of ideology to actual foreign policy is indicated by Stalin's and other Soviet leaders' fears that all "imperialist" powers would unite against the U.S.S.R. These fears led them to an exaggerated interpretation of Anglo-French hostility at Munich; to preference for a Nazi-Soviet pact instead of a proposed alliance with Britain and France a few months later; and to near-isolation, physically, at the time of the Nazi attack on the U.S.S.R. in 1941.

TRANSFORMATION OF THE INTERNATIONAL ENVIRONMENT

As a result of World War II, the international environment in which the Soviet Union has since operated was drastically changed. Only one of the three basic factors leading to this transformation was the result of Soviet initiative, however, and the general nature of the transformation was not foreseen by Soviet ideology.

The fundamental factor was the reduction of the number of great powers—i.e., those of roughly equivalent military capacity—from seven to two. As late as 1952 Stalin predicted that the major Axis powers, Germany and Japan, would soon re-emerge to fight another imperialist war with the United States; but, as discussed below, despite remarkable economic recovery these countries have not really regained great-power status. Their eclipse was, in fact, sealed by the "unconditional surrender" formula adopted at the Casablanca conference in 1943, where the U.S.S.R. was not even represented. The initiative was clearly U.S. President Franklin D. Roosevelt's, although he represented a strong current of Western democratic thinking that the aggressive crimes of the two Axis countries required their indefinite removal from the ranks of the major powers. The vacuum created by implementation of this decision (which Stalin after some hesitation accepted) was in-evitably filled by the stronger victors. Since France had been defeated and Italy's pretensions to great-power status were on the verge of demolition, these victors could only be the United States, the Soviet Union, and Great Britain. Indeed, for a brief period (1944–46) the Soviet leadership apparently did envisage a tripartite power distribution, with the principal confrontation between the latter two. Actually, however, com-plex factors—including dissolution of the British Empire, which was as strongly urged by the United States as by the U.S.S.R.—prevented British maintenance of great-power status. As a result, a bipolar distribution of power quickly emerged and has continued to dominate the postwar international scene.

In a bipolar environment Soviet options are fundamentally different from what they were in the multipartite interwar system. On the one hand, Soviet initiatives in the spread of Communism are more realistic, for the U.S.S.R. possesses such a large fraction of world military power that only determined resistance by the other "superpower," the United States, can act as an ultimate barrier. On the other hand, just because this bipolar balance often is perceived as a "zero-sum" situ-ation in which one side's gain is the other's loss, any major Soviet initiative is apt to arouse quicker and more determined resistance by the other "superpower" and middle powers. In other words, the closer the U.S.S.R. comes to a situation in which world domination is theoretically achievable, the warier (at least in principle) are the remaining powers. Consequently, unless the Soviet leaders are willing to risk an all-out war, they must calculate their moves and, particularly, weigh their words more carefully than they did when the U.S.S.R. ex-ercised only a small weight in the world balance.

The need for prudence has been immensely enhanced by the unprecedented increase in destructive force of weapons and their rapidity of delivery. At the same time, the overriding importance of nuclear weapons systems has constituted a *second factor* enhancing the position of the U.S.S.R. as the only real military peer of the United States. Although Soviet weaponry lagged far behind American until the late 1960's, the eventual Soviet ability to catch up in nuclear weapons has depended on advantages not shared by the remaining countries. While several countries have industrial and technological plants comparable in size to the Soviet Union's, none has the centralized state control which permits protracted, concentrated diversion of a major share of these resources to arms development. Consequently, while several countries have "gone nuclear" by producing bombs, none but the U.S.S.R. and the United States has so far been able to produce the massive range of alternative intercontinental delivery systems able to survive a first strike and inflict unacceptable damage on an opponent. The Soviet Union is also greatly favored in this effort at creating an "invulnerable deterrent" by its vast territory, which makes dispersion feasible. Quite possibly the Soviet experience of desperate resistance in World War II, when (in spite of losing about one-eighth of its population) the U.S.S.R. emerged relatively stronger than other countries, is also a factor. On the one hand, this experience strengthens the elite's resolve to maintain a powerful military force; on the other hand, it may give the elite confidence that the Soviet system could once again absorb gigantic losses, yet survive.

The *third factor* causing a drastic change in the U.S.S.R.'s environment after World War II was the extension of Soviet power into the heart of Central Europe. As suggested above, this extension was made possible by the vacuum created by the elimination of Germany as a power. The Soviet regime, however, deliberately chose to perpetuate its control over the entire area from the Russian border to Czechoslovakia's western frontier and the center of prewar Germany. The strategic implications of this choice—other effects are noted below—has been that the remaining portions of Central and Western Europe can only with great difficulty constitute a great power capable of self-defense. Since 1945 Soviet armies have been stationed less than one hundred miles from the Rhine River and only three hundred miles from the English Channel. When one compares these distances to the vast areas of maneuver and dispersion available to the U.S.S.R. and even the U.S., it is partially understandable why the great economic and demographic resources of Western Europe have not yet been matched by military capacity. Strategic geography renders the position of the Scandinavian and Mediterranean components of the North Atlantic Treaty Organization (NATO) even more precarious. Thus Soviet control of East-Central Europe, while undoubtedly to a considerable degree defensive in motivation, makes re-establishment of a real multipartite distribution of world power exceedingly difficult.

DEFENSIVE AND EXPANSIONIST ELEMENTS IN SOVIET POLICY

The dual offensive-defensive implications of Soviet occupation of East-Central Europe are the sharpest, ultimately perhaps the most tragic reflection of the nature of the U.S.S.R. as a highly penetrated political system. As was discussed in Chapter 7, the Soviet Union is not a national state, but (to use Vernon Aspaturian's term) an "arrested world state." From the start, Lenin based his system's claim to incorporate a diverse group of nations on the assertion that the Soviet state was only a step toward a Communist union of all nations. In fact, the frontiers actually attained at the end of the Russian Civil War (1920) included small segments of the Polish, German, Finnish and Romanian nations; conversely, large portions of the Ukrainian and Belorussian nations were left outside the U.S.S.R. Equally important, in terms of system interpenetrability, was the fact that the then independent Baltic nations, the Finns, and the bulk of the Poles themselves had constituted a part of the Czarist political system. Revolutionaries from these nations had been deeply involved in the internal struggles of the Bolsheviks and other political parties before the Revolution and during the Civil War. Stalin, at least, appears to have regarded severance of these national groups from the post–Civil War political system as a threat to his power. Conversely, the U.S.S.R. always had small cadres of devoted Communists ready for penetrating the neighboring political systems. The direct annexations of 1940–46, which incorporated nearly all Ukrainians and Belorussians, as well as the Baltic nations and more Romanians, Poles, and Finns into the U.S.S.R., did not eliminate its penetrability. In fact, these moves exacerbated the situation by arousing the animosity of the Poles, Finns, and Romanians, and even making many Czechoslovaks resentful, for the first time, of arbitrary Soviet expansion. Undoubtedly one reason Stalin insisted on establishing Communist governments in all of these border states (except Finland) was that he recognized that any non-Communist governments would be hostile, if only because of their lost territories. Thus, even when looked at from a defensive standpoint, the remedy for Soviet penetrability merely escalated the problem by requiring a still more drastic remedy—indirect domination of the European neighbors of the U.S.S.R.

In fact, the establishment of Communist regimes in East-Central Europe was never portrayed, even by Soviet spokesmen, as a primarily defensive move. Instead, Soviet leaders, while emphasizing that the Communist regimes could not have succeeded without the assistance of the Soviet Army, have consistently hailed their establishment as a demonstration of the expansive force of Communism. In other words, the foundation of a Communist "commonwealth of nations" in East Europe (including the U.S.S.R.) is proclaimed as an expansion of the multinational base for ultimate attainment of world Communism, the logical next step beyond the foundation of the multinational Soviet Union itself.

The above analysis suggests that, as in many other instances, Soviet proclamations exaggerate the consistency of ideological motivation (and in so doing frequently stimulate exaggerated alarm in the non-Communist world). Actually, the maintenance of a protective buffer zone on the Soviet frontier and the desire to avert the re-emergence of strong European rivals have continued to play as strong a role, very probably, in the Soviet leadership's determined support for East-Central European Communist regimes as has the desire to broaden the world base of Communism. The three motivations are so intimately interconnected, however, that it is hard to tell where one begins and the others end. Since the ideological justification for repeated Soviet intervention in East-Central Europe is identical to the legitimization of Moscow's domination of the non-Russian nationalities of the Soviet Union itself, any disruption of Communist control in the former area is likely to spread to the U.S.S.R. itself. That this possibility is not a purely theoretical matter was demonstrated during the Czechoslovak liberalization of 1967–68. Not only were Czech ideas spreading to the neighboring Ukraine, but Ukrainians were asking why, if the little Czechoslovak nation could enjoy such freedom, the 40 million Ukrainians in the second largest Soviet Republic could not obtain broad autonomy from Moscow. It is hardly surprising that Shelest, the Ukrainian Party first secretary (although possibly, as later hinted, "soft" in permitting manifestations of Ukrainian cultural distinction from the Russians), was extremely concerned about any relaxation of strict Leninist principles of proletarian internationalism.

The situation is complicated by the fact that several of the East-Central European economies are far more effective, at least in the provision of acceptable consumers' goods and services, than the cumbersome Soviet economy. As a result, East-Central European economic capacity is a valuable adjunct of Soviet power, but at the same time Soviet citizens who deal with East-Central Europe come to recognize their own system's severe limitations. Moreover, East-Central European populations inevitably are exposed to greater contact with the Western countries than is the Soviet population. Considerable proportions of the Czechs, East Germans, and Hungarians can, for example, receive direct television broadcasts from Western stations. It seems highly likely that East-Central Europeans are, therefore, the principal carriers of Western ideas and material expectations into the Soviet Union. The only way in which the Soviet regime can limit this contagion (while still utilizing the significant economic potential of the East-Central European countries) is to maintain firm Communist control there.

Soviet determination to retain control of these European areas, if it was ever in doubt, was harshly reaffirmed in the "Brezhnev Doctrine" following the 1968 Soviet invasion of Czechoslovakia. In principle, each member of the Communist commonwealth must adhere exclusively to the military alliance directed by Moscow; must reserve a monopoly of political power for its Communist party; and must retain centralized state direction of at least the "commanding heights" of its economy. Since the Soviet regime, in practice, determines whether these conditions are met, the northern tier of European Communist states (the German Democratic Republic, Czechoslovakia, Poland, and Hungary) which are strategically and economically most important, are actually satellites.*

Furthermore, in relation to Czechoslovakia in 1968 as to Hungary in 1956, the U.S.S.R. has firmly asserted the principle that, once a Marxist-Leninist regime comes to power in any country, the U.S.S.R. will prevent such a regime from being overthrown by any means. This implies that Communist dictatorships are fundamentally different from non-Communist dictatorships (even when the latter are equally antidemocratic),

* Bulgaria and the Mongolian People's Republic are also Soviet satellites.

for some combination of internal forces can conceivably over-throw the latter, while overthrow of a Communist regime is inconceivable as long as the U.S.S.R.'s guarantee is not questioned. In practice, the United States as well as the lesser non-Communist powers have not supported any overthrow of an avowedly Communist regime. Even when regimes in Yugoslavia, China, and Albania have openly quarreled (occasionally with considerable encouragement from Western governments) with the Soviet Union, none of these established Communist regimes has renounced Marxist-Leninism or admitted competing political forces. In one sense, this tacit acknowledgment of the Soviet guarantee (in effect long before the Brezhnev Doctrine was proclaimed) is one-sided, for, of course, the U.S.S.R. resolutely refuses to admit that it may not encourage replacement of a non-Communist regime by a Communist regime. With two exceptions (Cuba and North Vietnam), however, since the 1940's avowedly Communist regimes have not acquired independent state power. Increasingly, therefore, the Soviet guarantee of existing Communist regimes has in practice acquired defensive overtones, as the nature and timing of the Brezhnev Doctrine indicated.

THE AMBIGUOUS CHINESE FACTOR

Looming behind all of the Soviet efforts to maintain control of the East-Central European satellites is the question of Sino-Soviet relations. In fact, the immense though latent potential of China and the dramatic reversals in its relation to the U.S.S.R. have impressed the Soviet leadership so deeply that one may almost speak of a Soviet obsession with China.

The sweeping Communist victory in China in 1949 was, evidently, quite unanticipated by Stalin and his lieutenants. Despite the assistance the Chinese Communist leaders gave Soviet Far Eastern policy in the early 1950's, Stalin probably never accorded major importance to Peking. For a brief period in the mid 1950's, Khrushchev, on the other hand, emphasized and even exaggerated the significance of Chinese adhesion to Marxism-Leninism. The enormous Chinese population was cited as proof that nearly one-half of mankind had turned to Communism, and the great sweep of "red" on the maps of Eurasia visually symbolized the spread of Leninist regimes. At the same time, China seemed to be following the Soviet model of industrialization, and educational and cultural contacts between the largest Communist powers were intimate.

Beginning in 1957 or 1958 this impressive solidarity rapidly deteriorated. Apparently the principal immediate cause was divergence over relations with the principal non-Communist powers; Peking wanted the U.S.S.R. to take risks (primarily to attain Chinese objectives) that neither the current level of Soviet armaments nor the traditional caution of Soviet foreign policy justified. Today it seems evident that foreign observers exaggerated the long-range significance of this tactical divergence, however, for the fundamental cleavages between the Soviet and the Chinese Communist regimes have not been the result of a persistent Chinese intransigence toward "imperialists." On the contrary, the basic conflict appears to stem from the peculiar penetrability of the U.S.S.R. discussed above. In its simplest form, Soviet concern for Chinese Communist "deviation" arises from the Soviet need, also discussed above, to maintain strong controls in East-Central Europe lest the U.S.S.R. itself be infected. Although the Peking leadership backed Soviet suppression of the Hungarian rebellion, the Chinese Communists soon began "advising" that Soviet controls be loosened. In the early 1960's Peking supported Albanian and Rumanian divergences from Soviet policy; Chinese spokesmen bitterly accused the U.S.S.R. of "socialist imperialism" as a result of the Czechoslovak suppression.

In a more complex way the very existence of a drastically different "Chinese path" to Communism is a challenge to the peculiar nature of the Soviet system. The nature of this "path" is too complicated to be discussed fully here—certain features were noted in Chapter 2—but the essential danger lies in Chinese assertions (since 1958) that progress toward Communism can be made without the costly, cumbersome process of transforming the "base" by rapid urbanization and industrialization. Indeed, more recently Peking leaders have charged that this process in itself has frustrated Soviet efforts to attain Communism by giving rise to a selfish bureaucratic oligarchy little better than the capitalists. Because this critique (somewhat similar to criticism advanced by the Cuban Ernesto "Che" Guevara and his French theoretical aide, Régis Debray) is especially appealing to intellectuals and youths, it has gone a long way to destroy the remnants of Soviet ideological appeal outside the Soviet bloc. The Mao-Debray alternative is particularly attractive to young people—even in the Soviet satellites—because of its romantic emphasis on quick results and action against strong odds, as contrasted to cautious Soviet organizational techniques. The Maoist line is also more attractive to national revolutionary regimes that (like China's) are trying to integrate a fairly homogeneous population instead of (as in the U.S.S.R. and India) appealing to ethnically diverse elements.

Perhaps equally alarming to the Soviet leadership is the Chinese threat to the U.S.S.R.'s status as an Asian power, and thus as a putative world system transcending the purely European context. Insofar as these Soviet fears relate to short-range military dangers, they appear greatly exaggerated. Although Chinese troops have clashed stubbornly with Soviet frontier detachments, outside military opinion gives the underequipped Chinese forces little prospect of advancing into Soviet territory, or even into the Mongolian satellite. Soviet leaders express alarm at the imminent development of a Chinese nuclear force, but it will be many years before this force can be used for any purpose except near-suicidal reprisal against a Soviet attack. But the Soviet—or more precisely the Russian—mentality appears to be obsessed with a fear of "Asian hordes" like Genghis Khan's, which overran the East Slavic lands in the thirteenth century. Whether the top Soviet leadership really shares this atavism or encourages it to gain domestic support against the Chinese is uncertain, but the implicit appeal to East Slav solidarity against an Asian threat is in line with the alternative analyzed in Chapter 7. It may well be, too, that in some obscure way Russians identify the spectacular demographic ascendancy of Soviet Asians, which has become apparent in the past fifteen years, as another aspect of the "Asian hordes" threat. In any case, appeal to Slavic solidarity against specific Asian dangers is even more risky than the general alternative, discussed earlier, of emphasizing East Slav dominance in the U.S.S.R. Not only is the appeal invidious to non-Europeans in the Soviet "arrested world state," but it undermines Soviet efforts to present this "world state" as a model for the immense non-European populations of the Third World. For more than a decade the Chinese leadership has exploited this Soviet dilemma by arguing that the U.S.S.R. is not an Asian power and should not be admitted to the Asian-African bloc. Despite great cultural differences between the Chinese and Third World peoples, both generalized suspicion of white Europeans and appreciation of the relative similarity of China as a developing country seem to be working in the Third World in favor of the Chinese arguments against the U.S.S.R.

SOVIET PROSPECTS IN THE THIRD WORLD

In the long run, the Sino-Soviet rift may constitute the main reason why the Soviet regime has not been highly successful in taking advantage of the transformation of the Third World. Certainly the dissolution of the British, French, Netherlands, and Belgian colonial empires in the decade and a half following World War II fundamentally altered many aspects of international relations, with indirect effects (as noted above) on the power potential of Great Britain and other European states. Psychologically, this transformation has increased pressures on the more developed, predominantly white countries to broaden the circle of participation in international affairs (the League of Nations was virtually confined to European and American countries; the United Nations has an overwhelming Third World majority, including most Latin American representatives who perceive themselves as sharing the Third World's problems). The transformation has also brought increased demands (so far without notable success) for more even international sharing of material wealth as well. Occasionally, in the absence of universally accepted standards, perceived divergence of national interests among the greatly expanded body of "sovereign" states has made certain urgent proposals (e.g., sanctions against terrorists) virtually hopeless.

While the expansion in its state membership has greatly complicated the general international environment, the lack of power in the Third World severely limits its potential for fundamentally transforming the real external environment of the superpowers, including the U.S.S.R. There are few sizable military forces south of a line extending around the world roughly from the Rio Grande to the Himalayas. Those that do exist have been developed by states (Australia, South Africa, Israel) with European backgrounds, using equipment predominantly acquired from the United States or Europe; or (in the United Arab Republic, Cuba, the two Vietnams, India) such forces have at least been equipped and financed by the United States and European countries. Very few of the Third World states in the southern half of the globe have the technological capacity to develop and produce even the limited range of modern weapons systems which the middle-sized "Northern" countries can turn out. Equally important is the Third World's lack of economic power; low per capita output and uneven industrial development severely limit these countries' impact on the world economy.

All of these limitations mean that, from the Soviet point of view, any likely developments in the Third World cannot produce a drastic, short-range improvement in the prospects for attaining world Communism. The Chinese experience does, to be sure, suggest that a centralized, dynamic Communist regime may considerably enhance the military power of a developing nation. Economically, however, the effects are not so clear; and, of course, the general nature of the Chinese development has not been reassuring for the Soviet leadership. Consequently, the more immediate tangible prospects for Soviet policy in the Third World have been acquisition of strategic positions and denial of bases and material resources (mainly oil) to the Western powers. Still more significant has been the "demonstration effect" of the establishment of avowedly Marxist-Leninist regimes in Third World countries, as a proof that the world is indeed moving toward Communism.

Very soon after his Revolution succeeded Lenin turned to the underdeveloped countries—or, as he called them, the "semi-colonial" countries—particularly neighboring China, Turkey, and Iran. A characteristic of the penetrability of the Soviet system is that Mongol, Turkic, Iranian, and Armenian ethnic groups live astride Soviet frontiers with these Asian states, just as other ethnic groups straddle the U.S.S.R.'s European frontiers. As a result, Soviet policy toward its Asian neighbors, too, has been both defensive (to minimize the attraction independent Asian states may exert on Soviet citizens) and offensive, through the utilization of Soviet Asians to appeal to their fellow ethnics outside the U.S.S.R.

It was not until 1954, after Stalin's death, that the Soviet

Union made a major effort to penetrate Third World countries remote from the Soviet borders (previously arms aid had, however, been sent to distant countries of European background like Israel and Republican Spain). Under Khrushchev's aegis, large arms shipments were dispatched almost simultaneously to the U.A.R. (United Arab Republic, essentially Egypt) and Indonesia. During the next decade a number of other countries—principally Arab, but including several other Asian and African states—became Soviet military clients, although none became Marxist-Leninist. The crowning achievement, from the demonstration effect standpoint, was the vehement espousal of Leninism by the Cuban leader, Fidel Castro. Castro's adherence to Communism was a propaganda windfall for the Soviet leadership. As an "island of freedom" close to the United States, Communist Cuba appeared to be a striking confirmation of the thesis that the world was turning to Communism. During the early 1960's Castro was especially useful as a symbol to Khrushchev, then experiencing difficulties in maintaining his authority. Castro's appearance with the aging Khrushchev on the review stand in Red Square seemed to be a visible token that the latter's promise that the "present generation will live under Communism" was not an idle gesture.

Since Castro had attained power without any Marxist-Leninist apparatus (indeed, against the advice of the local Communists) his adherence to Leninism seemed to show that the tortuous path of creating a Marxist-Leninist party which could gradually oust other political elements was unnecessary, at least in some Third World countries. By 1963 Soviet writers were explicitly suggesting that certain developing countries (by then "developing" had replaced "semicolonial" as the Soviet term for the Third World) might move directly to "socialism," bypassing capitalism and without displacement of existing "national liberation" leaders. This optimistic prospect implied that differences between Third World states which resolutely opposed "imperialism" and accepted Marxist-Leninist prescriptions, and those which had come to power through real Communist-led revolutions might not be as fundamental as Leninists had previously asserted. This tentative blurring of distinction seemed to provide a possible Soviet escape from the fact, apparent to all observers by 1963, that the unity of the Communist "camp" itself was shattered. China and Albania were engaged in fierce verbal conflict with the U.S.S.R.—soon escalated to physical clashes on the Chinese-Soviet frontier; Yugoslavia was wholly independent; and Romania, North Vietnam, and North Korea were pursuing divergent policies. Under these circumstances the Soviet leadership had little reason to prefer a Communist client like North Korea, which refused to take sides against China and complicated Soviet negotiations with Japan and the United States, to a non-Communist client like the U.A.R., which appeared to be using Soviet military and economic assistance to further Soviet strategic objectives. Still, as indicated earlier, a residual distinction was maintained: Perpetuation of avowedly Communist regimes was guaranteed by Soviet power, and non-Communist clients were not.

During 1964-67 this prudent distinction assumed greater importance. In quick succession, three Soviet client dictators—Ben Bella in Algeria, Nkrumah in Ghana, and Sukarno in Indonesia—were overthrown, in the latter two cases at least by forces friendly to the Western powers. Soviet spokesmen stridently denounced "imperialist maneuvers," but the U.S.S.R. did not provide physical assistance to its ousted clients. At the same time, the United States began military reprisals against North Vietnam—but tacitly admitted that its Communist regime and its territorial integrity were inviolable. Conversely, Israel (an American client) replied to U.A.R. military harassment with a sweeping invasion and occupation of U.A.R. and Syrian territory. Whether the Soviet leaders wished to intervene forcibly to aid their defeated Arab clients is uncertain; although Soviet encouragement had been a major factor behind the anti-Israeli acts that provoked the hostilities. What is clear is that the U.S.S.R. was utterly unable to extend the principle of inviolability of the territorial integrity of Communist states to protect its non-Communist clients. An inevitable result was a sharp decline in Soviet prestige throughout the Third World, where many nationalist leaders assumed that the United States remained the only real world power.

SOVIET REASSESSMENTS

It appears very likely that during the mid-1960's the Soviet leadership was compelled to undertake a serious reassessment of its world position. The first tendency, apparently, was to ascribe the humiliating reverses in the Third World to inadequate Soviet military power. At the beginning of the 1960's Khrushchev's efforts to bluff the United States into thinking that the Soviet Union had acquired parity in intercontinental nuclear delivery capabilities was exposed. In 1962 the United States compelled him to give up his effort to recoup the situation by stationing short-range missiles in Cuba. This public display of United States military superiority was undoubtedly one reason why—in the face of American warnings—the U.S.S.R. refrained from assisting the U.A.R. against Israel five years later. Another factor contributing to Soviet impotence in the Middle East was the inability of the U.S.S.R. to project its own enormous land and air forces to an area even one thousand miles from its bases. Although there was a Soviet fleet in the Mediterranean, it lacked sizable amphibious troop-carrying capacity. More significant, the Soviet navy possesses no aircraft carriers, which could have provided fighter plane cover for a landing against the small but technically superior Israeli air force, which had virtually destroyed Arab air power. In contrast, in the Mediterranean as well as in the broader oceans, task forces built around large aircraft carriers provided the United States with the capacity to intervene effectively against moderately strong hostile forces based on land.

From 1965 on, the Soviet Union devoted immense resources to catching up with the United States in nuclear forces by building a superior intercontinental missile force and a nuclear submarine fleet approximately equal to the United States's. At the time of the 1962 Cuban crisis the U.S.S.R. could have inflicted immense damage on the United States, but the Soviet Union would have been destroyed as a political and economic system in an all-out war; today such conflict would mean complete destruction of both the United States and the Soviet Union. Nuclear parity makes conventional weaponry relatively more significant. In the areas of Europe and Asia close to its frontiers, the superiority of Soviet conventional forces is apparent. In more distant regions, the Soviet Union still has not overcome its lack of amphibious forces provided with mobile air cover, although steps have been taken to overcome these deficiencies by acquiring air bases on land in the Indian Ocean region and by starting construction of aircraft carriers. In these circumstances, exact ratios of intercontinental nuclear destructive capacity may be less important than the psychological effect of attainment of nuclear parity in strengthening the confidence of the Soviet elite. At the same time, however, Soviet leaders seem to realize that mutual nuclear destruction is the one catastrophic possibility which might "derail" the course of history toward Communism that Marx and Lenin predicted. Consequently, the contemporary power balance provides additional reasons for Soviet prudence in avoiding all-out war.

Even more important, from the psychological standpoint, was the clear evidence of United States retreat by 1968. With some hesitation, Soviet observers gradually concluded that the other superpower was facing a crisis of will. Protracted and bitter racial strife, a morale-shattering series of political assassinations, and dissatisfaction with American participation in the Vietnam war combined to reduce popular support for active policies abroad and maintenance of military superiority. Since American power had been the chief obstacle to Soviet foreign policy moves since 1946, American paralysis would open new possibilities for Soviet initiative. On the other hand, both the Soviet tradition of prudence in foreign affairs and the extreme dangers of nuclear destruction led to caution in testing these possibilities. Doubtless the Soviet leaders recall with trepidation how "unreliable" were American expressions of limited interest in South Korea in 1950; when invasion from North Korea actually occurred, it triggered (contrary to Soviet expectation) a massive American military response.

United States foreign policy in the early 1970's—perhaps calculatingly—revived this image of American unpredictability. In May, 1970, despite wide domestic protest, the United States government decided to destroy North Vietnamese bases in Cambodia by going to the aid of anti-Communist forces in that country. A few months later the United States threatened to intervene against Syria (still a Soviet client) if that country continued its intervention in the civil war in Jordan. In 1972 the United States, although warning against complete destruction of its ally Pakistan by another Soviet client, India, implicitly acquiesced in Pakistan's dismemberment. Later in the year, on the other hand, the United States sharply retaliated against massive North Vietnamese escalation of the invasion of South Vietnam. This whole pattern left the U.S.S.R. leadership uncertain as to just what steps the United States might take in any new crisis.

The Soviet Union did not immediately abandon its belief in the value of Third World clients as a result of the setbacks in the 1960's. As late as 1970 the U.S.S.R. was not only providing North Vietnam, Ceylon, the U.A.R., and other Arab states with very advanced weapons but also was dispatching thousands of Soviet soldiers and airmen to man these weapons. Increasingly, however, it became evident that all-out support of these clients would involve the U.S.S.R. in grave risks as well as heavy diversion of economic resources. A basic problem with Soviet acquisition of Third World clients has been that the U.S.S.R. has inevitably attracted dissatisfied, expansionist countries, since those favoring the territorial status quo have generally been aligned with the Western powers. It is significant that Indonesia under the pro-Soviet dictator Sukarno had immense territorial ambitions. Egypt has desired to expand in the Arab world as well as to defeat Israel. Even India, never reconciled to the partition of the Indian Subcontinent, is a territorially unsatisfied state. To put the matter another way, expansionist regimes try to use the U.S.S.R. as a shield and source of weapons to attain their own aims. Insofar as the U.S.S.R. itself is expansionist, these efforts to disrupt the status quo may be compatible with its interests. But the intransigent activities of some of the client states have caused disturbances at times and places that were gravely embarrassing for Soviet foreign policy. In the short run, at least, expansionist moves which clients consider vital may be sharply opposed to the long-run, prudent strategy of the U.S.S.R., both because of actual divergence of interests and because the client elites rarely have the experience and intelligence facilities which enable them to make prudent calculations.

One way to avoid clients' involving the U.S.S.R. in unacceptable risks would be for the Soviet center to exercise firm internal control over client policy-making elites. Such subordination, as expressed in the formulas of "democratic centralism" and "proletarian internationalism" is, indeed, the Soviet ideal. It appears that Khrushchev's enthusiasm, in the early 1960's, over the spread of avowedly Marxist-Leninist dictatorships was based in part on a calculation that such regimes would follow Soviet advice. In fact, however, the trend has been for long-established Marxist-Leninist regimes like those of North Korea and North Vietnam to reject Soviet counsel, and for the non-Communist pro-Soviet dictatorships (particularly in the Arab countries) to exclude all Marxist-Leninist influence in their domestic affairs as well as in foreign policy formation. These circumstances tend to blur the distinction between Communist and non-Communist clients and to require the U.S.S.R., if it wants to maintain a prudent international stance, to avoid giving "blank checks" to either.

Soviet Alternatives for the 1970's

The Soviet dilemma in dealing with client states has been greatly sharpened by Soviet desires to reach a broad understanding with the United States. Apart from diminishing the risk of accidental conflict, such an understanding might allow some diversion of Soviet resources to internal development. Trade with the United States, especially if accompanied by long-term credits, would provide the Soviet economy with key technical items, like computers, that the leadership requires (see Chapter 6) to maintain centralized control. American recognition of the East-Central European status quo might lessen Soviet difficulties in dominating its crucial satellites. The Soviet leadership has been eager to take steps to prevent Sino-American rapprochement from turning into a tacit anti-Soviet alignment. Between 1970 and 1973 it became increasingly apparent, however, that Soviet Third World clients constituted the principal obstacles to even a short-range *modus vivendi* with the United States. While maintaining its protective shield over his regime, the U.S.S.R. used its subsidies to Castro to compel him to moderate his belligerent pronouncements and to cease material support to guerrillas in the Western Hemisphere. In 1970 the Soviet Union acquiesced in American protection of Jordan against Syria and apparently warned other Arab states that the U.S.S.R. could not support an all-out attack on Israel or other clients of the United States. The U.A.R. in particular was kept on a "short leash" by denial of advanced weapons systems necessary to support such an attack. As a result, in 1972 its leadership publicly ordered most Soviet military personnel to leave the country. The Soviet regime apparently accepted both the psychological and the material costs of reduction of Soviet presence in the Arab world as a necessary counterpart to a reduction of risks for Soviet foreign policy. Soviet losses in this area had been, to be sure, partially offset by a large gain in Soviet prestige a few months earlier, when India, using Soviet equipment, crushed Pakistan. As indicated above, however, both India and the U.S.S.R. were constrained to limit the effects of this victory. In March, 1972, on the other hand, the North Vietnamese launched an all-out attack on South Vietnam, using Soviet-made tanks and artillery supplied many months earlier. Soviet acquiescence in the drastic American response, which involved interdiction of Soviet shipping as well as bombing of North Vietnam, seems to have been designed as a signal, both to the United States and to Soviet clients, that the latter could not expect Soviet support if they used Soviet-supplied weapons without Moscow's authorization.

In these cumulatively significant steps toward curbing its clients, the Soviet Union has been moving in the direction the United States took decades earlier, when it denied heavy weapons to an intransigent South Korean regime, required Anglo-French-Israeli evacuation of the Sinai area, cautioned Israel against excessive reprisals against the Arab states, and prevented Greek seizure of southern Albania. In other words, the United States has long pursued a policy of preventing states it arms from pursuing expansionist policies toward Soviet clients. In some circumstances (particularly Soviet support for Greek Communists in 1948–51 and for the North Korean invasion of South Korea in 1950) the U.S.S.R. under

Stalin refused to enforce parallel restraints. Both Khrushchev and the present Soviet leadership also declined to restrain clients. Today, the oligarchy ruling the U.S.S.R. seems to have been sufficiently impressed by the need for symmetrical agreements with the United States to have initiated a real, though tentative, departure in Soviet foreign policy—the acceptance of responsibility for client actions, whether the clients are Communist or not.

This new departure in foreign policy must be labeled tentative for the present because we cannot know if it represents more than a short-range adjustment to the realities of international relations. A major reason why the stability of this policy remains in question is the imminent turnover in Soviet leadership analyzed in Chapter 4. It is possible that increased prudence in the international arena merely reflects the concern of the aging oligarchy, which possesses neither the stamina nor the desire to take risky initiatives. A new, younger leadership might resume the bolder course Khrushchev pursued.

If, however, the Soviet elite adopts a long-range policy of restraining its clients as well as its own expansionist appetites, a fundamental alteration in the international situation may result. Since 1969 American foreign policy has encouraged the re-emergence of a multilateral balance, sometimes called the "pentagon of power," comprising China, Western Europe, and Japan, as well as the U.S.S.R. and the U.S.A. In order to achieve this objective, United States leadership is willing to accept a sharp reduction in American ability to control the course of international affairs. For reasons touched upon earlier in this chapter, this objective is difficult to attain; a long transitional period is inescapable. As a goal, however, it is fundamentally incompatible with the Communist prescription for a world state united under "proletarian internationalism." For the Soviet leadership to acquiesce in the emergence of a true multilateral balance would, therefore, mean that ideological prescriptions were being further down-graded in favor of traditional Russian national objectives. Such a multilateral alignment would, in fact, represent a retrogression to the interwar situation, when Soviet power was a relatively minor factor in the entire scope of world politics; but precisely because shifting combinations of great powers acted to minimize violent actions on the part of any one power, the security of the U.S.S.R. as a national state might be enhanced. At this point, however, the inherent instability of the U.S.S.R. as a multinational polity re-emerges as a barrier to long-term acceptance of a multilateral status quo, for such a balance enhances the tendency of smaller nations (both inside the U.S.S.R. and among its East-Central European satellites) to demand freedom of action.

Given the fundamental dilemma of Soviet policy arising from the penetrability of the Soviet system, it seems at least as likely that the Soviet elite will in the long run choose an alternative to the restraints implicit in acceptance of the U.S.-sponsored multilateral balance. One alternative is to resume, after a short breathing space, a generally expansionist policy designed to press rapidly toward a Communist world state dominated by Moscow.

As indicated earlier, the U.S.S.R. has moved a considerable distance toward strategic superiority in certain respects; an all-out effort might conceivably lead to general military dominance. Obviously a further sharp decline in American will to participate in world affairs, coupled with unilateral American restrictions on its own armaments, would enormously increase Soviet chances. Conceivably, lowered American concern for nuclear parity, combined with Soviet technological break-throughs, could even enable the Soviet leadership to envisage a first strike, which would limit Soviet losses to something comparable to those incurred in World War II. More likely would be a combination of (1) Soviet threats gradually reducing Western Europe to submission if American protection were withdrawn and (2) decisive Soviet expansion into the Third World through amphibious attacks on countries like Israel, South Africa, and Brazil.

Obviously such a strategy would appeal to a newer generation of ideologically oriented leaders in the U.S.S.R. Because of its predominantly military character, such a strategy would also appeal, if successful, to a stronger military component in the leadership. But the key word is "successful." Such a drastically expansionist policy would be extremely costly at best and would incur frightful risks of catastrophic American reaction.

A second alternative would permit—at least in principle— a lower level of economic costs and risks, while preserving some of the dynamic aspects of Soviet foreign policy, which acceptance of the multilateral status quo would sacrifice. Even in a relatively short run, the Soviet leadership could utilize détente with the United States and its major allies in Europe, Japan, and the Middle East to concentrate on re-establishing Soviet domination in the Communist sphere itself. Essentially, such a policy would mean destruction of the anti-Soviet regimes in Peking and Belgrade. While not so overtly hostile as the Chinese Communists since 1948, the Yugoslav regime's independent stance probably has done more to encourage centrifugal tendencies in the Soviet satellites and within the U.S.S.R. When elderly Marshal Josip Broz Tito dies, a new Communist leadership will face enormous difficulties in maintaining the unity of multinational Yugoslavia. Readiness of some nationalities to seek any outside support against their ethnic enemies, combined with latent sympathies among some Yugoslav Communists for the Soviet brand of Communism, may encourage forceful Soviet intervention. If this were successful, not only would Moscow have demonstrated that an independent Yugoslavia could not indefinitely pursue a "separate path" to Communism, but the U.S.S.R. would be in a position to suppress different types of deviation in neighboring Romania and Albania.

Suppression of the Chinese Communist deviation (and with it establishment of Soviet control over North Korea and perhaps North Vietnam) would be immensely more difficult, even after the death of Mao Tse-tung. For the next few years, at the cost of several million Soviet citizens killed by short-range Chinese nuclear reprisals, the U.S.S.R. could probably destroy Chinese nuclear and heavy industrial capacity and seize northern areas including Peking and Manchuria. Massive Soviet military preparations on the Chinese borders suggest that the present Soviet elite may envisage such a stroke. It would, however, entail immense risks. In the short run, a conflict involving nuclear weapons might spread to catastrophic, global proportions. Even if the U.S.S.R. were initially successful, however, protracted Chinese Communist resistance south of the Hwang River would involve Soviet forces in a struggle which they probably could not win against vast numbers of guerrillas. Such a war would mean an interminable drain on resources, putting further strains on the domestic situation of the U.S.S.R., while (as dissident writer Andrei Amalrik suggests) the example of Chinese resistance would encourage other nations in the Soviet sphere to dissidence.

Thus none of the basic alternatives for Soviet policy in the late 1970's is attractive for the Soviet leadership. From the point of view of the United States and its most important allies, there is little doubt that the first possibility, acquiescence in a status quo developing into a multilateral balance of power, though far from ideal, is much the most desirable. Attainment of this new balance will require, however, immense positive efforts by the principal non-Communist powers, as well as firmness in the essentially negative task of convincing the old and the new Soviet leadership that this alternative is the only safe one. Clearly, the United States leaders will need strong wills and resolute public support to demonstrate beyond question that a Soviet drive for a world Communist state is doomed to failure. But it is almost equally important, from the standpoint of American objectives, that the United States act to prevent establishment of complete Soviet control over all of East-Central Europe and East Asia, for (apart from the grave risks that Soviet military operations would entail for the whole world) such a monolithic power bloc would make a stable multilateral distribution of world power almost unattainable. What is most important is awareness that the role of the U.S.S.R. in international affairs, and ultimately its internal evolution, depend primarily not on Communist ideology or the wishes of Soviet leaders but on the constraining influences of the international environment that other leaders and other peoples construct.

SUGGESTED READING • CHAPTER 8

ASPATURIAN, VERNON V. *Process and Power in Soviet Foreign Policy.* Boston: Little, Brown, 1971. A comprehensive, up-to-date discussion of all aspects of the U.S.S.R. in international affairs.

BELOFF, MAX. *The Foreign Policy of Soviet Russia, 1929–1941.* 2 vols. London: Oxford University Press, 1947, 1949. Still the best treatment of the interwar period.

BRZEZINSKI, ZBIGNIEW. *The Soviet Bloc: Unity and Conflict.* Rev. ed. Cambridge: Harvard University Press paperback, 1971. An authoritative treatment of all phases of the Soviet takeover and control in East-Central Europe.

GOLDMAN, MARSHALL I. *Soviet Foreign Aid.* New York: Praeger, 1967. A thorough discussion of Soviet arms and economic assistance to states such as Egypt, India, and Indonesia.

HOFFMANN, ERIK P., and FLERON, FREDERICK (eds.). *The Conduct of Soviet Foreign Policy.* Chicago: Aldine-Atherton paperback, 1971. A collection of articles useful primarily from the methodological standpoint.

HORELICK, ARNOLD and RUSH, MYRON. *Strategic Power and Soviet Foreign Policy.* Chicago: University of Chicago Press, 1966. A detailed, reliable analysis of Khrushchev's arms policy, with particular emphasis on the Berlin and the Cuban crises.

MACKINTOSH, J. MALCOLM. *Strategy and Tactics of Soviet Foreign Policy.* London: Oxford University Press, 1962. The best analysis of Khrushchev's foreign policy.

RA'ANAN, URI. *The U.S.S.R. Arms the Third World.* Cambridge: MIT Press, 1969, An excellent analysis of the implications of Soviet arms aid.

SHULMAN, MARSHALL D. *Stalin's Foreign Policy Reappraised.* New York: Atheneum paperback, 1965. The most authoritative, up-to-date analysis of the Stalin period in world affairs.

ULAM, ADAM B. *Expansion and Coexistence: Soviet Foreign Policy, 1917–73.* 2d ed. New York: Praeger, 1974. The most comprehensive, up-to-date history.

WEEKS, ALBERT L. *The Other Side of Coexistence: An Analysis of Russian Foreign Policy.* New York: Pitman, 1970. A good analysis of recent developments, especially in Soviet-American relations.

WOLFE, THOMAS W. *Soviet Power and Europe, 1945–1970.* Baltimore: Johns Hopkins University Press paperback, 1970. A penetrating and authoritative analysis emphasizing military factors.

ZIMMERMAN, WILLIAM. *Soviet Perspectives on International Relations, 1956–1967.* Princeton, N.J.: Princeton University Press, 1969. An analysis of the interaction of ideological, structural, and environmental factors.

9

A SUMMING UP

It would be rash to assert that the expectations men have about politics play a more significant part in the Soviet system than in other political systems. Part of the apparent importance of Soviet political culture may arise from our inability to examine attitudes and personality structures in the U.S.S.R. directly. Nevertheless, at least from our limited perspective, the amalgam of Russian heritage and Marxist-Leninist ideology appears to have an enormous effect on behavior, particularly among the elite.

We have deliberately avoided any effort to describe in detail the link between the elements of the Russian heritage described in Chapter 1 and the specific features of the Soviet system. That such a connection exists is generally conceded, but few students of Russian history would agree on the exact way in which the heritage has influenced the present. One may assume that the tradition of subordinating the individual to the group—whether through the official despotism of the Czarist regime, the customs of the peasant *mir,* or the left-wing insistence on art for revolution's sake—has facilitated the imposition of Soviet totalitarianism. In Lenin's reinterpretation of Marxism we seem to see a direct influence (though possibly a subconscious one) of the Russian background. Sociological studies have shown that descendants of the pre-Revolution educated strata have been able, on the whole, to obtain places in the Soviet intelligentsia. One can expect, therefore, that the attitudes current in these strata have been passed on. However, like all great societies, Czarist Russia contained many contradictory elements; consequently, sweeping generalizations about its influence on the present are unwarranted. Despite these cautions, it *is* important for the student to realize that the present Soviet system has not been imposed on a blank slate.

The Marxist-Leninist component of contemporary Soviet political culture seems more evident. If one accepts the declarations of the regime at their face value, the ideology is the core of the system. Nor does the fact that major elements of the ideology have been altered and realtered by Lenin's successors negate this assumption, for Marxist-Leninism has always stressed the need for continual interaction of theory and practice. As the Soviet elite has changed, the psychological force of the doctrine has correspondingly altered. The Bolshevik revolutionary, dedicated to destroying the old order so as to be able to proceed to the rapid construction of a perfect society, has long since been replaced by the Party bureaucrat. Until recently, at least, the latter was able to find a connection between his personal progress from obscurity to power and the material accomplishments and enhanced prestige of the regime. The successes of the Soviet regime seemed narrow and philistine to many in the outside world and—as the spread of dissent indicates—to many sensitive persons in the U.S.S.R. To the officials who form the backbone of the regime, however, its achievements have been great enough to bolster their faith in the eventual fulfillment of the Marxist prophecy of the triumph of Communism.

Since 1961, however, this belief has suffered a number of severe shocks. At the beginning of the 1960's, open rupture with China and the forced withdrawal of Soviet missiles from Cuba shook confidence in the forward march of Communism. Later in the decade, Soviet occupation of Czechoslovakia was a tacit admission that even the existing sphere of Communist control depended on Russian military power. Reversals of Soviet allies in the Third World, culminating in Soviet imposition of curbs on its clients' expansionist ambitions, was an equally serious tacit admission that the Soviet regime was unwilling to incur severe risks to expand Communist influence. Continued failures of Soviet agriculture and the inability of Soviet technology to catch up with the achievements of the market economies resulted in fundamentally humiliating admissions of the continuing need—after nearly sixty years of Soviet power—for outside economic assistance. As a result, the series of agreements with the United States and other major non-Communist powers in 1972–73 had a twofold effect; on the one hand, they did acknowledge Soviet predominance in East-Central Europe; on the other hand, they amounted to a tacit renunciation of Soviet expansionist activity.

Because the historical inevitability of the spread of Communism throughout the world is a fundamental Leninist tenet, Soviet recognition of the status quo implies, at the least, an indefinite postponement of the millennial goals. Soviet statements continue to stress that the current line of "peaceful coexistence" does not mean the abandonment of the drive for world Communism—only the application of different tactics. But it is hard to believe that the elite itself is as convinced of its ultimate success as was the case thirteen years ago.

The past thirteen years have seen the development of what may be an even more fundamental danger for Marxist-Leninist ideology. In 1961, for the first time in the history of the Communist movement, a fairly definite timetable for attaining the millennial goals was set. Along with this timetable went a series of prescriptions for transitional measures during the following twenty years. Two-thirds of this time has elapsed, but many of the prescriptions, such as limitations on farmers' garden plots, opposition to personally owned housing and automobiles, and the use of "collective" bodies for enforcing discipline, have been abandoned. Instead, a Soviet writer emphasizes, "it is incorrect to assume that the socialist state of the

entire people is on the point of withering away and of handing
over all its functions to public organizations." Furthermore,
"socialism is not a brief state, but a definite phase, a prolonged
stage in the development of the Communist formation, one
that has its own periods and its own stages." * Thus, while the
regime still insists on the necessity of eventually eliminating
private property, material incentives, and state coercive agencies, there is no reference to a timetable that would make
these promises look realistic. The regime appears to hold as
firmly as ever, however, to one basic element of the materialist
aspect of Communist ideology—atheism. Belief in science as a
force that, under Communist control, can explain and accomplish everything fits in neatly with the concept of Marxism-
Leninism as the supreme science of society and with the
Communist official's self-image as an engineer of society. Just
as obviously, this creed of materialism rules out transcen-
dental belief; there is no clear evidence that attacks on religion
in the U.S.S.R. have abated.

The place of the Party also seems secure in the minds of
those who accept the ideology. Indeed, the ouster of Khrushchev (which may have been a consequence of waning confidence in the attainment of millennial goals) probably temporarily reinforced the symbolic importance of the Party as
such. Since then, there has been some increase in the operational importance of state institutions, indicated most recently
by the naming of top state bureaucrats to the Politburo. To
a limited extent, Leonid Brezhnev has gradually replaced
Khrushchev as a personal symbol of the Soviet regime. Nevertheless, the role of the Party as a legitimizing institution is
indispensable for the present elite. The fact that the life experiences of the present elite (in the Central Committee, the

* A. Yegorov, "The Party of Scientific Communism," *Kommunist*,
No. 2, January 1973, as translated in *Current Digest of the Soviet Press*,
XXV, No. 13, pp. 8–11.

Politburo, and Brezhnev personally) are grossly out of line with life experiences of the general Party membership and of the population as a whole reinforces the elite's eagerness to cling to Party orthodoxy. Most oligarchies have been conservative rather than dynamic, and an aged oligarchy is especially likely to be orthodox rather than innovative. At the same time, the relative harmony that has prevailed among Khrushchev's successors may well have convinced the elite that they have found mechanisms for avoiding the succession crises that formerly racked the Soviet system. Avoidance of drastic policy innovations, which reduces the scope of debate and differences among the elite, may make it easier to cope with the next succession. All of these factors suggest a period of retrenchment.

Whether a new elite generation, which must come to power very soon, will move from orthodox conservatism to reliance on a more pragmatic ideology, or whether a younger elite will seek to restore the dynamic aspects of Communism can only be a matter for speculation. In either case, the new elite generation will face problems that may undermine the stability of the Soviet system. Overt departure from Marxism-Leninism would make it hard to justify continued rule of non-Russians by Moscow, to say nothing of the effect it would have on the Soviet regime's position in East Central Europe. On the other hand, memories of the unfulfilled promises of 1961 will make it difficult to reinspire enthusiasm for the development of the "new man" of the Communist millennium.

Under Stalin's dictatorship, lack of enthusiasm among the Russian peasantry and more extreme disaffection among other national groups could be met by overwhelming force. In many ways, it was the availability of modern technology that made totalitarian control and indoctrination possible at that time. Large forces armed with modern weapons made effective resistance impossible, while the railroad network was used to shift uprooted populations to remote agricultural frontiers or to primitive quarters in the industrial centers. Utilizing modern means of communication and its ubiquitous security police, Stalin's regime in Moscow rooted out disaffection in 8 million square miles of territory. The printing press (and, to a lesser extent, the radio) made it possible quickly to transmit a uniform "line" to the army of propagandists and agitators. And the enormous cloacae of concentration camps silently eliminated the human "waste" that the regime felt the Soviet system could not expediently absorb. It is conceivable that a new elite could utilize similar methods for a short time. But, for all its defects, Stalin's regime retained the allegiance of an elite that equated its own success with the material successes of the system and was willing to undergo great hardships as well as to impose brutally harsh sacrifices upon the mass of the population. Considerable elements, especially workers in the Russian cities, continued to believe in the goals of Communism and to accept the means used to attain them. The limited consensus supporting coercion, rather than coercion itself, was the ultimate basis for Stalin's rule. It is most doubtful that a new elite could find even a limited consensus to serve as a basis for widespread and long-lasting coercion. If a new elite cannot do this, it may have to retreat to a territorially restricted Russian nation-state with a mixed economy and a stratified social system not markedly different from those prevailing in other modernized countries. In such a case, pressures for a pluralist political system would probably be strong, but we lack historical parallels to indicate whether or not such pressures in a modernized society could be resisted by a determined oligarchy.

On the other hand, it is always possible that the Soviet elite can achieve a break-through that will reinvigorate faith in millennial goals. The extent of domestic economic progress needed to constitute such a break-through is incalculable, but it scarcely seems attainable in the foreseeable future. A resounding Soviet success in international affairs, one that seems to bring world Communist domination in sight, might have the same reinvigorating effect. The present leadership appears to have temporarily renounced efforts to gain such a success. As discussed in Chapter 8, however, both the inherent tensions of the Soviet system and probable developments in peripheral areas like Yugoslavia may tempt the present Soviet leadership, or, more likely, its immediate successors. Such temptations to take a risky shortcut to restore Soviet dynamism may be overwhelming if Soviet leaders become convinced that other major powers have lost the interest and the will to play a counterbalancing role in world affairs. In the final analysis, the ultimate development of the Soviet system may be decided, therefore, by the kind of world order its critics create.

INDEX